Confucian Questions to Augustine

To. Mae

13. March. 2023.

Jun Soo Park

Confucian Questions to Augustine

Is My Cultivation of Self
Your Care of the Soul?

JUNSOO PARK

RESOURCE *Publications* • Eugene, Oregon

CONFUCIAN QUESTIONS TO AUGUSTINE
Is My Cultivation of Self Your Care of the Soul?

Copyright © 2020 JunSoo Park. All rights reserved. Except for brief quotations in critical publications or reviews, no part of this book may be reproduced in any manner without prior written permission from the publisher. Write: Permissions, Wipf and Stock Publishers, 199 W. 8th Ave., Suite 3, Eugene, OR 97401.

Resource Publications
An Imprint of Wipf and Stock Publishers
199 W. 8th Ave., Suite 3
Eugene, OR 97401

www.wipfandstock.com

PAPERBACK ISBN: 978-1-5326-5404-6
HARDCOVER ISBN: 978-1-5326-5405-3
EBOOK ISBN: 978-1-5326-5406-0

Manufactured in the U.S.A. 05/07/20

For Daniel, Timothy, and Esther

Contents

Acknowledgements — ix
Abbreviations of Augustine's Writings — x
Chronological Table: Confucius, Mencius, and Augustine in History — xv

1. **How to Acquire Virtues for Happiness** — 1
2. **Xue (學) and Moral Learning** — 35
3. **Si (思) and Contemplation** — 106
4. **Li (禮) and Sacrament** — 144
5. **Yue (樂) and Music** — 197
6. **Confucian Augustinianism** — 215

Bibliography — 231
Index — 241

Acknowledgements

THIS BOOK HAS BEEN developed from my PhD thesis submitted to the University of Edinburgh in Scotland. Above all, I would like to express my deepest gratitude for my supervisor, the Reverend Prof. Michael S. Northcott. His enthusiastic academic guidance, friendship, and patience reshaped me as a Christian ethicist. I am also indebted to his wife, Jill. Their love and support were a kind of family project.

I would like to say a very special thanks to St Michael's Parish Church of Scotland in Linlithgow, which gave me a great privilege to serve as assistant minister and to live in a historic manse close to Linlithgow Palace during my PhD. Following the doctorate and ministry in Scotland, I was inducted as Minister at St Andrew's United Reformed Church in Balham, London with vision being to enjoy God, follow Jesus, and live in the Holy Spirit.

I wish to acknowledge the institutions that helped make it financially feasible for me to undertake this project: the University of Edinburgh New College School of Divinity, the Catholic Foundation of Scotland, Kampen Theological University, and the Drummond Trust.

Finally, I am grateful to my lovely wife Bora and three young children: Daniel, Timothy, and Esther. As God's gifts they make my journey searching for truth happy. I hope this book will be a navigation for achievement of eternal happiness to my children, to whom this book is dedicated.

Thanks God!

JunSoo Park
St Andrew's Manse
London

Abbreviations of Augustine's Writings

IN ADDITION TO THE following, all abbreviations in this book are taken from: Allan d. Fitzgerald, *Augustine through the Ages* (Cambridge: Wm. B. Eerdmans Publishing Company, 2009). I have referred to Augustine's writings by abbreviated Latin in the notes. The following list is by chronological order in Augustine's works.

Abbreviations	Latin Titles	English Titles	Date
c. Acad.	Contra Academicos	Against the Skeptics	386
b. vita.	De beata vita	On the Happy Life	386
ord.	De ordine	On Order	386
sol.	Soliloquia	The Soliloquies	386/7
imm. an.	De immortalitate animae	On the Immortality of the Soul	386/7
mus.	De musica	On Music	387/391
mor.	De moribus ecclesiae catholicae et de moribus Manichaeorum	On the Catholic and the Manichaean Ways of Life	387/389
quant.	De animae quantitate	On the Greatness of the Soul	388/9
Gn. adv. Man.	De Genesis adversus Manichaeos	On Genesis, Against the Man	388/9

x

Abbreviations of Augustine's Writings

Abbreviations	Latin Titles	English Titles	Date
lib. arb.	*De libero arbitrio*	On Free Will	388–395
div. qu.	*De diversis questionibus octoginta tribus*	Eighty-Three Different Questions	388/395
mag.	*De magistro*	The Teacher	389
vera rel.	*De vera religione*	On True Religion	389/391
util. cred.	*De utilitate credendi*	On the Advantage of Believing	391
duab. an.	*De duabus animabus contra Manichaeos*	On the Two Souls, Against the Manichees	392/3
f. et symb.	*De fide et symbolo*	On Faith and the Creed	393
Gn. litt. imp.	*De Genesi ad littaram, imperfectus liber*	On the literal interpretation of Genesis, an Unfinished Book	393/4
s. Dom. mon.	*De sermone Domini in monte*	On the Sermon on the Mount	393/4
ex. Gal.	*Epistulae ad Galatas expositio*	Explanation: Epistle to the Galatians	394/5
ep. Rm. inch.	*Epistulae ad Romanos expositio inchoata*	Explanation: Epistle to the Romans	394/5
cont.	*De continentia*	On Continence	395
mend.	*De mendacio*	On Lying	395
Simpl.	*Ad Simplicianum*	To Simplicianus	396
agon.	*De agone christiano*	On the Christian Struggle	396
doc. Chr.	*De doctrina Christiana*	On the Christian Doctrine	396–426

Abbreviations of Augustine's Writings

Abbreviations	Latin Titles	English Titles	Date
en. Ps.	Enarrationes in Psalmos	Expositions on the Psalms	396–420
conf.	Confessiones	Confessions	397–401
c. Faust.	Contra Faustum Manichaeum	Against Faustus the Manichee	397–98
nat. b.	De natura boni	On the Nature of the Good	399
Trin.	De trinitate	On the Trinity	399–419
f. invis.	De fide rerum invisibilium	On Faith in the Unseen	400
op. mon.	De opere monachorum	On the Works of Monks	400
cat. rud.	De catechizandis rudibus	On catechizing Beginners	400
bapt.	De baptismo	On Baptism against the Donatists	400
b. conjug.	De bono coniugale	On the Good of Marriage	401
virg.	De sancta virginate	On Holy Virginity	401
Gn. Litt	De Genesi ad litteram	On the Literal Interpretation of Genesis	401–415
Jo. ev. tr.	In Johannis evangelium tractatus	Tractates on the Gospel of John	406–430
ep. Jo.	Tractatus in epistulam Ioannis ad Parthos	Tractates on the First Epistle of John	406–430
exc. urb.	De excidio urbis Romae	On the Sack of the City of Rome	410

Abbreviations of Augustine's Writings

Abbreviations	Latin Titles	English Titles	Date
un. bapt.	*De unico baptism contra Petilianum*	Concerning the One Baptism, Against Petilian	411
pecc. mer.	*De peccatorum meritis et remissione et de baptism parvulorum*	On the Merits and Forgiveness of Sins and on infant Baptism	412
f. et op.	*De fide et operibus*	On faith and Works	412/13
spir. et litt.	*De spiritu et littera*	On the Spirit and the Letter	412
civ. Dei.	*De civitate Dei*	City of God	413–27
nat. et gr.	*De natura et gratia*	On Nature and Grace	414/15
b. vid.	*De bono viduitatis*	On the Good of Widowhood	414
gr. et pecc. or.	*De gratia Christi et de peccato originali*	On the Grace of Christ and Original Sin	418
pat.	*De patientia*	On Patience	418
nupt. et conc.	*De nuptiis et concupiscentia*	On Marriage and Concupiscence	419/20
adul. conjug.	*De coniugiis adulterinis*	On Adulterous Marriage	419/20
an. et or.	*De anima et eius origine*	On the Soul and its Origin	419–421
cura mort.	*De cura pro mortuis gerenda*	On the Care of the Dead	420–422
c. Jul.	*Contra Julianum*	Against Julian	421
ench.	*Enchiridion ad Laurentium de fide spe et caritate*	A handbook on Faith, Hope, and Love	421–422

Abbreviations of Augustine's Writings

Abbreviations	Latin Titles	English Titles	Date
gr. et lib. arb.	De gratia et libero arbitrio	On Grace and Free Choice	426/27
retr.	Retractationes	Retractions	426/27
haer.	De haeresibus	On Heresies	428/29
c. Jul. imp.	Contra secundam Juliani: responsionem opus imperfectum	Incomplete Work Against Julian	429–430
ep.	Epistulae	Letters	386–429
s.	Sermones	Sermons	393–430
util. jejun.	De utilitate Jejunii	On the Usefulness of Fasting	429/430

Chronological Table: Confucius, Mencius, and Augustine in History[1]

c. Before 2070 BC	Legendary ages of the Sage-Kings such as Yao, Shun, and Yu
c. 2070–1600 BC	Legendary Xi Dynasty—Jie, the last king, a condemned tyrant
c. 1600–1045 BC	Shang or Yin Dynasty—Tang, the founding father of Zhou, the last king, a condemned tyrant
c. 1046–771 BC	Western Zhou—succeeding the Shang, the Zhou people adopted and then modified Shang practices in ancestor worship, patrilineal succession, bone divination, and social stratification. 'Ritual revolution' took place in 9th century.
770–256 BC	Eastern Zhou—the Zhou court is significantly weakened and China becomes a land of contending small states run by hegemons who nominally pledge loyalty to the Zhou court but are guided by self-interest and opportunism to increase their territory. It is also a period of great intellectual activity known for the 'Hundred Schools of Thought', a name for the numerous political, social, and cosmological theories that proliferated during this period.

1. Joachim Gentz, *Understanding Chinese Religions* (Edinburgh: Dunedin, 2013), ix; Xinzhong Yao, *An Introduction to Confucianism* (Cambridge: Cambridge University Press, 2000), xiv-xvi; Peter Brown, *Augustine of Hippo: A Biography*, Rev. ed. (Berkeley and Los Angeles: University of California Press, 2000), 3, 64, 178, 380.

770–476 BC	Spring and Autumn Period, a further division of the Eastern Zhou period; the name derives from *The Spring and Autumn Annals*, a chronicle of events in the state of Lu sometimes ascribed to Confucius.

551 ca. BC—birth of Confucius at Mount Ni, located southeast of Qufu in Lu state (in present-day Shandong province)

549 ca. BC—when Confucius is three years old, his father dies.

535 ca. BC—Confucius' mother dies when he is the age of 16 or 17 (other sources give this date as 527 BC, when he was 23 or 24 years old).

533 ca. BC—at the age of 19, Confucius marries a woman from the Qiguan family of the Song state. Around this time, he gained employment as manager of the state granary

532 ca. BC—birth of Confucius' son who is named Li after Duke Zhao of Lu sent a carp as a gift. Around this time Confucius was promoted to state husbandry manager.

522 ca. BC—around this time Confucius starts a private school and began to teach.

518 ca. BC—Confucius accepts Meng Yizi and Nangong Jinshu as disciples; Jinshu arranges for Confucius to travel to Luoyang, the Zhou capital, where he is attributed as meeting Laozi.

514 ca. BC—after conflict breaks out in Lu state, Confucius is forced to relocate briefly to the state of Qi.

516 ca. BC—Confucius returns to Lu.

501 ca. BC—Confucius became the chief magistrate of Zhongdu, present-day Wenshang county in Shandong Province.

500 ca. BC—Confucius becomes minister of justice and distinguishes himself at the conference between Lu and Qi at Jiagu.

497 ca. BC—Confucius leaves the state of Lu and heads east to Wei state, beginning his sojourns in several states to promote his ideas.

484 ca. BC—Confucius returned to his hometown, Qufu, in the state of Lu and focused on teaching and studying the Rites of Zhou.

479 ca. BC—death of Confucius at the age of 72 or 73. |

Chronological Table: Confucius, Mencius, and Augustine in History   xvii

475–221 BC	Warring States Period, a further layer of periodisation within the Eastern Zhou Dynasty marked by large-scale intense warfare made possible by administrative reforms designed to maximize individual states' ability to raise armies. During this period, Mencius and Xunzi lived. 372 ca. BC—Mencius was born. 324 ca. BC—Mencius moved from Ch'i. 319 ca. BC—Mencius returned from Liang. 319–312 ca. BC—Mencius became a scholar at the Jixia Academy. 312 ca. BC—Mencius Moved to Tsou. 289 ca. BC—Mencius died.
221–207 BC	Qin Dynasty—burning of books and the killing of Confucian scholars
206 BC–220 AD	Han Dynasty—Confucianism became the state orthodoxy Classics annotated Grand Academy established Old Text School; Confucianism was introduced to Vietnam, Korea. Indian Buddhism was introduced to China and interacted with Confucianism.
220–420	Wei-Jin Dynasties—Daoist Religion incorporated Confucian ethics.
386–581	Southern and Northern Dynasties—Buddhism flourished and debates between Confucianism and Buddhism intensified.
581–907	Sui-Tang Dynasties—Confucianism gradually regained its prestige; civil service examination system established; Nestorians came to China (635); Korean Silla Kingdom established Confucian Studies.

354–373	Augustine's Early Life

354—Augustine was born on 13 November in Thagaste in the province of Numidia in North Africa (today Souk Ahras in Algeria). He was the son of a pagan father, Patricius, and a Berber Christian mother, Monica. The family, which included two brothers and a sister, was respectable but somewhat impoverished.

354–365—the infancy and early schooling of Augustine in the local school.

366—Augustine's education continued at Madaura, a centre of education in Roman North Africa twenty miles south of Thagaste, where he was sent to study rhetoric at age twelve.

370—Augustine had to return home for a year while Patricius saved money for his further education. A year of idleness led the adolescent student into acts of dissipation and sexual adventure.

371—Augustine went to Carthage for first time to study.

372—Augustine's father died, baptised a Christian on his deathbed. He took a concubine.

373—Reading of *Hortensius*. Augustine's unnamed lover bore him a son, Adeodatus, "God-given." |
| 374–383 | Augustine's Teaching Career

374—Augustine returned home to Thagaste to teach grammar, the underlying foundation for the study of rhetoric. Monica, appalled at his alliance with the heretical Manichees, at first refused to allow him to enter her house. She prayed unceasingly for his conversion to the Catholic Church.

376—Augustine returned to Carthage following the death of a dear friend in Thagaste.

383—Augustine sailed for Rome to teach rhetoric. |

Chronological Table: Confucius, Mencius, and Augustine in History xix

384–390	Augustine's Conversion 384—Augustine moved to Milan and took up study of the Neoplatonists, especially Plotinus (205–270 CE). He was appointed as Professor of Rhetoric in Milan. He decided to become a catechumen in the Catholic Church of Milan after being impressed by the sermons of Bishop Ambrose. 385—Monica arrived in Milan. 386—Conversion (end of August) and going to Cassiciacum (September) 387—Returned to Milan (early March), Baptism, Vision of Ostia, Death of Monica 390—Death of Adeodatus and Nebridius
391–430	Bishop of Hippo 391—Arrived in Hippo to found monastery and ordained priest. 394—Augustine began combating Donatists for next eight years. 395—Augustine was consecrated as successor to Bishop Valerius. 396—Bishop Valerius died and Augustine succeeded him as Bishop of Hippo. He remained in this office until his own death in 430. 410—Conflict with Pelagius. 418—The Council of Carthage, with over two hundred bishops under Augustine's leadership, pronounced Pelagianism heretical. 430—Death and burial of Augustine on 28 August.

1

How to Acquire Virtues for Happiness

PURPOSE OF THIS STUDY

IN THIS BOOK, I compare the works of Confucius and Mencius with Saint Augustine. My purpose in so doing is to show Confucian Augustinianism as a new theological angle on Confucian-Christian ethics and modern Augustinianism such as Augustinian realism, Augustinian proceduralism, Augustinian civic liberalism, and Radical Orthodoxy by discovering analogies and differences in their respective understandings of character formation, and the development of moral virtues which lead to happiness.

There are excellent reasons for conducting such a comparative cross-cultural study of Confucius, Mencius, and Augustine. Above all, they not only highly influenced Chinese and Western culture respectively but also are of mutual influence in East Asia. It is persuasive that Confucius, Mencius, and Augustine have been regarded as key sources of ethics in the cultures of East and West given that their ethical thoughts have greatly influenced Confucianism and Western Christianity. Zhao demonstrates that "Confucianism is the mainstream of Chinese culture and Christianity is the cornerstone of Western culture. Chinese culture cannot be understood without understanding Confucianism, and nor can the Western spirit be interpreted without interpreting the spirit of Christianity."[1] Confucianism is an ethical religious tradition that has shaped the culture of China for 2,500 years, following which its influence subsequently spread to Korea, Japan and Vietnam.[2] Particularly, in the process of Confucian-

1. Yanxia Zhao, *Father and Son in Confucianism and Christianity: A Comparative Study of Xunzi and Paul* (Brighton: Sussex Academic Press, 2007), 7.
2. Ibid., 8.

ism's development Mencius has played a distinctive role in that "while Confucius laid the solid groundwork for Confucianism, Mencius clearly defined the principles, penetrated into their meanings more profoundly, and built a more comprehensive system."[3] Furthermore, the thinking of Confucius and Mencius has been regarded as orthodox in China, Korea, and Japan. Although still not directly visible in the social consciousness of modern Koreans and Japanese, it still profoundly shapes primary family life experiences. Thus, while the position of Confucianism in modern Chinese society has been challenged greatly since the Cultural Revolution, its influence is still profound, especially since the recovery of Chinese traditional culture from the end of the 1980s.[4] Therefore, the study of Confucianism, for Chinese Studies, has not only historical significance, but also modern relevance. Furthermore, Confucianism is a living tradition in a pluralistic global context in that the Confucian tradition becomes a heritage for the whole of humankind by the globalization of Confucianism in the appearance of Boston Confucianism represented by Robert Neville and John Berthrong. Confucianism is no longer a tradition restricted to the 'Sinitic', 'East Asian', or 'oriental' world as the sole possession of the ethnic Chinese.[5]

The relationship of Christianity and Western culture is a very close one and Christianity is now a major influence in Asian cultures, both within mainland China, and even more so in nations such as South Korea, Singapore and Taiwan which have significant influence from Confucianism.[6] In the West before the Enlightenment everything including science and philosophy was the 'maid' and 'servant' of Christian practice. Although the status of human rationality and reason greatly increased as a result of the Enlightenment, the ingrained influence of Christianity on Western society remains very strong.[7] It is noteworthy that Augustine has had a profound influence in the process of Christianity's development within Western civilization. For many centuries, from the Middle Ages to the present, as Drober depicts, Augustine has remained the most prominent and most widely studied author in western Christianity, second only

---

3. Carsun Chang, "The Significance of Mencius," *Philosophy East and West* 8, no. 1/2 (1958), 37.

4. Zhao, *Father and Son in Confucianism and Christianity*, 8.

5. Pan-Chiu Lai, "Chinese Culture and the Development of Chinese Christian Theology," *Studies in World Christianity* 7, no. 2 (2001), 234.

6. Zhao, *Father and Son in Confucianism and Christianity*, 8.

7. Ibid., 8.

to biblical writers such as Paul.[8] The roots of this extraordinary phenomenon go back to Augustine's own lifetime and are in part due to the fact that he did not produce the most immense literary corpus of all western Christianity for solely academic purposes.[9] Already, a good number of his contemporaries considered him to be both the most accomplished theologian and the most trustworthy pastor of their times.[10] These appreciations of Augustine's person and works have continued unabated for the last 1600 years. Considering the rapid growth of urban Chinese intellectuals converting to Protestantism formed by the Neoplatonic worldview of Augustine,[11] Confucian and Augustinian reasoning is necessary in the context of the Chinese church to engage religious dialogues and tackle public issues.[12]

According to Biggar, "recent Christian ethics has tended to present us with a choice between two options: either a conservative biblical and theological seriousness, which is shy of attending too closely to public policy; or liberal engagement with public policy, which is theologically thin and bland."[13] In contemporary American theological thought, there are two prominent schools: postliberalism and revisionism.[14] The term postliberalsim has been widely linked with the works of George Lindbeck, Ronald Thiemann, and various other representatives of the Yale School. Strongly influenced by nonfoundationalist thinkers such as Quine, Sellars, Geertz, and Wittgenstein, postliberals accept the position that we are largely determined by particular cultural-linguistic societies. The result of this kind of nonfoundationalism is the rejection of universals of any kind. In contrast, revisionist theology, widely associated with David Tracy and various other thinkers of the Chicago school, suggests all theological

8. Hubertus R. Drober, "Studying Augustine: an overview of recent research," in *Augustine and His Critics: Essays in Honor of Gerald Bonner*, ed. Robert Dodaro and George Lawless (London: Routledge, 2000), 18.

9. Drober, "Studying Augustine," 18.

10. Ibid., 19.

11. Alexander Chow, *Theosis, Sino-Christian Theology and the Second Chinese Enlightenment* (New York: Palgrave Macmillan, 2013), 170; Alexander Chow, "The East Asian Rediscovery of Sin," *Studies in World Christianity* 19, no. 2 (2013), 137.

12. Alexander Chow, "Calvinist Public Theology in Urban China Today," *International Journal of Public Theology* 8 (2014), 158.

13. Nigel Biggar, *Behaving in Public: How to do Christian Ethics* (Grand Rapids: W. B. Eerdmans Publishing Company, 2011), xvii.

14. Thomas Guarino, "Postmodernity and Five Fundamental Theological Issues," *Theological Studies* 57, no. 4 (1996), 680-82.

validity claims must have public attestation on the basis of Habermasian terms in their desire to justify theology in the educational marketplace, to establish the discipline as a legitimate academic and therefore public enterprise. Revisionism speaks of intertextuality, of a mutually critical correlation between Christian theology and other disciplines. Considering these extremes, Confucian and Augustinian reasoning could offer a middle way in the dimension of acquiring virtue rather than Heaven. Huang shows three models of Confucian theology according to understanding of Heaven in the Confucian tradition. In the Confucian classics *Book of Documents*, *Books of Poetry*, and *Analects*, Heaven is regarded as something transcendent of the world, similar to our Christian God. For Neo-Confucians, Heaven is the wonderful life-giving activity transcending the world within the world. For contemporary Confucians such as Xiong Shili, Mou Zongsan, and Tu Weiming, Heaven is something "immanently transcendent", the ultimate reality immanent in the world to transcend the world.[15] Contrary to Confucian theology on the understanding of Heaven, this intertextual reading having rich traditions, as Sebastian Kim demonstrates, offers theological implications in public spheres as an important part of indigenisation and doing theology in a multi-religious society.[16]

Furthermore, classical Confucians and Augustine have become more and more significant more in that their virtue ethics could be a radical alternative to that of the Aristotelian and Thomistic paradigms.[17] The revival of virtue ethics was prompted by Anscombe's article Modern Moral Philosophy in 1958.[18] In this article, she claims virtue can be a major alternative to utilitarian and Kantian ethics.[19] She points out that "anyone who has read Aristotle's *Ethics* and has also read modern moral philosophy must have been struck by the great contrasts between them."[20] She presents Aristotle as the role model of virtue ethics. This revival was

---

15. Yong Huang, "Confucian Theology: Three Models," *Religion Compass* 1, no. 4 (2007), 455.

16. Sebastian Kim, *Theology in the Public Sphere: Public Theology as a Catalyst for Open Debate* (London: SCM Press, 2011), 50.

17. Yao, *An Introduction to Confucianism*, 33.

18. Roger Crisp and Michael A. Slote, *Virtue Ethics* (Oxford: Oxford University Press, 1997), 3.

19. G. E. M. Anscombe, "Modern Moral Philosophy," in *Virtue Ethics*, ed. Roger Crisp and Michael Slote (Oxford: Oxford University Press, 1997), 44.

20. Ibid., 26.

further advanced by Alasdair MacIntyre who regards Thomistic virtue ethics as ideal.[21] The most significant point is that they proposed Aristotelian and Thomistic ethics as an ideal alternative to utilitarian and deontological theories. However, Aristotelian and Thomistic paradigms in the discussion of virtue ethics have been expanded into Chinese philosophy, particularly Confucianism, by mainstream philosophers such as Martha Nussbaum, Alasdair MacIntyre, and David Wong.[22] Moral instruction and ethical persuasion employed by Confucius and Mencius are even said to be able to provide a radical alternative to the Aristotelian and Thomistic paradigms.[23] The significance of moral formation of self, which is neglected in mainstream Kantian and Utilitarian ethics has been growing in the re-emergence of virtue ethics since Anscombe.[24]

Confucian Augustinianism could be a new type of Augustinianism as a middle way between the types of modern Augustinian liberalism and Radical Orthodoxy. According to Eric Gregory, there are four types in relation to modern Augustinian liberalism in the twentieth century.[25] The first type of modern Augustinianism is Augustinian realism.[26] Augustinian realists such as Reinhold Niebuhr and Robert Markus reconstructed Augustine's controversial doctrine of original sin and his dramatic narrative about two cities in order to temper the enthusiasm of democratic optimism and to support something like the secular order of liberalism. Given that Augustine's two cities exist in this present world mixed together,[27] Augustinianism tends to contrast secular with eternal rather than with sacred. Between World War I and the end of the Cold War, Augustinian realism was closely allied with another kind of realism indebted to Machiavelli and Weber. Its principal spokesperson in American politics was the Protestant theologian Reinhold Niebuhr. In Niebuhr's

---

21. Yuli Liu, *The Unity of Rule and Virtue: A Critique of a Supposed Parallel between Confucian Ethics and Virtue Ethics* (Singapore: Eastern Universities Press, 2004), 11.

22. David S. Nivison, *The Ways of Confucianism: Investigations in Chinese Philosophy* (Chicago: Open Court, 1996), 2.

23. Xinzhong Yao, *Confucianism and Christianity: A Comparative Study of Jen and Agape* (Brighton: Sussex Academic Press, 1996), 33.

24. Anh Tuan Nuyen, 'Can Morality Be Taught? Aquinas and Mencius on Moral Education,' in *Aquinas, Education and the East*, ed. Thomas Brian Mooney and Mark Nowacki (New York: Springer, 2013), 107.

25. Eric Gregory, *Politics and the Order of Love: An Augustinian Ethic of Democratic Citizenship* (Chicago: The University of Chicago Press, 2008), 1-2.

26. Gregory, *Politics and the Order of Love*, 10-11.

27. *civ. Dei.* 2.1.

version of politics, the central fact of human nature this side of the Eschaton is sin, and it is the purpose of government, not to eliminate sin, but to constrain or ameliorate its bad effects by passing laws. The background of Augustinian realism is a rough world threatened by fascism and Marxism and the failure of responses to these ideologies. Liberal democracy is the least bad form of government because it recognizes government's limited, sin-constraining role. In defending it, we need a realistic understanding of human nature and a willingness to use force and the threat of force in the interest of maintaining order and approximating justice. Sentimental attempts to drive a social ethic from the gospel commandment of love are dangerous. Augustinian realists offer a limited conception of politics as restraining evil, a conception that often travels with a troubling form of moral consequentialism. The second type of modern Augustinianism is Augustinian proceduralism which emerges in positive response to the massive influence of John Rawls' theory of "justice as fairness" in 1970s and 1980s.[28] With the Niebuhrian emphasis on sin this stresses the significance of fairness as a political virtue for a liberal society marked by conditions of pluralism. Augustinian proceduralists allow more positive political ideals, but themselves offer a minimalist conception of justice which privatizes important virtues such as friendship and compassion. The third type of modern Augustinianism is Augustinian civic liberalism emerged in 1990s by Jean Bethke Elshtain, Timothy P. Jackson, Rowan Williams, and Oliver O'Donovan on the roots of Paul Tillich, Martin Luther King Jr, Paul Ramsey, and Gustavo Gutierrez.[29] Augustinian civic liberalism emphasises love and civic responsibility.[30] Love of God and neighbour can play a central role in an Augustinian social vision. Instead of offering a new type of Augustinianism, Gregory just defends Augustinian civic liberalism by constituting a response both to critics of Augustine who defend liberal democracy (such as Hannah Arendt, Paul Ramsey, Martha Nussbaum, Robert M. Adams, and Timothy P. Jackson) and to fans of Augustine who attack liberal democracy (such as Alisdair MacIntyre, Stanley Hauerwas, Robert Kraynak, and John Milbank).[31] Civic liberalism is a virtue-oriented liberalism that aims to avoid individualistic and rationalistic assumptions about human nature as well as romantic or

---

28. Gregory, *Politics and the Order of Love*, 12.
29. Ibid., 12.
30. *civ. Dei.* 19.24.
31. Gregory, *Politics and the Order of Love*, 2.

totalitarian conceptions of political community.[32] This relies on a virtue-oriented rather than merely sin-oriented Augustinian politics.[33] Civic liberalism corresponds to liberal perfectionism in contemporary political philosophy. In political theory, liberal perfectionists include Joseph Raz, Vinit Haksar, Thomas Hurka, George Sher, and John Finnis. Civic liberals and liberal perfectionists allow ideal conceptions of human flourishing into the full light of the public square, conceptions that already shape practical deliberations of public decision-making and normatively evaluate the effects of liberal justice.[34] The fourth type of modern Augustinianism is antiliberal theology known as Radical Orthodoxy, which was launched by Cambridge theologians John Milbank, Catherine Pickstock and Graham Ward in 1999.[35] It can be called Augustinian Orthodoxy in that it highlights the use of a reading of St Augustine with the insights of postmodernism. John Milbank is the central figure associated with Radical Orthodoxy that emerged out of Anglican social thought (especially Christian socialism) as an intellectual, cultural, and ecumenical movement in the late 1980s. Radical Orthodoxy seeks to transcend liberal Protestant theology, conservative politics of free market capitalism, and liberal politics of welfare bureaucracy.[36] Returning to Neoplatonic and Augustinian texts, Radical Orthodoxy criticizes modern secularism and Kantian account of metaphysics by demonstrating the insufficiency of any account of reality that excluded religion or theology. Culture, participation, gift, liturgy, erotic desire and the body are key themes.[37] Radical Orthodoxy considers theology the queen of the sciences. Milbank places love at the center of his political Augustinianism whereas Stanley Hauerwas emphasizes patience.[38] Each type of modern Augustinianism stresses

---

32. Ibid., 10.

33. Ibid., 14.

34. Ibid., 10.

35. John Milbank, Catherine Pickstock, and Graham Ward, "Introduction: Suspending the Material: The Turn of Radical Orthodoxy," in *Radical Orthodoxy: A New Theology*, ed. John Milbank, Catherine Pickstock, and Graham Ward (London: Routledge, 1999), 2.

36. Gregory, *Politics and the Order of Love*, 125.

37. David Grumett, "Radical Orthodoxy," *The Expository Times* 122, no. 6 (2011), 261.

38. John Milbank, *The Future of Love: Essays in Political Theology* (Eugene: Cascade Book, 2009).

a distinct virtue: realists emphasize hope, proceduralists highlight justice, and civic liberals stress love.[39]

In particular, comparative study on the formation of moral self in Confucius, Mencius and Augustine has never been produced since previous research on their formation of moral self respectively has remained fragmented. In *Mencius and Aquinas*, for example, Yearley offers Mencius and Aquinas' theories of virtue, but he has nothing to say on their views on the acquisition of virtue by forming moral self.[40] In terms of Augustine's formation of moral self, in *Putting on Virtue*, Herdt deals with virtue's acquisition only within the Christian tradition. This indicates that it is high time that research on Confucius, Mencius and Augustine's formation of moral self be undertaken in the dimension of comparative ethics since comparative efforts can "lead to deeper understanding of the compared thinkers and perhaps to a re-assessment of the common readings of their thoughts."[41]

CHAPTER OVERVIEW

In this book, I deal with the formation of the virtuous self as described in the major texts of Confucius, Mencius and Augustine. This book is divided into six chapters. In the chapter 1, I outline the project, and position it in the scholarly literature on comparative virtue ethics as well as the formation of moral self of Confucius, Mencius, and Augustine. And then I describe inter-textual reasoning as the research methods according to the hermeneutics of Gadamer. From the chapter 2 to 5, I compare Confucius and Mencius' *xue* (學), *si* (思), *li* (禮), and *yue* (樂) with Augustine's moral learning, contemplation, sacrament, and music. In the chapter 6, I show Confucian Augustinianism as a new theological perspective on Confucian-Christian ethics and Augustinianism in the light of this research.

---

39. Gregory, *Politics and the Order of Love*, 2.

40. Nuyen, 'Can Morality Be Taught? Aquinas and Mencius on Moral Education,' 107.

41. Ibid., 107.

TYPES OF CONFUCIAN-CHRISTIAN DIALOGUES

In this book, I compare the theoretical descriptions of the formation of the moral self, the acquisition of the virtues, and virtuous practices in Confucius, Mencius and Augustine. Although no systematic study directly on the topic of the comparison between classical Confucians and Augustine's teachings on the formation of moral self is available, some relevant research has already been undertaken by both Chinese and Western scholars. Their works can be categorized into three types: the first is Ricci's missiological apologetics and a conceptual bridge, the second contribution can be found in Ching's theological approach and New-Confucianism, and the last is Yearley's academic approach and its influences.

Ricci's Missiological Apologetics and a Conceptual Bridge

In terms of the comparison of Confucianism and Christianity there are three kinds of approaches: missiological apologetics, theological, and academic. The first approach was exemplified by the Jesuit missionary to China, Matteo Ricci. Although many missionaries have historically attempted to introduce different forms of Christianity to China, Roman Catholic missionaries such as Ricci who entered China, and engaged Confucianism in the sixteenth century, are regarded as a significant starting point of comparing between Confucian and Christian thoughts.[42] In a long fresco of a monument built by the Chinese government at the beginning of the twenty-first century in order to celebrate individuals who have made significant contributions to the progress of civilization during the several thousand years of Chinese history only two Westerners are represented: Marco Polo (1254-1324) and Matteo Ricci (1552-1610).

---

42. "The history of these comparisons, whether seen from the Chinese or the Western sides, often tells us more about the people doing the comparisons than about the civilizations being compared, however. Both the foreign and the familiar civilization can resemble chameleons: they assume a protective coloration to meet the threats posed by a strange and potentially hostile environment. For example, the West often has fluctuated between excessive praise of China and excessive condemnation of it. Enlightenment thinkers often saw in China the rational, areligious society that they hoped to create in the West, while nineteenth century missionaries often saw in China a backward and heathen society that they hoped to cure by introducing Western ideas and religion." Lee H. Yearley, "A Comparison between Classical Chinese Thought and Thomistic Christian Thought," *Journal of the American Academy of Religion* 51, no. 3 (1983), 427.

Ricci is mentioned in the fresco as "the promoter of cultural exchanges."[43] Ricci is rightly considered the earliest known European to have discovered Confucianism. But long before Jesuits could have dreamt of going to China, other Christian missionaries from the West had preceded them. As Nestorian Monument in Chinese and Syriac in 781 shows, Nestorians monks from the west had found their way to Ch'ang-an, capital of the T'ang dynasty from the seventh century, but these few travelers could not exert much influence on Chinese culture or society due to Buddhism that had already experienced several centuries of integration in Chinese culture.[44] In the thirteenth century, furthermore, the Franciscan friars came to Mongol China, but they not only lived there for a shorter period than the Nestorians, but also did not pay much attention to Confucianism as a Chinese religion or philosophy.[45] The lay Roman Catholic Marco Polo, who stirred Europe with accounts of his experiences in Mongol China, described the Chinese as pagans.[46] Europe, hence, did not seem to know of Confucianism until the seventeenth century, until the reports and writings of the Jesuit missionaries. The Jesuits commended cultural accommodation as the missionary method for attempting to introduce Christianity to China. Hence Ricci as "the founder of Western sinology" translated extensive parts of Confucius' *Four Books* into Latin. Ricci also developed the first system for Romanizing Chinese, and he tested the effectiveness of his work as teaching materials on newly arrived European Jesuits.[47] He served as a bridge between two different cultures on the basis of the Confucian classics.

The Jesuit mission to China in the late sixteenth and seventeenth centuries represented the first significant intellectual encounter between Chinese thought and religion and Western Christianity.[48] In the nineteenth and twentieth centuries, Protestant missionaries, in part because of their extensive charitable works such as hospitals and schools, and in part because of the extent of European colonial and trade interventions

---

43. Jean-Paul Wiest, "Matteo Ricci: Pioneer of Chinese-Western Dialogue and Cultural Exchanges," *International Bulletin of Missionary Research* 36, no. 1 (2012), 17.

44. Michael Loewe, "Imperial China's Reactions to the Catholic Missions," *Numen* 35, no. 2 (1988), 179.

45. Julia Ching, *Confucianism and Christianity: A Comparative Study* (Tokyo: Kodansha International in cooperation with the Institute of Oriental Religions, 1977), 13.

46. Ching, *Confucianism and Christianity*, 13.

47. Wiest, "Matteo Ricci," 18.

48. Loewe, "Imperial China's Reactions to the Catholic Missions," 181.

in mainland China, brought an even more forceful impact to bear on the majority of the Chinese population than had been felt in the earlier stages.[49] Yet, Protestant missionaries as non-conformists did not produce more fruitful works than Ricci in the aspect of East-West cultural exchange. Ricci was respectful of Chinese culture, many of those who came after were not, and especially not the British.[50] Arguably this was because of the toxic effects of European and especially British trade practices in China and the Opium Wars of of 1839-1842 with England and 1858-1860 with France. Even though the Opium Wars opened China's physical door to the West by gunboats and diplomatic pressure, the Chinese mind could not be opened by such methods.[51] The various treaty arrangements led to religious conflict. As the consequence of the treaties after 1860, the French state, as protector of foreign priests and Chinese Catholics, became frequently involved in so-called 'missionary cases' (*jiao'an* 教案) which was used in relation to anti-Christian agitation during the last four decades of the nineteenth century. For example, a popular movement labelled 'Boxer' managed an incursion near the provincial capital of Chengdu, notably Jintang, and included a brief penetration of Chengdu itself which resulted in the figure of 1,500 to 2,000 for the number of Catholics killed or missing in Sichuan in 1902.[52] While it can be argued that anti-missionary conflict was to some extent part of the growing resistance by the Chinese people to the increasing pressures exerted by the foreign powers, it should also be recognized that anti-Christian violence tended to be intimately linked to existing tensions within and among local systems.[53] Hundreds of major *jiao'an* were solved only after involvement of the foreign legations.

Scholars have asked why Ricci adopted cultural accommodation in his organization of the Jesuit mission to China. One theory is that before

49. Ibid., 181; Michael Greenberg, *British Trade and the Opening of China 1800-42* (Cambridge: Cambridge University Press, 1951), 104.

50. Ryan Dunch, "Beyond Cultural Imperialism: Cultural Theory, Christian missions, and Global Modernity," *History and Theory* 41, no. 3 (October 2002), 303.

51. Tang Edmond, "The Cosmic Christ: The Search for a Chinese Theology," *Studies in World Christianity* 1, no. 2 (1995), 132; Michael Northcott, "Christianity in Asia," in *International Encyclopedia of the Social & Behavioral Sciences*, 2nd, ed. James D. Wright (Amsterdam: Elsevier, 2015), 532.

52. Ernest P. Young, *Ecclesiastical Colony: China's Catholic Church and the French Religious Protectorate* (Oxford: Oxford University Press, 2013), 98.

53. R. G. Tiedemann (ed), *Handbook of Christianity in China*, vol. 2 (Leiden: Brill, 2009), 303.

arriving in China, Ricci stayed at Goa, the capital of the Portuguese Indies, until the spring of 1582. There he observed the ineffectiveness of Portuguese mission by military force. At that time Western missionaries believed in the superiority of European culture and attempted to impose their own cultural patterns. This attitude unfortunately endured among many until the middle of the twentieth century. During the sixteenth century, however, a few individual missionaries, most notably Bartolomé de Las Casas in South America, and Jesuit missionaries, including Ricci, in China and Japan, did acknowledge the richness of local cultures.[54] Impressed by the achievements in Japanese and Chinese literature, politics, and philosophy, Jesuit missionaries decided to make this culture the foundation of their missionary project. Valignano masterminded this new approach, which was based on the concept of a multi-polar world whose center was no longer Europe. Ricci and many of the early China Jesuits adopted pioneer Valignano's new model for the church's mission in Asia.[55] Thus, Ricci determined to win the respect of Chinese scholars and officials in intellectual terms in two ways. He set out to acquire a familiarity with those aspects of Chinese culture in which they had been professionally trained, so that he could bring references to traditional Chinese literature to bear in his arguments. At the same time, he strove to impress his Chinese friends with the achievements of the western intellect. Roland Allen argues that the accommodation of Christian culture to local cultures was the original missionary method of the Apostle Paul in his mission to the Gentiles. Paul attempted to accommodate the truth of Christianity to Hellenistic thinking in the cultural center of the Mediterranean world (*Acts* 17:16-34).[56] Ricci's approach to non-Christians on this account resembled that of the early Christian church. He went to China to spread the Catholic religion, but he carefully avoided the pitfalls of cultural confrontation.[57] Instead, he followed a policy of cultural accommodation in an effort to reconcile two disparate systems of faith and thought. Ricci was, as Wiest argues, "re-engaging with the theological

---

54. Wiest, "Matteo Ricci," 17.

55. Ibid., 17.

56. Roland Allen, *Missionary Methods: Paul's or Ours?* (Michigan: Wm. B. Eerdmans Publishing Company, 1956), 62. Clayton Croy, "Hellenistic Philosophies and the Preaching of the Resurrection (*Acts* 17:18, 32)," *Novum Testamentum* 39, no. 1 (1997), 21.

57. Wiest, "Matteo Ricci," 19.

tradition of the Greek Fathers, such as Clement of Alexandria, who brought the heritage of Homer and Plato to the service of Christian thought."[58]

While Ricci adopted Confucianism as a contact point with Christianity, he was less accommodating, though not wholly resistant, to Buddhism and Daoism. In late Ming society and government, Buddhism and Daoism penetrated deeply into the political as well as the everyday life of Ming people.[59] By the end of the fifteenth century, the total number of Buddhist and Daoist priests exceeded half a million, and there were more than a thousand Buddhist monasteries in Beijing, usually sponsored by eunuchs and court officials. Even Buddhism received some patronage by the Ming imperial court, and individual monks were able to exercise influence in court politics. Daoist priests were also put into high official positions in the government and were allied with the eunuchs. Daoism, which originated with the works of Master Lao-tze in the six century BC, put heavy emphasis on physical health and developed techniques for healing, meditation, increased fertility, and the seeking of longevity. In this religious background of late Ming, Ricci made the first efforts of missionary accommodation by dressing as a Buddhist bonze and using a vocabulary borrowed from Buddhism to teach the Christian Gospel, arriving at Macao, a Portuguese colony located on the southeast coast of China.[60] However, after Ricci was instructed by his Superior, Father Valignano, to receive language training, he soon gave up that outlook for two reasons. First, he realized that the Chinese treated them not as Christian missionaries but as monks from one of the Buddhist sects. Second, he discovered that government officials and prominent people looked down upon them because religious leaders were not a well-respected class in China.[61] From his perspective, the dominant value system was not Buddhism, but Confucianism. Besides, he devoted long years to the study of Chinese and of Confucian classics, and became persuaded that there was more compatibility between Christianity and Confucianism, particularly the early teachings of Confucius himself, with reverence for a supreme being and sublime moral exhortations.[62] The more Ricci studied

58. Ibid., 19.

59. Chung-Yan Joyce Chan, "Commands from Heaven: Matteo Ricci's Christianity in the Eyes of Ming Confucian Officials," *Missiology* 31, no. 3 (2003), 270-71.

60. Ching, *Confucianism and Christianity*, 14.

61. Chan, "Commands from Heaven," 273.

62. Ching, *Confucianism and Christianity*, 14.

the classical Chinese texts, the more he understood from Confucian teachings that, in ancient times, the Chinese were devoted worshippers of the Lord of Heaven, the equivalent of the Creator God in Christianity.[63] Therefore, he had to distinguish clearly for his readers what was right and wrong regarding the doctrine about God, the human body and soul, heaven and hell, and how Christian teachings differed from Buddhist and Daoist thought. Ricci regarded Buddhism and Daoism as false religions that led people astray from the true God. Ricci was determined to point out the errors of their teachings so that the Chinese would return to the true ancient religion. He realized that the most effective means of propagating his ideas among learned Chinese was through writing.

Ricci published *The True Meaning of the Lord of Heaven* (*Tianzhu shiyi* 天主實義) in Beijing in 1603. It is regarded as the first significant work on the history and theology of Chinese Christianity by a Catholic scholar, and in it Ricci uses a Chinese way of thinking to introduce Christianity to Chinese intellectuals (rather like Schleiermacher attempted in the eighteenth century in commending Christianity to German romantics in his *Speeches on Religion*).[64] He began the *True Meaning of the Lord of Heaven* with an intelligent analogy that captures the essence of Confucian philosophy, which also explains why God exists and why there can only be one true God. Throughout the book, quotations from Confucian classics are used as support and commentary for Ricci's presentation of the Christian doctrines. Ricci draws heavily upon Chinese literary and historical allusions, showing himself a sympathetic scholar of ancient and current Chinese texts, and able to use Chinese ways of argumentation. Ricci was aware of the tie between the Chinese religious system and its bureaucratic political structure based on the Confucian concept of the Mandate of Heaven and the five relationships. By making this analogy between the earthly ruler and the Ruler of heaven and earth, Ricci established common ground between Christianity and Confucian values.[65] As with Augustine's early works such as *Contra Academicos* and Confucius' *Analects*, the discourse takes the form of a dialogue. In order to show that most Chinese did not realize they had followed the erroneous doctrines of Buddhism and Daoism, and had departed from the true meaning of the ancient religious beliefs of Confucianism, some parts of

---

63. Chan, "Commands from Heaven," 274.
64. Wiest, "Matteo Ricci," 19.
65. Chan, "Commands from Heaven," 276.

The True Meaning of the Lord of Heaven focus on an anti-Buddhist and anti-Daoist polemic. Ricci refuted Lao-tzu's teaching of nothingness as the Way/Eternal principle and Buddha's teaching on void as the means to enlightenment. He argued that God is not an abstract principle or merely a cosmic force but a personal God who exhibits virtues, goodness, and character.[66] In particular, Ricci spent several sections of the text refuting what he argued were the false doctrines of Buddhism such as soul reincarnation, fasting and good works, and the concepts of heaven and hell. Arguing against the hierarchical understanding of soul, Ricci attacked the reincarnation doctrine. He argued that, since different creatures possess different souls that are not interchangeable, reincarnation is an impossible idea. The human soul is not extinguished and different from the souls of birds and beasts. Ricci then gave three more reasons why the idea of reincarnation was deceitful and superstitious: no one is able to remember their former lives; there is no evidence of soul transfer; and human abuse of animals shows that animals could not possibly be a human in a former life.[67]

Ricci used the original Confucian texts of Confucius and Mencius to refute the wrong beliefs in Buddhism and Daoism rather than Confucian writings in subsequent centuries.[68] Under the rapid spread of Daoism and the new doctrines of Buddhism in the beginning of the Sui (581-618) and Táng Dynasties (618-907), Confucian Learning lost its supremacy.[69] To overcome contemporary challenges, new generations of Confucian scholars produced Neo-Confucianism. In terms of the intensity of reform, the scholars of the Song-Ming Dynasties attempted to make more radical modifications in the classical Confucian teachings, whereas Tang Confucians such as Han Yu (768-824) took human nature as his starting point and attempted to establish the orthodox transmission of the Confucian tradition.[70] Neo-Confucianism was formed in an effort to systematically answer the questions raised by Buddhism and Daoism, so that it gave rise to "fundamental transformation of Confucian doctrines which thereby enabled Neo-Confucians to construct a comprehensive and complicated doctrinal system containing an evolutionary cosmology, a humanistic

---

66. Ibid., 274.
67. Matteo Ricci, *The True Meaning of the Lord of Heaven*, 5.2.
68. Ricci, *The True Meaning of the Lord of Heaven*, 5.7.
69. Yao, *Confucianism and Christianity*, 96.
70. Ibid., 96.

ethics and a rationalistic epistemology."[71] For instance, Zhu Xi and Wang Yang-ming's thoughts show how Buddhism and Daoism influenced to Neo-Confucianism. In order to compete with the ever-growing popular Buddhist and Daoist thought, Zhu Xi (1130-1200) incorporated the Buddhist idea of 'human nature' into Confucian ethics and developed a new interpretative framework for Confucianism that dominated the Chinese intellectual circle for more than four centuries.[72] Wang Yang-ming (1472-1529), the most influential Neo-Confucian scholar in the Ming Dynasty, incorporated the Buddhist and Daoist concepts of the "heavenly principle" and "true self" into his interpretation of Confucianism and suggested that when one clears away one's selfish desires, one will be able to attain the realization of perfect goodness, which is the ultimate revelation of the Absolute in self.[73] Hence, Ricci regards the doctrines of Zhu Xi and Wang Yang-ming as a corrupted form of ancient Confucianism.[74] Given that ancient Confucianism is a sociopolitical ethics, Neo-Confucianism is different from it. Thus, Ricci upheld the ancient teaching of Confucius and Mencius rather than Neo-Confucianism influenced by Buddhism and Daoism.[75]

In this context, Ricci focused on virtue as a contact point between Confucianism and Christianity. He affirmed the humanistic elements of Confucian teachings and employed the ethical aspects of Christianity to

71. Yao, *Confucianism and Christianity*, 97.
72. Chan, "Commands from Heaven," 271.
73. Ibid., 271.
74. Ricci, *The True Meaning of the Lord of Heaven*, 2.6.
75. In terms of human nature, Ricci advocates Mencius' theory that man's inborn nature is good rather than Xunzi's theory that all people are born with natural tendencies toward waywardness. Ricci proposes how he understands Mencius's doctrine on human nature as follows; "In ancient times, there were debates on whether human nature is good or not. Who has ever made doubt existence of not being good in the principle? Mencius said human nature is not the same as that of cows and dogs. An interpreter said as follows; in terms of nature humans secure righteousness, whereas beasts obtain eccentricity. However, the principle cannot be not only divided into two but also one-sidedness. In this context, sages in ancient times thought human nature are not the same as the principle." (Ricci, *The true meaning of the Lord of Heaven*, 7.1. "古有岐人性之善不 誰有疑理爲有不善者乎 孟子曰 人性 與牛犬性不同 解者 曰 人詩性之正 禽獸詩性之偏也 理則無二無偏 是古之賢者 固不同性於理矣。") Just as Ricci argues that human souls are different from the souls of birds and beasts, Mencius demonstrates that human nature has innate goodness in contrast to the "eccentricity" of breasts. Particularly, that humans aspire to love for other people reflects human nature is innately good. In this context, Ricci proposes Mencius' theory on human nature has something common with God's love of Christianity.

How to Acquire Virtues for Happiness 17

establish common points of contact in the dimension of virtue.[76] His cultural accommodation strategy made the comparison possible. Ricci's first Chinese publications were primarily ethical teachings through which he hoped to appeal to both the literati class and the common people. One of his works on ethics produced in the Chinese language was the *Twenty-Five Tracts*, which contain teachings on how to cultivate virtue and wisely use time, and a discussion pertaining to natural philosophy.[77] He deals with how the Lord of Heaven talked about them by adopting the vocabulary of treasured Confucian virtues and expounding a Christian understanding of those virtues. For instance, in *the True Meaning of the Lord of Heaven*, he attempts to interpret Confucius' benevolence (*ren* 仁) as God's love of Christianity; "Benevolence is not only loving for the Lord of Heaven but also loving for people."[78] This indicates that thought of ancient Confucianism is included to that of Christianity.[79] His missiological apologetics seems to be less balanced than modern attempts to compare China and the West.[80] However, his work is still valuable in that Ricci provided support and evidence with regard to the possibility of comparing Confucian culture and Christianity.[81] As a result of his introduction on Confucianism to Europe, even Leibniz proposed that "it would appear almost necessary that Chinese missionaries should be sent to us to teach us the use and practice of natural religion, just as we send missionaries to them to teach them revealed religion" with enthusiastic desire for Europe and China to learn from each other in the period of Enlightenment.[82] This shows that a

---

76. Ricci, *The true meaning of the Lord of Heaven*, 1.1.

77. Chan, "Commands from Heaven," 275.

78. Ricci, *The true meaning of the Lord of Heaven*, 7.7. "仁也者，乃愛天主與夫愛人者"

79. Ibid., 7.8. According to Panikkar's classification of religious dialogues, Ricci's approach can be regarded as "inclusivism". Raimundo Panikkar, *The Intrareligious Dialogue* (New York: Paulist Press, 1999), 6.

80. Yearley, "A Comparison between Classical Chinese Thought and Thomistic Christian Thought," 427.

81. "The famous Jesuit missionary and head of the China mission, Matteo Ricci, believed that there were traces of Christianity in Chinese culture and customs, including evidences of the cross among the Chinese. By this belief, Ricci confirmed the translatability of Western concepts and ideas into Chinese, the possibility of shared understanding of the notion of God and other spiritual realities across the boundaries of language, geography, culture and time." Zhao, *Father and Son in Confucianism and Christianity*, xi.

82. Ibid., xii; David E. Mungello, "Leibniz's Interpretation of Neo-Confucianism," *Philosophy East and West* 21, no. 1 (1971), 4.

comparative study of Confucianism and Christianity not only is possible but also fruitful in improving dialogue as to shared values.[83]

Ching's Theological Approach and New-Confucianism

The second approach to dialogue between Confucianism and Christianity is Julia Ching's theological one. Theological approach needs to be understood in the context of the New-Confucianism movement of the twentieth century. In contrast to the popularity of Confucianism in Europe in the period of the Enlightenment, Confucianism in China has fallen into a state of crisis as the influence of Western culture has gradually penetrated every corner of modern Chinese society from the first half of the nineteen century.[84] Even as the Communist People's Republic of China removed Confucianism from both the government and social custom, Confucianism seemed to disappear from Chinese society.[85] In spite of such persecutions, a movement in China for the revival of Confucianism called "New Confucianism" or "the Third Epoch of Confucian Humanism" took place in the 1920s and 1930s when scholars tried to identify the unique value of Confucianism in the wake of the systematic introduction of modern Western culture into China and the revival was hugely promoted in the 1970s and 1980s by industrial success in nations based on Confucian culture.[86] Along with the growth of New-Confucianism some works on comparison between Confucianism and Christianity have been produced by Chinese Christian scholars such as Zhao Ziehen, Xu Baoqian, and Wu Leichuan. They argue that Christianity can be developed into a practicable religion within a Chinese cultural context through greater sensitivity to Confucian teaching practices. New-Confucian scholars such as Mou Zongsan produced an intensive discussion of the relationship between Confucianism and Christianity.[87] Mou Zongsan (1909-95), the second generation of New Confucianism, not only pointed out that a renewed Confucianism ought to include a place for democratic theory, the development of ecumenical and modern

---

83. Zhao, *Father and Son in Confucianism and Christianity*, xii, 7.
84. Ibid., viiii.
85. Ibid., viiii.
86. Jiyuan Yu, *The Ethics of Confucius and Aristotle : Mirrors of Virtue* (New York: Routledge, 2007), 2.
87. Zhao, *Father and Son in Confucianism and Christianity*, 190.

scientific learning, but also defended the religious nature of the Confucian Way (*rudao* 儒道). Mou hypothesized that if Confucianism is a religion, it "should perfect the duties of the proper way of everyday life."[88] He presents the moral cultivation of the five cardinal virtues, social rituals, and pedagogies for "the proper conduct of daily life" as the case for the Confucian Way. According to Zhao, Christian studies and comparative studies between Confucianism and Christianity have been made mainly outside mainland China such as Taiwan and Hong Kong while it is still a new theme for research in mainland China. It is noteworthy that there is a limited number of comparative studies between Confucianism and Christianity even though conflicts between Chinese and Western culture evoke greater necessity for comparative work between these two cultures.[89] In this context, Ching's *Confucianism and Christianity* offers relevant insights in comparing Confucius and Mencius with Augustine. In terms of method, above all, Ching's approach is significantly theological in comparing the two traditions Her work is "a study of Confucianism in the light of certain perspectives borrowed from Christianity" through "theological horizon."[90] According to Yearley, there are two ways to examine religions on a single continuum: theological and academic.[91] He pays attention to the questions they ask as the most revealing way to distinguish theologians and academicians. For him, a theologian is the one who raise questions in "a traditional religious community" while the academician is the one whose question arise in the "university community."[92] He thinks that they are distinguishable even though those two communities do intertwine in complex.[93]

In accordance with his classification, Ching's questions and answers are obviously theological: "Have we the same God? The assumption so far has been, Yes, Yahweh is the God of Israel, and also the universal God, just as the Lord-on-High represents the God of the Shang house, becoming by extension the God of all. Yahweh is a personal God, full of

---

88. John H. Berthrong, "Chinese (Confucian) Philosophical Theology," in *The Oxford Handbook of Philosophical Theology*, ed. Thomas P. Flint and Michael C. Rea (Oxford: Oxford University Press, 2011), 17.

89. Zhao, *Father and Son in Confucianism and Christianity*, 190.

90. Ching, *Confucianism and Christianity*, xviii.

91. Lee H. Yearley, "Confucianism and Christianity," *Philosophy East and West* 29, no. 4 (1979), 509.

92. Ibid., 510.

93. Ibid., 510.

power and mercy, just as the Lord-on-High is father and mother of the people."[94] In terms of God, Ching relatively focuses on similarities rather than differences in order to show contact points between Confucianism and Christianity. Ching offers "historical encounters" between the two religions through Matteo Ricci as the first step to contribute to the theological self-understanding of Christians by making Confucianism better known and understood.[95] Hoping to provide structures for a religious dialogue, Ching describes her task as "an examination of the internal structure of Confucian thought in view of suggesting ways by which each of the two traditions might be better understood in light of the other."[96] Ching regards Confucianism as being more compatible with Christianity than Buddhism because of its shared ethical concern.[97] She seeks to define the concern by comparing the two traditions under topical headings which represent the focal points of discourse about human experience. Given that she regards Christianity and Confucianism as religious traditions grounded in the New Testament teachings and classical text-the so-called Five Classics and Four Books respectively,[98] the problem arises of how these traditions can be historically linked. For this task, she argues that Christianity and Confucianism can only engage in a dialogue about man.[99] She ultimately focuses on a comparison of two kinds of "humanism."[100] More specifically, Ching shows the possibility of comparing between Mencius and Augustine in the problem of evil.[101] Mencius and Augustine commonly deal with the problem of evil, but their approaches for solving evil are different.[102] Mencius regards the cause of evil as the formation of bad habits while Augustine sees the doctrine of sin as offence against God.[103] Along with the problem of evil, Ching offers Confucian benevolence as a significant contact point with Christianity. She argues Confucian *ren* can be parallel with the Christian virtue of love or charity (*agape*) since it has been translated as "human-heartedness,

94. Ching, *Confucianism and Christianity*, 143.
95. Ibid., 12, 215.
96. Ibid., xix.
97. Ibid., xxiii.
98. Ibid., xviii.
99. Ibid., 30.
100. Ibid., 30, 87, 93, 138.
101. Ibid., 75.
102. Ibid., 73.
103. Ibid., 75.

benevolence, love."[104] Although she acknowledges the differences between them in that Christian teaching of charity is related to "God's love for man" and the Confucian teaching of *ren* is based on "human nature itself", she further emphasized love as "a universal virtue."[105] She presents that Confucian rumination on benevolence can provide insight in understanding further the Christian God of Love. Confucians need a more articulate theory of human fallibility and Christians a more profound inquiry into human goodness.[106]

Yearley's Academic Approach and Its Influences

The third approach to dialogue between Confucianism and Christianity is Yearley's academic one. According to Anscombe, the cause of the decline of virtue ethics in modern western philosophy resulted as a consequence of the dominance of Christianity influenced by legalistic notions of Torah since the concepts of being bound, permitted, or excused became deeply embedded in our language and thought for many centuries.[107] According to her argument, philosophical interest in virtue and the virtues can be traced back to Aristotle in ancient Greece and rule-based moral theories became dominant after ancient Rome by a more legalistic way of thinking about morality based on Christianity.[108] However, Anscombe's critique of Christianity is not reasonable at least in comparative studies on Confucianism and Christianity. Rather those who adopted missiological apologetics or a theological approach in comparing with Confucianism maintained a continued interest in virtue ethics to utilize it as a contact point bridging both religions, while western philosophers have tended to neglect it.[109] If there are some differences between previous comparative studies and modern comparative studies in accordance with the revival of virtue ethics in the aspect of philosophy, different approaches on virtue ethics just exist. At least, virtue ethics has been continuously dealt with as an important theme in comparative studies on both religions.

---

104. Ibid., 93.
105. Ibid., 93.
106. Ibid., 103, 139.
107. Anscombe, "Modern Moral Philosophy," 30.
108. Liu, *The Unity of Rule and Virtue*, 1.
109. Ibid., 11.

In contrast to those who adopted missiological apologetics or a theological approach, modern comparative religious ethicists try to be neutral in comparing Confucianism and Christianity. Yearley calls such ethicists "academicians" who are closer to the "disinterested inquirer," distinguishing them from theologians who are closer to the "cunning apologist."[110] Such an academic approach as comparative religion in the West traces its origins to Max Müller formed in the context of the aftermath of colonialism and evolutionism in the nineteenth century.[111] His call for a "science of religion" led to the view that religion could be investigated under the critical, historical, and comparative criteria provided by science. As a result, religion was treated with the same intellectual scrutiny as were other cultural and natural phenomena. Its new scientific theory was used by liberal theology as a powerful polemic for placing Christianity at the top of the evolutionary ladder.[112] Furthermore, after the First World War, the decline of evolution theory and rise of phenomenology of religion adopting the Husserlian principle of neutrality in questions of value (*epoche*) accelerated the academic approach in studying cultural history and the uniqueness of religious traditions. In *epoche* the comparatist could describe the material without the value judgments of the previous generation.[113] Comparative religion is different from comparative theology since faith is a necessary factor in the latter and not in the former, but the fields are not entirely separated in that the comparative theologian also needs to be an academic scholar in the context of a religious study.[114]

In *Mencius and Aquinas*, Yearley as an academician shows "striking differences" between Mencius and Aquinas, even though he analyses their virtue theories and the concept of courage as their common ground. He acknowledges that they have some resemblances, but these are rather insignificant due to thin resemblances.[115] At first, he points out there are general differences between Mencius and Aquinas; e.g., propriety (*li*),

---

110. Yearley, "Confucianism and Christianity," 509.

111. Eric J. Sharpe, *Comparative Religion: A History* (London: Duckworth, 1986), 45.

112. Walter H. Capps, *Religious Studies: The Making of a Discipline* (Minneapolis: Fortress Press, 1995), 271.

113. Capps, *Religious Studies*, 110.

114. Francis X. Clooney SJ, "Comparative Theology," in *The Oxford Handbook of Systematic Theology*, ed. Kathryn Tanner, John Webster, and Iain Torrance (Oxford: Oxford University Press, 2007), 12.

115. Lee H. Yearley, *Mencius and Aquinas: Theories of Virtue and Conceptions of Courage* (Albany: State University of New York Press, 1990), 171.

fate (*ming*), and attention (*ssu*) are lacking in Aquinas; revelation, church, or sacraments are not found in Mencius.[116] In particular, he makes an emphasis on the differences of cultural context between Mencius and Aquinas such as world view and family.[117] Furthermore, he describes how different the ideas of virtue of Mencius and Aquinas are.[118] For Aquinas, the acquired cardinal virtues are practical wisdom, justice, courage, and moderation; they differ from the theological virtues of faith, hope and charity. For Mencius, the list is considerably different, as it includes propriety, intelligent awareness, righteousness, and benevolence. He attempts to show the difference of benevolence between Mencius and Aquinas by distinguishing Aquinas' beneficence (*beneficentia*) and benevolence (*benevolentia*).[119] In terms of benevolence, missionary Ricci, who adopted Thomism as his theology, regards it as a concept of bridging between Confucianism and Christianity. In contrast, Yearley as an academician focuses on finding dissimilarities rather than resemblances even in comparing the concept of love.

Yearley's method has been influential for contemporary comparative scholars. Yao takes a central concept, *ren*, from the thought of the greatest Chinese who ever lived, Confucius, and then goes on to a careful comparison between *ren* and a correspondingly central concept in Christianity, *agape*. Both *ren* and *agape* may be broadly translated as love, but love takes many forms. He explores in detail the nuances of *ren* and *agape*. This indicates Yao focuses on the list of virtues in virtue theories. His method is the same as that of Yearley in that he is more interested in showing differences rather than similarities.[120] For instance, Yao shows "humanism" and "theism" as the central difference by expounding the doctrine of Confucius and Jesus.[121]

Stalnaker focuses on how to attain virtue by examining personal formation of both thinkers. He is interested in finding similarities in that he adopts a method similar to that of Neville's comparative categories, here termed "bridge concepts," that serve as the basic cross-cultural tools

---

116. Ibid., 4.
117. Ibid., 170.
118. Ibid., 40.
119. Ibid., 40.
120. Yao, *Confucianism and Christianity*, 54.
121. Ibid., 66.

for making the comparison.[122] In terms of methodology, furthermore, he criticizes the understanding of Yearley's "secondary theories" that "may hinder the analysis of human flourishing offered by sophisticated religious thinkers such as Xunzi and Augustine."[123] Stalnaker argues, on the contrary, such theories that can offer a "weak holism" are essential and constitutive of that analysis.[124] Stalnaker presents Augustine's spiritual exercises such as liberal arts, Bible study, fasting, and prayer,[125] but he loses sight of the importance of epistemology as the starting point of the formation of moral self in Augustine's earlier writings after his conversion.

Norden also attempts a comparison in accordance with Yearley's method. Norden focuses on how to overcome evil, like Stalnaker who links it with human nature, but he explains the problem of evil in relation to world view. For Augustine, everything in existence is created and preserved by God and Created entities share in God's being and perfection, but in differing degrees and none matches God's reality or perfection.[126] The world view of Confucians like Mencius is, like that of Augustine, "hierarchical." However, Norden points out "this hierarchy is not expressed in terms of degrees of being, nor does Mencius recognise any radical division in reality between the material and the immaterial realms."[127] Mencius world view is described as organism. Cosmologically, the highest place in the hierarchy is occupied by Heaven. Heaven sometimes seems to have some anthropomorphic characteristics, but Mencius does not talk about Heaven in the way one talks to the personal God of the Old and New Testaments.[128] For Norden, differences of Augustine and Mencius on world view are only used as a good illustration of the sort of logical incompatibility and untranslatability that MacIntyre discusses.[129] More important, Norden shows through the differences between them they can help each other in solving their problems. Two competing

---

122. Aaron Stalnaker, *Overcoming Our Evil: Human Nature and Spiritual Exercises in Xunzi and Augustine* (Washington: Georgetown University Press, 2006), 26.

123. Ibid., 295.

124. Ibid., 295.

125. Ibid., 211-233.

126. Bryan W. Van Norden, "Mencius and Augustine on Evil: A Test Case for Comparative Philosophy," ed., *Two Roads to Wisdom?: Chinese and Analytic Philosophies* (Chicago: Open Court Press, 2001), 320.

127. Ibid., 322.

128. Ibid., 322.

129. Ibid., 335.

traditions can explain narratives of one another and attempt to present through these narratives how the other tradition's problems are insoluble from within that tradition, but can be both diagnosed and circumvented from within the first tradition.[130] He takes note that they attempt to give an explanation for human wrongdoing.[131] He claims that Mencius cannot explain why Augustine so acted by using the resources of his own philosophical psychology while Augustine can demonstrate his own actions by using his notion of human will.[132]

METHOD

Intertextual Reasoning

Any comparative ethical study faces fundamental challenges due to its essential characters. Comparative religious ethics brings together ethical traditions that have developed in relative isolation from one another and that are defined quite broadly along cultural and regional lines. This indicates scholars in comparative ethical study ought to be able to cover the vast range of texts and their intellectual and historical contexts. Even religions that are major sources for comparative ethical study are essentially divergent rather than convergent, so that there seems to be little room for communication between religions.[133] Naturally, one who is skeptical of comparative religious ethics might raise a question about how a practitioner can bring distant ethical statements into interrelation and conversation. In order to solve these problems, methods about how to bridge two different traditions in a comparative ethical study are significantly important.

In this book, intertextual reasoning is used as a main research method for comparing works of Confucius and Mencius with Augustine. Intertextual reasoning is not entirely separated from missiological, theological, and academic approaches. Intertextual reasoning is missiological in that its approach, as Matteo Ricci shows, offers a conceptual bridge through virtue. According to Fingarette, for Confucius ritual propriety, humaneness, reciprocity, loyalty, learning, music, familial social relationships, and

---

130. Ibid., 315.
131. Ibid., 335.
132. Ibid., 335.
133. Yao, *Confucianism and Christianity*, 1.

obligations are constantly recurring themes in the *Analects*.[134] However, for Confucius all of these themes are not the main frame of cultivating virtue. As Confucius shows that "self-cultivation begins with studying the *Book of Poetry*, is established by ritual propriety, and is perfected by music,"[135] the main frames of cultivating virtue are moral learning, ritual propriety, and music. Along with these three methods, Mencius stresses self-reflection in acquiring virtue according to his understanding of human nature. Confucius and Mencius' *xue* (學), *si* (思), *li* (禮), and *yue* (樂) offer a framework for comparison with Augustine's moral learning, contemplation, sacrament, and music for acquiring virtue. Intertextual reasoning also adopts a theological approach in that it is, as Clooney argues, "constructive theology" on the basis of faith and theological grounds in an interreligious context of theology.[136] According to David Tracy, "on strictly theological grounds, the fact of religious pluralism should enter all theological assessment and self-analysis in any tradition at the very beginning of its task."[137] Tracy illuminates four major processes in a comparative theology: "reinterpreting central religious symbols in a religiously pluralistic world; providing theological interpretation with new foundations comprised of both tradition and contemporary pluralism; addressing questions of religious pluralism on explicitly theological grounds; and finally, in light of these, reviewing tradition by a hermeneutics of suspicion and critique and by a hermeneutics of retrieval."[138] Intertextual reasoning also seeks academic approach in that comparative theologians need to be an academic scholars proficient in the study of religion when they are engaged in the study of a religious tradition.[139] Given that Confucianism and Christianity have developed in relative isolation from one another, the problem about how Confucius and Mencius (fifth and fourth century BC), and Augustine (354-430), a medieval Christian, can be bridged must be fundamentally faced. The ethics of ancient Confucians and Augustine did not take place in a vacuum, so it is necessary to take into account all kinds of context such as

134. Herbert Fingarette, *Confucius: The Secular as Sacred* (Long Grove: Waveland Press, 1972), 2.

135. *Analects*, 8.8. Translation adapted from Legge. 子曰：「興於詩，立於禮。成於樂。」

136. Francis X. Clooney, *Comparative Theology: Deep Learning Across Religious Borders* (Chichester: Wiley-Blackwell, 2010), 42.

137. Ibid., 6.

138. Ibid., 6.

139. Ibid., 12.

social, political, cultural, and theoretical backgrounds in ancient China and Rome that affect Confucius, Mencius, and Augustine respectively.[140] The focus of this comparison, however, is on what each set of ethics actually says, that is, on the ideas and arguments in ethical texts of each side for the sake of avoiding bold and ill supported comparative generalizations.[141] In one word, the essential method employed is textual analysis, by which I will turn to the original texts of Confucius, Mencius, and Augustine in order to analyze their direct and indirect meanings and implications.[142]

In this book, I compare Confucius and Mencius' *xue* (學), *si* (思), *li* (禮), and *yue* (樂) with Augustine's moral learning, contemplation, sacrament, and music as methods for acquiring virtue. These are conceptual bridges in comparing them. Yet, in order to operate the conceptual bridge properly, a couple of distinct problems should be solved: untranslatability and incommensurability. In a conceptual framework, untranslatability and incommensurability may both be present between the claims or theses of two competing traditions. Here the difficulty is not with understanding the claims of another culture but with judging their truth or falsity. Two radically different conceptual schemes have different standards of rationality; they license different inferences and take different kinds of beliefs as obvious or unassailable. Thus, if we do manage to translate a sentence S from language A into language B, S may turn out to be obviously false in A and obviously true in B. There is no third, "neutral" standpoint from which we can adjudicate such differences.[143] When cultures and their respective conceptual schemes differ radically, it is often the case that a given sentence of the language of one culture cannot be translated straightforwardly into a sentence of the language of the other.[144] Concepts and expressions found in one language presuppose a matrix of beliefs or social practices of the culture which have no counterpart in the other.[145]

This is inextricably linked with the matter of neutrality. Many scholars point out the limit of neutrality in intertextual reading. Clooney points out its limit in that faith is a necessary in comparative theology

---

140. Yu, *The Ethics of Confucius and Aristotle*, 17.

141. Ibid., 17.

142. Zhao, *Father and Son in Confucianism and Christianity*, xii.

143. John Jenkins, "Yearley, Aquinas, and Comparative Method," *Journal of Religious Ethics* 21, no. 2 (1993), 380.

144. Jenkins, "Yearley, Aquinas, and Comparative Method," 380.

145. Ibid., 380.

unlike comparative religion.[146] Sugirtharajah also critiques the problem of neutrality. From the vantage point of "postcolonial criticism," Sugirtharajah classifies three different modes of relating the Bible to Asian culture and religion in colonial history: "orientalist mode" advocating the promotion and revival of the native texts, "Anglicist mode" replacing the indigenous texts by integrating the colonized into the culture of the colonizer, and "nativistic mode" attempting to recover the vernacular forms as a corrective measure. For him, postcolonial reading is "an emancipatory reading of the texts."[147] For Archie C. C. Lee the purpose of cross-textual reading is to realise an iconoclastic role for the Bible in order to shape a Christian identity in a multi-scriptural context.[148] Pointing out the limit of objective reading of the Bible, Yeo presents "intersubjective reading."[149] Pieris criticizes three categories such as exclusivism, inclusivism, and pluralism in the academic magisterium in the West since these categories do not make sense in Asia where there is a common struggle against poverty and destitution of the masses.[150] Hence, many adherents of metacosmic religions (Buddhists, Hindus, Muslims, and Christians) have learned to re-interpret their beliefs according to some of the liberative elements in the cosmic religiosity of their co-believers who belong to the poorer classes.[151] In this context, Pieris shows new categories such as syncretism, synthesis, and symbiosis.[152] According to him, syncretism is a haphazard mixing of religions. That does not exist among the poor, but is attributed to them by observers. Synthesis is the creation of a tertium quid out of two or more religions, destroying the identity of each component religion. For him, Christian uniqueness reflects both the process and product of a symbiosis. It indicates one's conversion to the common heritage of all religions (beatitudes) and also a conversion to the

146. Francis X. Clooney, "Comparative Theology," 12. Cf. Oliver O'Donovan, *Resurrection and Moral Order: An Outline for Evangelical Ethics* (Leicester: Apollos, 1994), 77.

147. R. S. Sugirtharajah, *Asian Biblical Hermeneutics and Postcolonialism: Contesting the Interpretations* (Sheffield: Sheffield Academic Press, 1999), 3-24.

148. Archie C. C. Lee, "Cross-Textual Hermeneutics and Identity in Multi-Scriptural Asia," in *Christian Theology in Asia*, ed. Sebastian C. H. Kim (Cambridge: Cambridge University Press, 2008), 200.

149. K. K. Yeo, *Musing with Confucius and Paul: Toward a Chinese Christian Theology* (Cambridge: James Clarke & Co, 2008), 53.

150. Aloysius Pieris, "Interreligious Dialogue and Theology of Religions: An Asian Paradigm," *Horizons* 20, no. 1 (1993), 107.

151. Ibid., 110.

152. Ibid., 113-14.

specificity of one's own religion as dictated by other religionists. It can be regarded as interreligious dialogue.

In *Truth and Method*, Gadamer argues the idea of a perfect translation is entirely illusory due to "prejudice" that is a soil where our judgment is grown.[153] Gadamer insists the translator must show his colors owing to the limitation of perfect translation.[154] As he shows that "every translator is an interpreter,"[155] translation is a process of "re-creation of text" as follows:

> Let us again start by considering the extreme case of translation from a foreign language. Here no one can doubt that the translation of a text, however much the translator may have dwelt with and empathized with his author, cannot be simply a re-awakening of the original process in the writer's mind; rather, it is necessarily a re-creation of the text guided by the way the translator understands what it says.[156]

It is natural for a translator to be often painfully aware of his inevitable distance from the original.[157] For Gadamer, translating as interpretation which requires a laborious process of understanding is not mere reconstruction but "fusion of horizons."[158] Gadamer states:

> In this sense understanding is certainly not concerned with "understanding historically"-i.e., reconstructing the way the text came into being. Rather, one intends to understand the text itself. But this means that the interpreter's own thoughts too have gone into re-awakening the text's meaning. In this the interpreter's own horizon is decisive, yet not as a personal standpoint that he maintains or enforces, but more as an opinion and a possibility that one brings into play and puts at risk, and that helps one truly to make one's own what the text says. I have described this above as a "fusion of horizons."[159]

---

153. Hans-Georg Gadamer, *Truth and Method*, 2nd ed. trans. Joel Weinsheimer and Donald G. Marshall (London: Continuum, 2004), xi.
154. Ibid., 386.
155. Ibid., 387.
156. Ibid., 386.
157. Ibid., 386.
158. Ibid., 374.
159. Ibid., 388.

Fundamentally, Gadamer's "fusion of horizons" is the matter of language; "All understanding is interpretation, and all interpretation takes place in the medium of a language that allows the object to come into words and yet is at the same time the interpreter's own language."[160] Thus, he makes an emphasis on "the reciprocal relationship that exists between interpreter and text" in bridging the gulf between languages.[161] For him, translating a foreign language is an "extreme case of hermeneutical difficulty."[162] In terms of "fusion of horizons", for instance, the classical Chinese term *tian* (天) in Augustine and Mencius is a representative example as follows:

> Consider the Classical Chinese term *tian* 天, which is standardly rendered as 'Heaven' in English, and as *caelum* in Latin. However, *tian* often refers to a sort of higher power, which is responsible for implanting an ethical sense in humans, and for managing some of the things that we might describe as 'fate'. On this basis, it might seem more appropriate to translate *tian* as 'God' or *Deus*. However, many of the characteristics that are central to Augustine's conception of God are either absent or significantly less prominent in Mencius's conception of *tian*. For example, Mencius would never have conceived of *tian* as 'eternal' in the precise way that Augustine conceives of God as eternal (that is, as existing outside of time). Furthermore, Mencius's *tian* seems less personal than Augustine's God. One cannot imagine Mencius crying out to *tian* in the manner that Augustine (or Job) cries out to God. Clearly, there is no possibility of translation as "same-saying" between Augustine's Latin and Mencius's Chinese.[163]

It might seem that there could not be untranslatability between the languages of Augustine and Mencius, given that Augustine wrote in Latin, and the *book of Mencius* has been translated into Latin. Clearly, the classical Chinese term *tian* might seem like God or *Deus*. Yet, Mencius's *tian* seems less "eternal" and "personal" in comparison with Augustine's concept of God. It indicates, as Gadamer argues, perfect translation

---

160. Ibid., 389.
161. Ibid., 387.
162. Ibid., 387.
163. Norden, "Mencius and Augustine on Evil: A Test Case for Comparative Philosophy," 317.

between Augustine's Latin and Mencius's Chinese is impossible but "fusion of horizons" as a process of interpretation is possible.

In terms of translation, MacIntyre's understanding is similar to that of Gadamer. In *Whose Justice? Which Rationality?*, MacIntyre also holds that not all languages are intertranslatable; "those situations in which the task of translation is from the language of one community whose language-in-use is expressive of and presupposes a particular system of well-defined beliefs into the different language of another such community with beliefs which in some key areas are strongly incompatible with those of the first community."[164] However, in understanding MacIntyre's claim about translatability, it is important to keep in mind both what he means by "translation" and the relationship he sees between language and beliefs. MacIntyre is not denying that it is possible for a speaker of any given natural language to learn any other natural language. Nor is MacIntyre denying that it is possible to modify an existing language so that it comes to have expressive resources that had previously only existed in some other language. In fact, MacIntyre writes:

> when Greek philosophy came to be written in Latin, those who continued the Greek tradition of philosophical enquiry had to be able to recognize ... the previous singularly unphilosophical character of Latin, thus acknowledging the extraordinary achievement of those who like Cicero both translated from Greek and neologized Latin, so that it acquired new resources.[165]

MacIntyre illustrates the difference between being able to understand a tradition and being able to translate all its claims into the language of another tradition by pointing to the possibility of "bilinguals"—people who, for example, might have been raised within one community and its tradition, and then through migration or conquest, become a member of another community and its different tradition. Such bilinguals might very well understand each tradition, and such understanding might include knowledge of those parts of each that cannot be translated into the language of the other. Such bilinguals would not encounter the sort of radical incommensurability constituted by incomprehensibility, but they may be unable to resolve conflicts of belief between the traditions, instead having

---

164. Alasdair C. MacIntyre, *Whose Justice? Which Rationality?* (Notre Dame: University of Notre Dame Press, 1988), 379.

165. Ibid., 372.

to relativize the claims of each in some such form as "seems true to this particular community" or "seems justified to this particular community."

Particularly, there could be a problem of translation in translating the *Analects, Mean, Great Learning,* and *Book of Mencius,* since these works have been translated into English by many scholars. As Yao states that "translation of the Confucian classics often reflects a personal involvement in re-experiencing the philosophy behind the texts,"[166] different translators have different understandings of the Confucian philosophy, and therefore their translations are different. In order to present the Confucian tradition in the best way, he emphasizes that "we cannot possibly adopt single translations exclusively."[167] In treating the *Analects, Mean, Great Learning,* and *Book of Mencius,* I will make selective use of the translations rendered respectively by James Legge, Raymond Dawson, D.C. Lau, and Irene Bloom with occasional changes according to my own understanding and judgment. The references to the original sources and to their English translators are given in the footnotes when necessary and also in the bibliography. More importantly, I compare Confucius and Mencius' *xue* (學), *si* (思), *li* (禮), and *yue* (樂) with Augustine's moral learning, contemplation, sacrament and music by presenting their similarities within differences and differences within similarities chapter by chapter, and then in conclusion I offer Confucian Augustinianism as a new theological perspective on Confucian-Christian ethics in the light of this research.

Continuity between Augustine's Early and Later Works

For this task, Augustine's early works on the formation of moral self are intensively expounded. It is because such works make possible a dialogue with ancient Confucians. As Drober shows that "the most recent and comprehensive bibliography on Augustine contains the titles of some 20,000 of a total of about 50,000 estimated publications worldwide, and the annual bibliography published in the *Revue des études Augustiniennes* adds some three to five hundred items to this number each year,"[168] there is a great deal of bibliography on Augustine's thinking, based on his many books and treatises. It may be that too much is made of his two most

---

166. Yao, *An Introduction to Confucianism,* 14.
167. Ibid., 14.
168. Drober, "Studying Augustine," 19.

famous books such as *Confessions* and *City of God* even though there are many other works as follows:

> *Confessions* and *City of God* are, therefore, by no means only accidentally the most studied of all the numerous works of Augustine, comprising some 15 per cent of all publications concerning Augustine. In second place, but trailing by a long distance, follow the Sermons and the Letters, adding another 7 per cent between them. Following next are *De trinitate*, *De doctrina Christiana*, and his biblical commentaries on John and the Psalms, together sharing a further 8 per cent of scholarly literature devoted to Augustine. This statistic reveals a fundamental feature of all Augustinian scholarship: it is by no means evenly distributed.[169]

Drober points out that most of research on Augustine concentrates on his later works. The shortage of research on Augustine's earlier works written before 390s may weaken the possibility of comparative enterprise since his later works do not make any room for pagan virtue. It is noteworthy that research on Augustine's formation of moral self has been largely neglected at least since the Reformation, for the intellectual concern provoked by his doctrine of predestination led to intensive critical scrutiny of his late, anti-Pelagian writings.[170] In his early works, Augustine's method of cultural accommodation is similar to that of Ricci in that he brought Platonism to support Christian thought to criticize Manichaeism and skepticism in his works from 386 to 396.[171] With regard to this matter, Brown demonstrates differences between early and later Augustine, focusing on his interpretation of St Paul.[172] According to

169. Ibid., 19.
170. Stalnaker, *Overcoming Our Evil*, 197.
171. Brown, *Augustine of Hippo*, 79, 139.
172. "By June 394, he was giving 'lectures' on the Epistle to the Romans to his friends at Carthage ... Augustine did not 'discover' Paul at this time. He merely read him differently. Previously, he had interpreted Paul as a Platonist: he had seen him as the exponent of a spiritual ascent, of the renewal of the 'inner' man, the decay of the 'outer'; and, after his baptism, he had shared in Paul's sense of triumph: 'Behold all things have become new.' The idea of the spiritual life as a vertical ascent, as a progress towards a final, highest stage to be reached in this life, had fascinated Augustine in previous years. Now, he will see in Paul nothing but a single, unresolved tension between 'flesh' and 'spirit'. The only changes he could find were changes in states of awareness of this tension: ignorance of its existence 'before the Law'; helpless realisation of the extent of the tension between good and evil 'under the Law'; a stage of utter dependence on a Liberator 'under grace'. Only after this life would tension be resolved,

Brown, early Augustine interpreted Paul as a Platonist with an emphasis of "spiritual ascent." However, Harrison objects that Augustine changed his thinking after reading St Paul's epistles in the 390s:

> In the last chapter we suggested that if one is to speak of a revolution in Augustine's thought then one should look for it in 386, at the moment of his conversion, and not in the 390s when his thought is held by many scholars to have undergone a landslide, as a result of reading St Paul, which resulted in the destruction of the positive optimism of the early works and the construction from the rubble of an uncompromising doctrine of original sin, of mankind's inability to know, will, or do good without grace, and of the predestination of the elect.[173]

Although Augustine acknowledges in his later works, that he placed too much emphasis on reason in his early works,[174] Augustine did not insist humankind can "know, will, or do good without grace" in his early writing. In later works he makes an emphasis on progressing only through Jesus Christ. For instance, when it comes to virtues in early Augustine's works, he shows the love of God as a supreme virtue in the context of Plato's cardinal virtues.[175] In this context, contrary to previous trends, I will primarily expound Augustine's earlier works related to the formation of moral self. By offering a great deal of ideas on the formation of moral self such as the inner teacher, divine illumination, mimesis of Christ, monastic community, friendship, contemplative life, baptism, marriage, and music as a liberal discipline, Augustine's early works can provide conceptual bridges for comparing with that of Confucius and Mencius.

'When death is swallowed up in victory.' It is a flattened landscape: and in it, the hope of spiritual progress comes increasingly to depend, for Augustine, on the unfathomable will of God." Brown, *Augustine of Hippo*, 144-145.

173. Carol Harrison, *Rethinking Augustine's Early Theology: An Argument for Continuity* (Oxford: Oxford University, 2005), 20.

174. *retr.* 1.1.4, 1.3.2, 1.10.1.

175. *mor.* 15. 25. "that temperance is love giving itself entirely to that which is loved; fortitude is love readily bearing all things for the sake of the loved object; justice is love serving only the loved object, and therefore ruling rightly; prudence is love distinguishing with sagacity between what hinders it and what helps it. The object of this love is not anything, but only God, the chief good, the highest wisdom, the perfect harmony."

2

Xue (學) and Moral Learning

INTRODUCTION

CONFUCIUS, MENCIUS AND AUGUSTINE all discuss at some length the role of moral education in the formation of the moral or virtuous self. For them, moral learning is internal, communitarian, and transcendental. In this chapter, I first explicate Confucius' account of moral learning (*xue* 學). This includes the matter of how self-cultivation is connected with becoming the man of virtue to bring about benevolent government, the matter of how practice is involved with Heaven and filial piety, the matter of sex, poverty, and happiness in moral learning, and the role of tradition and imitation. Then I move to Mencius' account of moral learning. This deals with how self-cultivation contributes to benevolent government in connection with will, how human unity is formed in relation to filial piety and schooling, the influence of environment and asceticism in moral learning, and how Heaven is related to imitation and tradition. And then I proceed to show Augustine's account of moral learning. This is expounded in the dimension of divine illumination and friendship.

CONFUCIUS' MORAL LEARNING

Self-Cultivation, Man of Virtue, and Benevolent Government

Confucius and Mencius' self-cultivation theories were formed in the context of political crisis. The Zhou (周) Dynasty is largely divided into the Western Zhou (西周, 1027-771 BC) and the Eastern Zhou (東周, 770-256 BC), which is again divided into the Spring and Autumn period

(春秋, 770-481 BC) and the Warring States period (戰國, 480-221 BC). Confucius (孔子, ca. 551-479 BC) lived in the Spring and Autumn period and then Mencius (孟子, ca. 372-289 BC) and Xunzi (荀子, ca. 323-238 BC) lived in the Warring States period.[1] Just as after the death of Socrates, his school of thought was further developed by Plato and Aristotle, thus becoming the orthodoxy of western philosophy, the school of Confucius was developed by Mencius and Xunzi, and became the orthodoxy of Chinese philosophy. Confucius as founder of the *Ru* (儒) School of Chinese thought laid emphasis on virtue (德) as a solution to the situation in *Analects* (論語), *Great Leaning* (大學), and *Doctrine of the Mean* (中庸) which were collected by his followers. He states that "exalting virtue consists of making loyalty and good faith into one's main principles and moving towards tightness," he deals with how to exalt virtue and clear up confusions.[2] He firmly believed that the Way (道) could make a contribution to solving such disorderly chaos.[3] As he lamented that people are not interested in virtue in his time,[4] he points out the necessity of moral education for cultivating virtue since "when the man of high station is well instructed, he loves men; when the man of low station is well instructed, he is easily ruled."[5] Thus, he insists that it is not necessary to distinguish classes in teaching:[6]

> When the Master went to Wei, Ran You drove his carriage. The Master observed, "How numerous are the people!" You said, "Since they are thus numerous, what more shall be done for

---

1. The term Confucianism (儒教 *rujiao*) is a Jesuit invention based on the Latinization of the Chinese name *Konfuzi* (Confucius). Virtually, the exact meaning of *rujiao* in Chinese is "Teaching of the Ru", not "Teaching of Confucius". Ru refers to a class of ritual specialists to which Confucius belonged and with whom his teachings are associated. Even though the Chinese designation for Confucius' teaching refers to this professional group, Confucius is regarded as the founder of the "Teaching of the Ru" and as the editor of their canonical works. Gentz, *Understanding Chinese Religions*, 53.

2. *Analects*, 12.10., trans. Raymond Dawson (Oxford: Oxford University Press, 2008). 子張問崇德、辨惑。子曰：「主忠信，徙義，崇德也。愛之欲其生，惡之欲其死。既欲其生，又欲其死，是惑也。『誠不以富，亦祇以異。』」

3. *Analects*, 6.17. As translated in Dawson. 子曰：「誰能出不由戶？何莫由斯道也？」

4. *Analects*, 15.4. 子曰：「由！知德者鮮矣。」

5. *Analects*, 17.4. trans. James Legge (Oxford: Clarendon Press, 1893). 子之武城，聞弦歌之聲。夫子莞爾而笑，曰：「割雞焉用牛刀？」子游對曰：「昔者偃也聞諸夫子曰：『君子學道則愛人，小人學道則易使也。』」子曰：「二三子！偃之言是也。前言戲之耳。」

6. *Analects*, 15.38. 子曰：「有教無類。」

them?" "Enrich them," was the reply. "And when they have been enriched, what more shall be done?" The Master said, "Instruct them."[7]

For Confucius the formation of moral self is an important aspect in nurturing ordinary people as well as in achieving economic sufficiency. For him it is defined as cultivating the Way which is in accordance with human nature conferred by Heaven.[8] He opposes the death penalty. Regarding four abominations, Confucius states:

> To put the people to death without having instructed them—this is called ruthlessness. To require from them, suddenly, the full tale of work, without having given them warning—this is called harshness. To issue orders as if without urgency, at first, and, when the time comes, to insist on them with severity—this is called oppressiveness. And, generally, in the giving of pay or rewards to men, to do it in a stingy way—this is called acting the part of a mere official.[9]

If so, who can rightly govern and teach people? Confucius thinks the one who rectify one's own self can participate in government and instruct others.[10] In other words, truly virtuous ministers can properly govern and teach others. To rectify one's own self refers to cultivating one's own character. In terms of rectifying (正), he urges ministers to take the initiative in being virtuous since people will follow their character; "Ji Kang asked Confucius about government. Confucius replied, to govern means to rectify. If you lead the people with correctness, who will dare not to be correct?"[11] .. "The Master said: If one's character is rectified, then things will get done without orders being issued; but if one's character is not rectified, then although orders are issued they are

---

7. *Analects*, 13.9. Translation adapted from Dawson and Legge. 子適衛，冉有僕。子曰：「庶矣哉！」冉有曰：「既庶矣。又何加焉？」曰：「富之。」曰：「既富矣，又何加焉？」曰：「教之。」

8. *Doctrine of the Mean*, 1.1. 天命之謂性。率性之謂道。修道之謂教。

9. *Analects*, 20.2. Translation adapted from Dawson and Legge. 子張曰：「何謂四惡？」子曰：「不教而殺謂之虐；不戒視成謂之暴；慢令致期謂之賊；猶之與人也，出納之吝，謂之有司。」

10. *Analects*, 13.13. 子曰：「苟正其身矣，於從政乎何有？不能正其身，如正人何？」

11. *Analects*, 12.17. 季康子問政於孔子。孔子對曰：「政者，正也。子帥以正，孰敢不正？」

not followed."[12] More specifically, rectifying indicates the superior is fond of ritual propriety (禮), righteousness (義), good faith (信).[13] Confucius stresses the influence of virtuous men to inferiors, he likens them to wind and grass respectively.

> Ji Kang asked Confucius about government, saying, "What do you say to killing the unprincipled for the good of the principled?" Confucius replied, "Sir, in carrying on your government, why should you use killing at all? Let your evinced desires be for what is good, and the people will be good. The relation between superiors and inferiors is like that between the wind and the grass. The grass must bend, when the wind blows across it."[14]

In terms of politics, this indicates that Confucius seeks benevolent government (仁政) rather than government depending on punishment since possession of all under heaven belongs not to a skillful man at war but to the man of virtue. When Nangong Kuo put a question to Confucius about differences between Yi and Ao who were skillful at archery (but neither managed to die a natural death) and Yu and Ji who personally sowed the crops but gained possession of all under the kingdom, Confucius regards Kuo as the man of virtue.[15] Who is the man of virtue? For Confucius, the man of virtue is the complete man (成人). Confucius shows ways for becoming a complete man through self-cultivation in relation to understanding, being free from desires, courage, ritual propriety, music, and truthfulness as follows:

> Suppose a man with the knowledge of Zang Wu Zhong, the freedom from covetousness of Gong Chuo, the bravery of Zhuang of Bian, and the varied talents of Ran Qiu; add to these the

---

12. *Analects*, 13.6. Translation adapted from Dawson. 子曰：「其身正，不令而行；其身不正，雖令不從。」

13. *Analects*, 13. 4. 樊遲請學稼，子曰：「吾不如老農。」請學為圃。曰：「吾不如老圃。」樊遲出。子曰：「小人哉，樊須也！上好禮，則民莫敢不敬；上好義，則民莫敢不服；上好信，則民莫敢不用情。夫如是，則四方之民襁負其子而至矣，焉用稼？」

14. *Analects*, 12.19. 季康子問政於孔子曰：「如殺無道，以就有道，何如？」孔子對曰：「子為政，焉用殺？子欲善，而民善矣。君子之德風，小人之德草。草上之風，必偃。」

15. *Analects*, 14.5. 南宮适問於孔子曰：「羿善射，奡盪舟，俱不得其死然；禹稷躬稼，而有天下。」夫子不答，南宮适出。子曰：「君子哉若人！尚德哉若人！」

accomplishments of the rules of ritual propriety and music—
such a one might be reckoned a complete man.[16]

He defines a complete man as one who thinks of righteousness when given the opportunity of gain and is prepared to give up his life when faced with danger as well as not forgetting an old agreement.[17] For Confucius the formation of moral self is the matter of self-cultivation to become the man of virtue (君子). He states that "what the superior man seeks, is in himself. What the mean man seeks, is in others."[18] This indicates being the man of virtue is the matter of self-cultivation (修己), through which the man of virtue can show reverence and tranquility to others; "Zi Lu asked what constituted the man of virtue. The Master said, The cultivation of himself in reverence . . . He cultivates himself so as to bring tranquility to others . . . He cultivates himself so as to bring tranquility to all the people. Self-cultivation so as to bring tranquility to the hundred surnames—even Yao and Shun were still solicitous about this."[19]

Practice, Heaven, and Filial Piety

What are the specific methods for self-cultivation in Confucius? Confucius states that people are close to one another by nature and they diverge as a result of repeated practice.[20] Confucius offers practice (習) in relation to human nature (性). Confucius did not, as Zi Gong said, clearly express an opinion on human nature and the way of Heaven.[21] Seen in the light of later discussions by Mencius, Xunzi, and others about whether human nature is originally good or bad, Confucius

---

16. *Analects*, 14.12. Translation adapted from Legge. 子路問成人。子曰：「若臧武仲之知，公綽之不欲，卞莊子之勇，冉求之藝，文之以禮樂，亦可以為成人矣。」

17. Cf. *Analects*, 14.12. 曰：「今之成人者何必然？見利思義，見危授命，久要不忘平生之言，亦可以為成人矣。」

18. *Analects*, 15.21. 子曰：「君子求諸己，小人求諸人。」

19. *Analects*, 14.42. Translation adapted from Dawson and Legge. 子路問君子。子曰：「脩己以敬。」曰：「如斯而已乎？」曰：「脩己以安人。」曰：「如斯而已乎？」曰：「脩己以安百姓。脩己以安百姓，堯舜其猶病諸！」

20. *Analects*, 17.2. As translated in Legge. 子曰：「性相近也，習相遠也。」

21. *Analects*, 5.13. As translated in Legge. "The Master's personal displays of his principles and ordinary descriptions of them may be heard. His discourses about human nature, and the way of Heaven, cannot be heard." 子貢曰：「夫子之文章，可得而聞也；夫子之言性與天道，不可得而聞也。」

seems not to be specific about what human nature is. However, Confucius partly shows some evidences that human nature is good. At first, he explains the possibility of virtue in human nature in relation to heaven; "Heaven produced the virtue that is in me."[22] What is Heaven for Confucius? He states that he began studying at fifteen and then he eventually understood the decrees of Heaven as follows:

> At fifteen, I set my heart on learning. At thirty, I stood firm. At forty, I had no doubts. At fifty, I knew the decrees of Heaven. At sixty, my ear was an obedient organ for the reception of truth. At seventy, I could follow what my heart desired, without transgressing what was right.[23]

This indicates for Confucius Heaven is an essential object of study because studying Heaven is inextricably linked to being the man of virtue; "If one does not understand fate, one has no means of becoming the man of virtue. Without an acquaintance with the rules of ritual propriety, it is impossible for the character to be established. Without knowing the force of words, it is impossible to know people."[24] For example, Confucius praises Yao because by imitating Heaven he could institute elegant regulations:

> Great indeed was Yao as a ruler! How majestic was he! It is only Heaven that may be deemed great, but only Yao modelled himself upon it. How vast was his virtue! The people could find no name for it. How majestic was he in the works which he accomplished! How glorious in the elegant regulations which he instituted![25]

Confucius regards the man of virtue as the one who is in awe of the decree of Heaven as well as great men and the words of sages.[26] What is Heaven? This is a significantly controversial issue. According to Fung, Heaven in ancient Confucianism can be classified into five different

---

22. *Analects*, 7.23. As translated in Dawson. 子曰：「天生德於予，桓魋其如予何？」

23. *Analects*, 2.4. Translation adapted from Dawson and Legge. 子曰：「吾十有五而志于學，三十而立，四十而不惑，五十而知天命，六十而耳順，七十而從心所欲，不踰矩。」

24. *Analects*, 20.3. Translation adapted from Dawson and Legge. 子曰：「不知命，無以為君子也。不知禮，無以立也。不知言，無以知人也。」

25. *Analects*, 8.19. Translation adapted from Dawson and Legge. 子曰：「大哉，堯之為君也！巍巍乎！唯天為大，唯堯則之。蕩蕩乎！民無能名焉。巍巍乎！其有成功也；煥乎，其有文章！」

26. *Analects*, 16.8. 孔子曰：「君子有三畏：畏天命，畏大人，畏聖人之言。小人不知天命而不畏也，狎大人，侮聖人之言。」

meanings: physical, anthropomorphic, fatalistic, naturalistic, and ethical Heaven. For Confucius Heaven is anthropomorphic whereas for Mencius Heaven is fatalistic and for Xunzi Heaven is naturalistic.[27] Confucius indicates his sincere respect for Heaven which remained for him a responsive over-all authority.[28] Following Confucius, Mencius elaborates a theory which affirms benevolence as the universal nature of man and traced its ultimate source to Heaven.[29] Thus, man's heart is a microcosm of Heaven through which a union with Heaven is made not only possible but also necessary. Unlike Mencius, Xunzi treats human nature as evil and highlights ritual propriety as the way of maintaining an orderly society. For Xunzi, Heaven, in combination with Earth, indicates the natural world.[30] Confucius' understanding of Heaven as an anthropomorphic *Shang Ti* (上帝) is similar to the religious belief of a large part of the common people of China, and had probably existed since early times. For example, in the *Shih Ching, Shu Ching, Tso Chuan* and *Kuo Yü* Heaven (天) and God (帝) are frequently mentioned. Among them, many indicate an anthropomorphic *Shang Ti*, "a name which literally translated means Supreme Emperor, seems to have been the highest and supreme authority, who presided over an elaborate hierarchy of spirits (神), who were secondary to him and paid him allegiance."[31]

Confucius emphasizes that ritual propriety (禮) can be possible in support of benevolence. This indicates that ritual propriety can be conducted when human nature is good as follows:

> Zi Xia asked, saying, What is the meaning of the passage—The pretty dimples of her artful smile! The well-defined black and white of her eye! The plain ground for the colours? The Master said, The business of laying on the colours follows (the preparation of) the plain ground. Ceremonies then are a subsequent thing? The Master said, It is Shang who can bring out my meaning. Now I can begin to talk about the odes with him.[32]

27. Yu-lan Fung, *A History of Chinese Philosophy: The Period of the Philosophers*, trans. Derk Bodde (Peiping: H. Vetch, 1937), p. 31.

28. Pei-Jung Fu, "The Concept of 'T'ien' in Ancient China: With Special Emphasis on Confucianism," (Ph.D. diss., Yale University, 1984), 133.

29. Ibid., 151.

30. Ibid., 167.

31. Fung, *A History of Chinese Philosophy*, 31.

32. *Analects*, 3.8. As translated in Legge. 子夏問曰：「『巧笑倩兮，美目盼兮，素以為絢兮。』何謂也？」子曰：「繪事後素。」曰：「禮後乎？」子曰：「起予者商也！始可與言詩已矣。」

From the perspective of Fung, for Confucius Heaven may have a right to bestow virtue to humans. Like Fung, Guo Moruo and H.G. Creel claim that Shang Di was originally the high god of the Shang people. Such a hypothesis has been widely accepted and is often repeated.[33] However, Graham claims that for Confucius Heaven seems to take part in functions of fate and nature as well as those of deity. According to him, Confucius focuses on its alignment with moral goodness, its dependence on human agents to actualize its will, and the variable, unpredictable nature of its associations with mortal actors.[34] Furthermore, the matter of Heaven is, as Allen argues, related to the discussion of Sang Di (上帝) which is called the most powerful spirit in the oracle bone inscriptions of the Shang Dynasty (B. C. ca. 1600-1050) and is variously translated in English as "high lord, lord on high, high god, supreme thearchy, and even God."[35] Allan pays attention to the fact that Shang Di is closely connected to Heaven and the terms are sometimes used interchangeably in the transmitted textual tradition from the Western Zhou (ca. 1050-771 BC) on. She raises a question on why Sang Di should be translated into God given that *Tian* (天) literally means 'sky' even though *Tian* is conventionally translated as 'heaven' when it is associated with spiritual power. She points out that the matter of translations of God and heaven derives from reconceptualization of this relationship into a familiar Judeo-Christian one.[36] Contrary to Fung, Allan suggests that "Shang Di was originally the spirit of the pole star. As such, it was the one celestial body which was higher than the ten suns, with whom the Shang ancestors were identified. Tian-the sky-was the location of the Shang Di and the other ancestral spirits. Thus, it was a wider term that came to serve as a euphemism for Shang Di or, more broadly, for Shang Di and all the celestial phenomena and spirits who were under his aegis."[37]

---

33. Sarah Allan, "On the Identity of Shang Di 上帝 and the Origin of the Concept of a Celestial mandate (*Tian Ming* 天命)," *Early China* 31 (2007), 1.

34. A. C. Graham, *Disputers of the Tao: Philosophical Argument in Ancient China* (La Salle: Open Court, 1989).

35. Allan, "On the Identity of Shang Di 上帝 and the Origin of the Concept of a Celestial mandate (*Tian Ming* 天命)," 1.

36. Ibid., 1.

37. Ibid., 2. cf. *Analects*, 2.1. As translated in Legge. "The Master said, He who exercises government by means of his virtue may be compared to the north polar star, which keeps its place and all the stars turn towards it." 子曰：「為政以德, 譬如北辰, 居其所而眾星共之。」

In particular, it is noticeable that Confucius links study (學) to practice (習); "to learn something and at times to practice it—surely that is a pleasure?"[38] This shows that practice must be linked to learning in the context of self-cultivation. For him, the purpose of moral learning is not for obtaining reputation but for cultivating self; "In ancient times, men learned with a view to their own improvement. Nowadays, men learn with a view to the approbation of others."[39] For Confucius, study is the essential part of self-cultivation. He believed that study and the cultivation of virtue were aspects of the same process. Hence, he states that "if one loves humaneness but does not love learning, the consequence of this is folly; if one loves understanding but does not love learning, the consequence of this is unorthodoxy; if one loves good faith but does not love learning, the consequence of this is damaging behavior; if one loves Straightforwardness but does not love learning, the consequence of this is rudeness; if one loves courage but does not love learning, the consequence of this is rebelliousness; if one loves strength but does not love learning, the consequence of this is violence."[40]

Confucius insists on the importance of order in study. He places emphasis on practicing "filial piety" (孝) and "fraternal submission" (弟) as the roots of humaneness prior to studying literature since if the roots are firmly planted, the Way grows.[41] He submits that "a youth, when at home, should be filial, and, abroad, respectful to his elders. He should be earnest and truthful. He should overflow in love to all, and cultivate the friendship of the good. When he has time and opportunity, after the performance of these things, he should employ them in polite studies (文)."[42] For him, the man of virtue is the one who concerns himself with the root (本). After studying literature, he shows how to preserve what he studied; "If the scholar is not grave (重), he will not call forth any veneration, and his learning will not be solid. Hold faithfulness (忠) and sincerity (信) as

---

38. *Analects*, 1.1. As translated in Dawson. 子曰：學而時習之，不亦說乎？

39. *Analects*, 14.24. As translated in Legge. 子曰：「古之學者為己，今之學者為人。」

40. *Analects*, 17.7. As translated in Dawson. 子曰：「由也，女聞六言六蔽矣乎？」對曰：「未也。」「居！吾語女。好仁不好學，其蔽也愚；好知不好學，其蔽也蕩；好信不好學，其蔽也賊；好直不好學，其蔽也絞；好勇不好學，其蔽也亂；好剛不好學，其蔽也狂。」

41. *Analects*, 1.2. 君子務本，本立而道生。孝弟也者，其為仁之本與！

42. *Analects*, 1.6. As translated in Legge. 子曰：「弟子入則孝，出則弟，謹而信，汎愛眾，而親仁。行有餘力，則以學文。」

first principles, has no friends who are not up to his own standard. When you have faults, do not fear to abandon them."[43]

Sex, Poverty, and Happiness

As Confucius confessed that "in a community of ten households there will certainly be someone as loyal and trustworthy as I am, but not someone so fond of learning as I am," his aspiration for moral learning was intense.[44] Hence, he was always concerned about the failure to cultivate virtue, the failure to put into practice what he has learnt, hearing what is right and being unable to move towards it, being unable to change what is not good.[45] What makes him worry about failing to cultivate virtue? Confucius laments that it is difficult to find the one who loves virtue as much as he loves sex,[46] and hence one of the challenging obstacles for study is the matter of sex particularly in youth:

> There are three things which the man of virtue guards against: in the time of his youth, when his vital powers have not yet settled down, he is on his guard in matters of sex; when he reaches the prime of life and his vital powers have just attained consistency, he is on his guard in matters of contention; and when he becomes old and his vital powers have declined, he is on his guard in matters of acquisition.[47]

This indicates, as Bell argues, that the elderly have greater capacity for moral judgement in that they are less enslaved by sexual desire.[48] As sexual desire decreases with age, there may be less conflict between the desire for sex and the desire to do good. The improvement of moral

---

43. *Analects*, 1.8. As translated in Legge. 子曰：「君子不重則不威，學則不固。主忠信，無友不如己者，過則勿憚改。」

44. *Analects*, 5.28. As translated in Dawson. 子曰：「十室之邑，必有忠信如丘者焉，不如丘之好學也。」

45. *Analects*, 7.3. As translated in Dawson. 子曰：「德之不脩，學之不講，聞義不能徙，不善不能改，是吾憂也。」

46. *Analects*, 9.18. As translated in Legge. "I have not seen one who loves virtue as he loves sex." 子曰：「吾未見好德如好色者也。」

47. *Analects*, 16.7. Translation adapted from Dawson. 孔子曰：「君子有三戒：少之時，血氣未定，戒之在色；及其壯也，血氣方剛，戒之在鬥；及其老也，血氣既衰，戒之在得。」

48. Daniel A. Bell, *China's New Confucianism: Politics and Everyday Life in a Changing Society* (Princeton: Princeton University Press, 2008), 153.

judgement with age derives from the fact that elderly do not typically experience conflict between sexual desire and the desire to do good to the same extent as younger people even though this is not to imply that the desire for sex is entirely extinguished for elderly people. It is easier to control and subordinate to moral principles compared to male adolescents. Hence, at seventy years old, Confucius notes that he can give free reign to his heart's desires, meaning that there is less of a conflict between what he wants to do and what he should do.[49] That is why Confucius places emphasis on paying attention to sexual desire in learning virtue in youth.

In addition, he emphasizes overcoming the matter of poverty in pursuing moral learning as well as sexual desire. For example, he demonstrates that the reasons why he acquired many abilities in menial matters resulted from humble circumstances in his early years and having no official employment when he became older.[50] This indicates that poverty could not hinder his love for study. For him, in other words, study is not the matter of environment but will (志); "The prosecution of learning may be compared to what may happen in raising a mound. If there want but one basket of earth to complete the work, and I stop, the stopping is my own work. It may be compared to throwing down the earth on the level ground. Though but one basketful is thrown at a time, the advancing with it is my own going forward."[51] As Confucius claims that the forces of a large state may be robbed of their commander, but the will of an ordinary man cannot be taken from him,[52] he shows the importance of will. That is why the man of virtue who unites the love of study with sincere faith can hold firm to death in pursuit of the Way.[53] Even about the relation between will and the Way, he claims that "man can enlarge the Way, but it is not true that the Way enlarges man."[54] Such understanding of poverty is linked to his understanding of the man of virtue (君子) as the scholar or public servant (士) "whose mind is set on truth, but who is ashamed

---

49. Ibid., 153.

50. *Analects*, 9.6,7. 大宰問於子貢曰：「夫子聖者與？何其多能也？」子貢曰：「固天縱之將聖，又多能也。」子聞之，曰：「大宰知我乎！吾少也賤，故多能鄙事。君子多乎哉？不多也。」 牢曰：「子云，『吾不試，故藝』。」

51. *Analects*, 9.19. As translated in Legge. 子曰：「譬如為山，未成一簣，止，吾止也；譬如平地，雖覆一簣，進，吾往也。」

52. *Analects*, 9.26 子曰：「三軍可奪帥也，匹夫不可奪志也。」

53. *Analects*, 8.13. 子曰：「篤信好學，守死善道。

54. *Analects*, 15.29. As translated in Dawson. 子曰：「人能弘道，非道弘人。」

of bad clothes and bad food, is not at all fit to be consulted."[55] The man of virtue is concerned about the Way and is not concerned about poverty because hunger is a possible outcome when one ploughs while official salary is a possible outcome when one studies. The object of the man of virtue is not food but the Way (道).[56] In other words, for Confucius "the man of virtue is the one who does not seek to satisfy his appetite to the full when he eats and avoid comfort when he is at home. He is diligent in deed and cautious in his speech, and he associates with possessors of the Way and is put right by them. He may simply be said to love to learn."[57] To be sure, given that Confucius said that "to avoid resentment when one is poor is difficult, but to avoid arrogance when one is rich is easy,"[58] even for the man of virtue poverty must be difficult. Nevertheless, he stresses that "the scholar who cherishes the love of comfort is not fit to be deemed a scholar"[59] since the man of virtue reaches out for what is above by thinking of virtue but the small man reaches out for what is below by thinking of comfort.[60] As a result, the man of virtue remains firm in the face of suffering, but if the small man suffers, he is carried away on a flood of excess.[61] It is because he thinks true happiness does not depend on wealth; "Even in the midst of eating coarse rice and drinking water and using a bent arm for a pillow happiness (樂) is surely to be found; riches and honors acquired by unrighteous means are to me like the floating clouds."[62] In this perspective, Confucius praises Bo Yi and Shu Qi who died of hunger at the foot of the Shou Yang Mountain, criticizing the Duke Jing of Qi who had a thousand teams, each of four horses but did

---

55. *Analects*, 4.9. Translation adapted from Dawson and Legge. Legge translates *shi* (士) as "scholar" while Dawson translates it as "public servant." 子曰：「士志於道，而恥惡衣惡食者，未足與議也。」

56. *Analects*, 15.32. 子曰：「君子謀道不謀食。耕也，餒在其中矣；學也，祿在其中矣。君子憂道不憂貧。」

57. *Analects*, 1.14. Translation adapted from Dawson and Legge. 子曰：「君子食無求飽，居無求安，敏於事而慎於言，就有道而正焉，可謂好學也已。」

58. *Analects*, 14.10. As translated in Dawson. 子曰：「貧而無怨難，富而無驕易。」

59. *Analects*, 14.2. As translated in Legge. 子曰：「士而懷居，不足以為士矣。」

60. *Analects*, 4.11. 子曰：「君子懷德，小人懷土；君子懷刑，小人懷惠。」；*Analects*, 14.23. 子曰：「君子上達，小人下達。」

61. *Analects*, 15.2. 子曰：「君子固窮，小人窮斯濫矣。」

62. *Analects*, 7.16. As translated in Dawson. 子曰：「飯疏食飲水，曲肱而枕之，樂亦在其中矣。不義而富且貴，於我如浮雲。」

not have a single virtue.⁶³ Hence, like them Confucius himself wanted to be assessed by people as follows; "he is the sort of person who gets so worked up that he forgets to eat, is so happy that he forgets anxieties, and is not aware that old age will come."⁶⁴ Considering he states that "those who understand a thing are not equal to those who are fond of it, and those who are fond of it are not equal to those who delight in it,"⁶⁵ he truly delighted in study beyond loving it. Hence, he said that he may die in the evening without regret if he hears the Way in the morning.⁶⁶

Tradition, Imitation, and Friend

In terms of the object of moral learning, Confucius commends tradition instead of exploring extraordinary things, feats of strength, disorder, spiritual beings, and death.⁶⁷ For example, when Zilu asked about serving ghosts, spirits, the dead, Confucius replied that it is meaningless curiosity if one does not understand life and is not capable of serving men.⁶⁸ According to Fingarette Confucius is not just a traditionalist. He regards Confucius as visionary in that Confucian vision is not merely a political vision, but philosophical and religious one.⁶⁹ For Confucius, such topics were not his object of moral learning. Confucius clearly identified his identity as the bearer of tradition; "I transmit but do not create. Being fond of the truth, I am an admirer of antiquity. I venture to be compared with our old Peng."⁷⁰ The confidence of his identity bestowed by Heaven was exposed in the face the of threat of death by the people of Kuang. When Confucius was intimidated there, he states that "when King Wen

63. *Analects*, 16.12. 齊景公有馬千駟，死之日，民無德而稱焉。伯夷叔齊餓于首陽之下，民到于今稱之。其斯之謂與？

64. *Analects*, 7. 19. As translated in Legge. 葉公問孔子於子路，子路不對。子曰：「女奚不曰，其為人也，發憤忘食，樂以忘憂，不知老之將至云爾。」

65. *Analects*, 6.20. 子曰：「知之者不如好之者，好之者不如樂之者。」

66. *Analects*, 4.8. 子曰：「朝聞道，夕死可矣。」

67. *Analects*, 7.21. 子不語怪，力，亂，神。

68. *Analects*, 11.12. As translated in Dawson. "Zilu asked about serving ghosts and spirits. The Master said: 'If one is not yet capable of serving men, how can one serve ghosts?' He ventured to ask about the dead, and the Master said: 'If one does not yet understand life, how does one understand death?'" 季路問事鬼神。子曰：「未能事人，焉能事鬼？」敢問死。曰：「未知生，焉知死？」

69. Fingarette, *Confucius*, 69.

70. *Analects*, 7.1. As translated in Dawson. 子曰：「述而不作，信而好古，竊比於我老彭。」

died, was culture not still here? If Heaven had intended to put an end to this culture, later mortals would not have been able to share in it. If Heaven is not yet putting an end to this culture, what have the people of Kuang got to do with me?"[71] This shows that he considered himself a transmitter of tradition. To be sure, Confucius himself is said to have lost both of his parents in his youth. However, one may suppose that he could early on understand well enough the legacies of the antiquity of both his own distinguished lineage as well as that of the venerable state which his ancestors of the previous several generations had come to serve with some distinction.[72]

Why did Confucius emphasize the study of tradition? The answer is inextricably linked to his understanding of how to acquire knowledge. Confucius states:

> Those who are born with the possession of knowledge come first. Those who know things from study come next. Those who study things although they find them difficult come next to them. Those who do not study because they find things difficult, that is to say the common people, come last.[73]

This seems to value innate knowledge. However, given that he states that "I am not one who was born in the possession of knowledge but one who is fond of antiquity, and earnest in seeking it there,"[74] he virtually stressed the importance of knowing things from study rather than having knowledge at birth; "There may be those who act without knowing why. I do not do so. Hearing much and selecting what is good and following it; seeing much and keeping it in memory—this is the second style of knowledge."[75] When there was an ordinary person putting a question to him, he tried to look at both sides of the question and go into it thoroughly rather than pretending to have knowledge.[76]

---

71. *Analects*, 9.5. As translated in Dawson. 子畏於匡。曰：「文王既沒，文不在茲乎？天之將喪斯文也，後死者不得與於斯文也；天之未喪斯文也，匡人其如予何？」

72. Scott Bradley Cook, "Unity and Diversity in the Musical Thought of Warring States China," (Ph.D. diss., University of Michigan, 1995), 118.

73. *Analects*, 16.9. Translation adapted from Dawson. 孔子曰：「生而知之者，上也；學而知之者，次也；困而學之，又其次也；困而不學，民斯為下矣。」

74. *Analects*, 7.20. 子曰：「我非生而知之者，好古，敏以求之者也。」

75. *Analects*, 7.28. As translated in Legge. 子曰：「蓋有不知而作之者，我無是也。多聞擇其善者而從之，多見而識之，知之次也。」

76. *Analects*, 9.8. 子曰：「吾有知乎哉？無知也。有鄙夫問於我，空空如

Xue (學) and Moral Learning

Confucius offered the Zhou dynasty as the ideal model of tradition for study; "Zhou had the advantage of viewing the two past dynasties, so how splendid is his culture! I follow Zhou."[77] It is because he considered the virtue of Zhou perfect virtue, particularly, highly admiring the duke of Zhou:[78]

> Shun had five ministers, and the empire was well governed. King Wu said, "I have ten able ministers." Confucius said, "Is not the saying that talents are difficult to find, true? Only when the dynasties of Tang and Yu met, were they more abundant than in this of Zhou, yet there was a woman among them. The able ministers were no more than nine men. King Wen possessed two of the three parts of the empire, and with those he served the dynasty of Yin. The virtue of the house of Zhou may be said to have reached the highest point indeed."[79]

What kinds of materials did Confucius suggest for acquiring moral knowledge in study? Regarding this question, Yan Hui shows as follows:

> Yan Hui, in admiration of the Master's doctrines, sighed and said, "I looked up to them, and they seemed to become more high; I tried to penetrate them, and they seemed to become more firm; I looked at them before me, and suddenly they seemed to be behind. By orderly method our Master skillfully leads people on step by step. He broadens my knowledge with literatures (文) and restrains me with ritual propriety (禮). When I wish to give over the study of his doctrines, I cannot do so, and having exerted all my ability, there seems something to stand right up before me; but though I wish to follow and lay hold of it, I really find no way to do so."[80]

也，我叩其兩端而竭焉。」

77. *Analects*, 3.14. As translated in Legge. 子曰：「周監於二代，郁郁乎文哉！吾從周。」 cf. Joel J. Kupperman, "Tradition and Community in the Formation of Character and Self," in *Confucian Ethics: A Comparative Study of Self, Autonomy, and Community*, ed. Kwong-Loi Shun and David B. Wong (Cambridge: Cambridge University Press, 2004), 115.

78. *Analects*, 7.5. 子曰：「甚矣吾衰也！久矣吾不復夢見周公。」

79. *Analects*, 8.20. As translated in Legge. 舜有臣五人而天下治。武王曰：「予有亂臣十人。」孔子曰：「才難，不其然乎？唐虞之際，於斯為盛。有婦人焉，九人而已。三分天下有其二，以服事殷。周之德，其可謂至德也已矣。」

80. *Analects*, 9.11. Translation adapted from Legge. 顏淵喟然歎曰：「仰之彌高，鑽之彌堅；瞻之在前，忽焉在後。夫子循循然善誘人，博我以文，約我以禮。欲罷不能，既竭吾才，如有所立卓爾。雖欲從之，末由也已。」

Confucius enlarged Yan's knowledge with classical writings as well as restraining him with ritual propriety. The fact that literature, ethics, loyalty, and truthfulness were four things which the Master taught indicates he was highly concerned about virtue, not bookishness,[81] since his goal was to create the man of virtue. Hence, he states that "set your heart on the Way, base yourself on virtue, rely on benevolence, and take your relaxation in the arts (藝)."[82] The arts as subjects conducted in the Zhou dynasty that Confucius greatly admired refer to "Six Disciplines" (六藝) such as ritual propriety (禮), music (樂), archery (射), chariot-riding (御), calligraphy (書), and computation (數). As he never refused instruction to anyone who brought a simple present of dried meat for entering his school,[83] he taught large numbers of students by using the Six Disciplines with class distinctions which brought about widespread use of moral education in China.

In particular, Confucius highlighted the value of studying the *Book of Poetry* (詩經) due to its multiple usefulness as follows:

> My disciples, why do you not study the *Book of Poetry*? The *Odes* serve to stimulate the mind. They may be used for purposes of self-contemplation. They teach the art of sociability. They show how to regulate feelings of resentment. You use them at home to serve one's father, and one uses them in distant places to serve one's ruler. From them we become largely acquainted with the names of birds, beasts, plants, and tree.[84]

The *Book of Poetry* not only helps one to be stimulated, to observe, to be sociable, to express grievances, and to practice filial piety and loyalty, but also gains much knowledge about environment. This results from the nature of the *Book of Poetry*; "In the *Book of Poetry* are three hundred pieces, but the design of them all may be embraced in one sentence—Having no depraved thoughts."[85] Even the *Book of Poetry* led Confucius

---

81. *Analects*, 7.25. 子以四教：文，行，忠，信。

82. *Analects*, 7.6. Translation adapted from Legge. 子曰：「志於道，據於德，依於仁，游於藝。」

83. *Analects*, 7.7. 子曰：「自行束脩以上，吾未嘗無誨焉。」

84. *Analects*, 17.9. As translated in Legge. 子曰：「小子！何莫學夫詩？詩，可以興，可以觀，可以群，可以怨。邇之事父，遠之事君。多識於鳥獸草木之名。」 cf. Michael Northcott, *The Environment and Christian Ethics* (Cambridge: Cambridge University Press, 1996), 254.

85. *Analects*, 2.2. As translated in Legge. 子曰：「詩三百，一言以蔽之，曰『思無邪』。」

to use the standard pronunciation.[86] Therefore, he taught the *Book of Poetry* to his son prior to the rules of ritual propriety as follows:

> Chen Kang asked Bo Yu, saying, "Have you heard any lessons from your father different from what we have all heard?" Bo Yu replied, "No. He was standing alone once, when I passed below the hall with hasty steps, and said to me, 'Have you learned the *Book of Poetry*?' On my replying 'Not yet,' he added, 'If you do not learn the *Book of Poetry*, you will not be fit to converse with.' I retired and studied the *Book of Poetry*. Another day, he was in the same way standing alone, when I passed by below the hall with hasty steps, and said to me, 'Have you learned the rules of ritual propriety?' On my replying 'Not yet,' he added, 'If you do not learn the rules of Propriety, your character cannot be established.' I then retired, and learned the rules of Propriety. I have heard only these two things from him." Chen Kang retired, and, quite delighted, said, "I asked one thing, and I have got three things. I have heard about the *Book of Poetry*. I have heard about the rules of ritual propriety. I have also heard that the superior man maintains a distant reserve towards his son."[87]

This indicates the *Book of Poetry* played an important role in educating Confucius' son. Why did Confucius stress the *Book of Poetry* in relation to ritual propriety? In other words, what did Confucius ultimately teach through the *Book of Poetry*? For Confucius, loyalty (忠) and reciprocity (恕) are an all-pervading unity in his doctrine.[88]

What is Confucius' idea about how to study? At first, he presents it by defining the nature of study; "Even if one studies as if it will not be attained, one is still afraid of failing to reach it."[89] This indicates the importance of continuously reviewing what one studied; "If a man keeps cherishing his old knowledge, so as continually to be acquiring new, he may be a teacher of others."[90] In terms of how to study, Confucius offers

---

86. *Analects*, 7.18. 子所雅言, 詩、書、執禮, 皆雅言也。

87. *Analects*, 16.13. Translation adapted from Legge. 陳亢問於伯魚曰：「子亦有異聞乎？」對曰：「未也。嘗獨立，鯉趨而過庭。曰：『學詩乎？』對曰：『未也。』『不學詩，無以言。』鯉退而學詩。他日又獨立，鯉趨而過庭。曰：『學禮乎？』對曰：『未也。』『不學禮，無以立。』鯉退而學禮。聞斯二者。」陳亢退而喜曰：「問一得三，聞詩，聞禮，又聞君子之遠其子也。」

88. *Analects*, 4.15. 子曰：「參乎！吾道一以貫之。」曾子曰：「唯。」子出。門人問曰：「何謂也？」曾子曰：「夫子之道，忠恕而已矣。」

89. *Analects*, 8.17. As translated in Dawson. 子曰：「學如不及，猶恐失之。」

90. *Analects*, 2.11. As translated in Legge. 子曰：「溫故而知新，可以為師矣。」

his disciple Yan Hui as an excellent example. When Confucius was asked by the Duke Ai about which of the disciples loved to study, he replied that Yan Hui is the one who loved to study as well as not transferring his anger on those who did not deserve it and not repeating a fault.[91] Even Zi Gong thought that he cannot be compared to Hui in that he hears one point and knows all about a subject.[92] For Confucius, Hui is the one who did not flag when Confucius was speaking to him, His mind did not stray from benevolence for as long as three months contrary to the rest of them who attained it only occasionally.[93] Furthermore, Confucius rated highly Hui's ability of self-study with cleverness; "I have talked with Hui for a whole day, and he has not made any objection to anything I said—as if he were stupid. He has retired, and I have examined his conduct when away from me, and found him able to illustrate my teachings. Hui!—He is not stupid."[94] Above all, Confucius praised how he was honed by hardships; "Admirable indeed was the virtue of Hui! He lived in a squalid alley with a tiny bowlful of rice to eat and a ladleful of water to drink. Other men would not endure such hardships, but Hui did not let his happiness be affected. Admirable indeed was the virtue of Hui!"[95] In other words, Hui was the man of virtue.

With regard to the method of study, more specifically, Confucius also emphasizes the importance of finding a good teacher and imitating his words and deeds since it is one of the best ways to learn the practice of virtue; "The mechanic, who wishes to do his work well, must first sharpen his tools. When you are living in any state, take service with the most worthy among its great officers, and make friends of the most virtuous among its scholars."[96] When Zi Zhang enquired about the way of the good man (善人), Confucius clearly replied that if he does not tread in

---

91. *Analects*, 6.3. 哀公問：「弟子孰為好學？」孔子對曰：「有顏回者好學，不遷怒，不貳過。」

92. *Analects*, 5.9. 子謂子貢曰：「女與回也孰愈？」對曰：「賜也何敢望回。回也聞一以知十，賜也聞一以知二。」子曰：「弗如也！吾與女弗如也。」

93. *Analects*, 6.3. 不幸短命死矣！今也則亡，未聞好學者也。」

94. *Analects*, 2.9. As translated in Legge. 子曰：「吾與回言終日，不違如愚。退而省其私，亦足以發。回也，不愚。」

95. *Analects*, 6.11. As translated in Legge. 子曰：「賢哉回也！一簞食，一瓢飲，在陋巷。人不堪其憂，回也不改其樂。賢哉回也！」

96. *Analects*, 15.10. As translated in Legge. 子貢問為仁。子曰：「工欲善其事，必先利其器。居是邦也，事其大夫之賢者，友其士之仁者。」

the footsteps of others, he cannot enter the chamber of the sage."[97] Hence, he states that "When we see men of worth, we should think of equaling them; when we see men of a contrary character, we should turn inwards and examine ourselves."[98] If so, where can we find such teachers? Confucius shows that "when I walk along with two others, they may serve me as my teachers. I will select their good qualities and follow them, their bad qualities and avoid them."[99] Namely, such teachers can be easily found around us. For him, a source of such teachers is friends (友); "Regard loyalty (忠) and sincerity (信) as your main concern. Do not make friends of those who are not up to your own standard. When you have faults, do not shrink from correcting it."[100] Which types of friends are commendable for Confucius? He outlines both the advantageous and injurious types of friendship. According to him, beneficial friends are those who are upright, and sincere, while harmful friends are those who are ingratiating good at seeming pliant.[101] This indicates that we may meet harmful friends as well as beneficial ones. How to cope with that? Confucius advises that "Loyally provide your friend with information and guide him skillfully. If you find him impracticable, stop. Do not disgrace yourself."[102]

For Confucius, moral learning is not limited to the individual dimension. Moral learning as the method of self-cultivation finds its true end in the political dimension, given that the man of perfect virtue pursues this not only for himself but also for others:

> Zi Gong said, "Suppose the case of a man extensively conferring benefits on the people, and able to assist all, what would you say of him? Might he be called humane?" The Master said: "Why only humane? He would undoubtedly be a sage. Didn't even Yao and Shun have to take pains over this? Now the humane man, wishing himself to be established, sees that others are

---

97. *Analects*, 11.20. As translated in Legge. 子張問善人之道。子曰：「不踐跡，亦不入於室。」

98. *Analects*, 4.17. As translated in Legge. 子曰：「見賢思齊焉，見不賢而內自省也。」

99. *Analects*, 7.22. 子曰：「三人行，必有我師焉。擇其善者而從之，其不善者而改之。」

100. *Analects*, 9.25. Translation adapted from Dawson and Legge. 子曰：「主忠信，毋友不如己者，過則勿憚改。」

101. *Analects*, 16.4. 孔子曰：「益者三友，損者三友。友直，友諒，友多聞，益矣。友便辟，友善柔，友便佞，損矣。」

102. *Analects*, 12.23. Translation adapted from Dawson and Legge. 子貢問友。子曰：「忠告而善道之，不可則止，無自辱焉。」

established, and wishing himself to be successful, sees that others are successful. To be able to take one's own familiar feelings as a guide may definitely be called the method of humaneness."[103]

Confucius regards the one who benefits people far and wide, and is capable of bringing salvation to the multitude, as a sage. The reason why he called such man a sage is that he knew how hard it is to practice what he studied. Confucius stated that "in terms of studying literatures I am comparable with others, but as to myself being a man of virtue in practice, I have never yet managed to achieve that."[104] Even he argued that "though a man may be able to recite the three hundred odes, but if he is given a post in government and cannot successfully carry out his governmental charge, and if he is sent to far places and cannot react to the circumstances as he finds them, then even if he has learnt to recite many of them, of what use is this to him?"[105] In spite of the difficulty of practicing what one studied, he enthusiastically wished what he studied can be contributed to government; "Zi Gong said, There is a beautiful gem here. Should I lay it up in a case and keep it? or should I seek a good price and sell it? The Master said, Sell it! Sell it! But I would wait for one to offer the price."[106] For Confucius, such desire seems to be natural since he struggled to "find a man who has studied for three years without coming to be good."[107] To be sure, this does not indicate his scholarship is just fixed to achieve high social positions. He stressed, the determined scholar and the man of virtue even sacrifice their lives to preserve perfect virtue without seeking to live at the expense of injuring their virtue.[108] As

---

103. *Analects*, 6.30. Translation adapted from Dawson and Legge. 子貢曰：「如有博施於民而能濟眾，何如？可謂仁乎？」子曰：「何事於仁，必也聖乎！堯舜其猶病諸！夫仁者，己欲立而立人，己欲達而達人。能近取譬，可謂仁之方也已。」

104. *Analects*, 7.33. Translation adapted from Dawson. 子曰：「文，莫吾猶人也。躬行君子，則吾未之有得。」

105. *Analects*, 13.5. As translated in Legge. 子曰：「誦詩三百，授之以政，不達；使於四方，不能專對；雖多，亦奚以為？」

106. *Analects*, 9.13. As translated in Legge. 子貢曰：「有美玉於斯，韞匵而藏諸？求善賈而沽諸？」子曰：「沽之哉！沽之哉！我待賈者也。」

107. *Analects*, 8.12. As translated in Legge. 子曰：「三年學，不至於穀，不易得也。」

108. *Analects*, 15.9. 子曰：「志士仁人，無求生以害仁，有殺身以成仁。」; *Analects*, 17.13. 子曰：「鄉原，德之賊也。」

a practical example for this, he urged to "recompense injury with justice, and recompense kindness with kindness."[109]

This section shows that Confucius' moral learning is realistic in that he focused on acquiring virtue as a solution for solving political chaos. For him, Heaven is an object of moral learning because it produces virtue in relation to human nature. Practicing filial piety (孝) and fraternal submission (弟) is to cultivate moral self. Contrary to Augustine who emphasizes grace for forgiving sins, Confucius presents will (志) for overcoming sexual desire and poverty.

MENCIUS' MORAL LEARNING

Self-Cultivation, Benevolent Government, and Will

As Mencius claims that "the Empire has its basis in the state, the state in the family, and the family in one's self,"[110] the starting point of his formation of moral self is based on self-cultivation. He warns that if a man does not practice the Way, he will not have his way even with his own wife and children.[111] Beyond the dimension of family, for him the best way to bring orders to the Empire is that the man of virtue cultivates his character. It is because he thought the trouble with people is what they require from others is great, while the burden they lay upon themselves is light. His moral education is significantly political.[112] Hence, he stresses the man of virtue

---

109. *Analects*, 14.34. As translated in Legge. 或曰：「以德報怨，何如？」子曰：「何以報德？以直報怨，以德報德。」

110. *Mencius*, 4A5. trans. D. C. Lau (London: Penguin Books, 2004). 孟子曰：「人有恆言，皆曰『天下國家』。天下之本在國，國之本在家，家之本在身。」cf. *Great Learning*, 8.1.

111. *Mencius*, 7B9. 孟子曰：「身不行道，不行於妻子；使人不以道，不能行於妻子。」

112. Graham shows differences between Confucius and Mencius in the concept of benevolence (仁) and ritual propriety (禮); "The greatest is still *jen*, but the word has narrowed and clarified in meaning. Confucius had inherited it as a word like English 'noble' covering everything distinctive of the man of breeding; seeking the unifying principle behind it he found pure benevolence, the disinterested concern for others, but for him this was not yet the whole sense of the word. By the time of Mencius, however, *jen* is directly translatable by 'benevolence'. Another difference is that we no longer have the impression with Mencius that all moral concepts depend for their meaning on the context of ceremony. *Li* 'ceremony' is now the inward sense of good manners, and stands beside *jen* in a set of four cardinal virtues inside the heart, the benevolent and the right, ceremony and wisdom (*jen yi li chih* 仁義禮智)." Particularly,

secures good words and principles as specific methods for ruling the Empire; "Words which are simple, while their meaning is far-reaching, are good words. Principles which, as held, are compendious, while their application is extensive, are good principles. The words of the man of virtue enshrine great principles."[113] In this context, he offers self-cultivation as a prerequisite for moral education for others; "anciently, men of virtue and talents by means of their own enlightenment made others enlightened. Nowadays, it is tried, while they are themselves in darkness, and by means of that darkness, to make others enlightened."[114] He regards those who rectify others by rectifying themselves as the great men.[115]

Mencius explains his moral education in the relation between a king and his people. According to the modes of labor, he argues that the methods of moral education need to be differentiated. Mencius states:

> Then, is it the government of the kingdom which alone can be carried on along with the practice of husbandry? Great men have their proper business, and little men have their proper business … Some labor with their minds, and some labor with their strength. Those who labor with their minds govern others; those who labor with their strength are governed by others. Those who are governed by others support them; those who govern others are supported by them. This is a principle universally recognized.[116]

---

jen can be translated to benevolence is noticeable, given Graham shows the importance of benevolent government as well as human nature in Mencius' thought. He presents "unlike Confucius, who sees the reform of government in terms of a judicious selection between the rituals of the Hsia, Shang, and Chou, Mencius wants political and economic measures." However, Graham does not show how benevolent government can be related to human nature endowed by Heaven in moral education. Graham, *Disputers of the Tao*, 113.

113. *Mencius*, 7B32. Trans. James Legge (New York: Dover Publications, 1970). 孟子曰：「言近而指遠者，善言也；守約而施博者，善道也。君子之言也，不下帶而道存焉。君子之守，修其身而天下平。人病舍其田而芸人之田，所求於人者重，而所以自任者輕。」

114. *Mencius*, 7B20. Translation adapted from Legge. 孟子曰：「賢者以其昭昭，使人昭昭；今以其昏昏，使人昭昭。」

115. *Mencius*, 7A19. 「有大人者，正己而物正者也。」

116. *Mencius*, 3A4. As translated in Legge. 「然則治天下獨可耕且為與？有大人之事，有小人之事。且一人之身，而百工之所為備。如必自為而後用之，是率天下而路也。故曰：或勞心，或勞力；勞心者治人，勞力者治於人；治於人者食人，治人者食於人：天下之通義也。」

Mencius shows the government of the kingdom is carried by those who labor with their minds in order to rule those who labor with their strength. For Mencius, those who labor with their minds are kings and government officials, and those who labor with their strength are people. Hence, his moral education paid great attention to the matter of how to make kings virtuous; "He who, using force, makes a pretense to benevolence is the leader of the princes. A leader of the princes requires a large kingdom. He who, using virtue, practices benevolence is the sovereign of the kingdom. To become the sovereign of the kingdom, a prince need not wait for a large kingdom."[117] Mencius argues when one subdues men by virtue, in their hearts' core they are pleased, and sincerely submit, as was the case with the seventy disciples in their submission to Confucius. When one by force subdues men, they do not submit to him in heart.[118] Mencius stresses the rise and fall of states are determined by benevolence in support of evidences of his previous three dynasties as follows:

> the Three Dynasties won the Empire through benevolence and lost it through cruelty. This is true of the rise and fall, survival and collapse, of states as well. If the sovereign be not benevolent, be cannot preserve the throne from passing from him. If the Head of a State be not benevolent, he cannot preserve his rule. If a high noble or great officer be not benevolent, he cannot preserve his ancestral temple. If a scholar or common man be not benevolent, be cannot preserve his four limbs. Now they hate death and ruin, and yet delight in being not benevolent—this is like hating to be drunk, and yet being strong to drink wine![119]

Given that Mencius stresses the importance of benevolence in government, this passage above shows the importance of human will, just as Confucius shows calamity and happiness in all cases are determined by men's own seeking as follows:

> A man must first despise himself, and then others will despise him. A family must first destroy itself, and then others will

---

117. *Mencius*, 2A3. Translation adapted from Lau and Legge. 孟子曰：以力假仁者霸，霸必有大國，以德行仁者王，王不待大。

118. *Mencius*, 2A3. 以力服人者，非心服也，力不贍也；以德服人者，中心悅而誠服也，如七十子之服孔子也。

119. *Mencius*, 4A3. As translated in Legge. 孟子曰：「三代之得天下也以仁，其失天下也以不仁。國之所以廢興存亡者亦然。天子不仁，不保四海；諸侯不仁，不保社稷；卿大夫不仁，不保宗廟；士庶人不仁，不保四體。今惡死亡而樂不仁，是猶惡醉而強酒。」

destroy it. A State must first smite itself, and then others will smite it. This is illustrated in the passage of the Tai Jia, When Heaven sends down calamities, it is still possible to escape them. When we occasion the calamities ourselves, it is not possible any longer to live.[120]

Mencius demonstrates that there is no difference between killing with a knife and killing with misrule. He stresses the king, as the parent of his people, ought to take care of his people.

> King Hui of Liang said, "I wish quietly to receive your instructions." Mencius replied, "Is there any difference between killing a man with a stick and with a sword?" The king said, "There is no difference!" "Is there any difference between killing him with a knife and killing him with misrule?" "There is no difference," was the reply. Mencius then said, "In your kitchen there is fat meat; in your stables there are fat horses. But your people have the look of hunger, and on the wilds there are those who have died of famine. This is leading on beasts to devour men. Beasts devour one another, and men hate them for doing so. When a prince, being the parent of his people, administers his government so as to be chargeable with leading on beasts to devour men, where is his parental relation to the people?"[121]

As the *Book of History* states that "Heaven having produced the inferior people, made for them rulers and teachers, with the purpose that they should be helpful to God,"[122] Mencius thinks that the purpose of a ruler is to protect his people in supporting God. Mencius insists that "the people are the most important element in a nation; the spirits of the land and grain are the next; the sovereign is the lightest."[123] In this context, he claims that a king without benevolence and righteousness could be

---

120. *Mencius*, 4A8. As translated in Legge. 夫人必自侮，然後人侮之；家必自毀，而後人毀之；國必自伐，而後人伐之。《太甲》曰：『天作孽，猶可違；自作孽，不可活。』此之謂也。

121. *Mencius*, 1A4. As translated in Legge. 梁惠王曰：「寡人願安承教。」 孟子對曰：「殺人以梃與刃，有以異乎？」 曰：「無以異也。」 「以刃與政，有以異乎？」 曰：「無以異也。」 曰：「庖有肥肉，廄有肥馬，民有飢色，野有餓莩，此率獸而食人也。獸相食，且人惡之。為民父母，行政不免於率獸而食人。惡在其為民父母也？」

122. *Mencius*, 1B3. As translated in Legge. 《書》曰：『天降下民，作之君，作之師。惟曰其助上帝，寵之。

123. *Mencius*, 7B14. 孟子曰：「民為貴，社稷次之，君為輕。」

expelled and killed by his people;[124] "He who outrages the benevolence proper to his nature, is called a robber; he who outrages righteousness, is called a ruffian. The robber and ruffian we call a mere fellow. I have heard of the cutting off of the fellow Zhou, but I have not heard of the putting a sovereign to death, in his case."[125] Mencius notes that this principle might be applied to officers in evidence of Tseng Tzu's saying that "what you mete out will be paid back to you."[126] When the king puts in practice a benevolent government, his people will love him and all above them, and will die for their officers. In addition, Mencius thinks that when a king is virtuous that is morally educational for the people; "If the sovereign be benevolent, all will be benevolent. If the sovereign be righteous, all will be righteous."[127]

Therefore, for Mencius, a king who seeks to practice a benevolent government is a prerequisite for preserving his Empire and has significant advantages. Mencius shows if a king puts in place a benevolent government, no power will be able to prevent his becoming sovereign since the flowing progress of virtue, as Confucius said, is more rapid than the transmission of royal orders by stages and couriers.[128] For Mencius, a benevolent king is one who is not fond of killing and the king can settle the Empire by uniting it because all the people of the nation will unanimously give it to him.[129] He explains the advantage of benevolent government to King Hsiang of Liang as follows:

> Does your Majesty understand the way of the growing grain?
> During the seventh and eighth months, when drought prevails,

---

124. *Mencius*, 1B6. 孟子謂齊宣王曰：「王之臣有託其妻子於其友，而之楚遊者。比其反也，則凍餒其妻子，則如之何？」王曰：「棄之。」曰：「士師不能治士，則如之何？」王曰：「已之。」曰：「四境之內不治，則如之何？」王顧左右而言他。

125. *Mencius*, 1B8. As translated in Legge. 曰：「賊仁者謂之賊，賊義者謂之殘，殘賊之人謂之一夫。聞誅一夫紂矣，未聞弒君也。」

126. *Mencius*, 1B12. 孟子對曰：「凶年饑歲，君之民老弱轉乎溝壑，壯者散而之四方者，幾千人矣；而君之倉廩實，府庫充，有司莫以告，是上慢而殘下也。曾子曰：『戒之戒之！出乎爾者，反乎爾者也。』夫民今而後得反之也。君無尤焉。君行仁政，斯民親其上、死其長矣。」

127. *Mencius*, 4B5. As translated in Legge. 孟子曰：「君仁莫不仁，君義莫不義。」

128. *Mencius*, 2A3. 行仁政而王，莫之能禦也。孔子曰：『德之流行，速於置郵而傳命。』

129. *Mencius*, 1A6. 卒然問曰：『天下惡乎定？』吾對曰：『定于一。』『孰能與之？』對曰：『天下莫不與也。』

the plants become dry. Then the clouds collect densely in the heavens, they send down torrents of rain, and the grain erects itself, as if by a shoot. When it does so, who can keep it back? Now among the shepherds of men throughout the nation, there is not one who does not find pleasure in killing men. If there were one who did not find pleasure in killing men, all the people in the nation would look towards him with outstretched necks. Such being indeed the case, the people would flock to him, as water flows downwards with a rush, which no one can repress.[130]

Mencius expects that people will naturally flock to the benevolent king if benevolent government is carried like rain in a drought. It is Heaven's desire.[131] According to him, when right government prevails in the kingdom, princes of little virtue are submissive to those of great, and those of little worth to those of great. When bad government prevails in the kingdom, princes of small power are submissive to those of great, and the weak to the strong. He stresses that they who accord with Heaven are preserved, and they who rebel against Heaven perish. Mencius states:

> There is an appointment for everything. A man should receive submissively what may be correctly ascribed thereto. Therefore, he who has the true idea of what is Heaven's appointment will not stand beneath a precipitous wall. Death sustained in the discharge of one's duties may correctly be ascribed to the appointment of Heaven. Death under handcuffs and fetters cannot correctly be so ascribed.[132]

In this context, Mencius warns that "if men of virtue and ability be not confided in, a State will become empty and void. Without the rules of propriety and distinctions of right, the high and the low will be thrown into confusion. Without the great principles of government and their various business, there will not be wealth sufficient for the expenditure."[133]

---

130. *Mencius*, 1A6. As translated in Legge. 『王知夫苗乎？七八月之間旱，則苗槁矣。天油然作雲，沛然下雨，則苗浡然興之矣。其如是，孰能禦之？今夫天下之人牧，未有不嗜殺人者也，如有不嗜殺人者，則天下之民皆引領而望之矣。誠如是也，民歸之，由水之就下，沛然誰能禦之？』

131. *Mencius*, 4A7. 孟子曰：天下有道，小德役大德，小賢役大賢；天下無道，小役大，弱役強。斯二者天也。順天者存，逆天者亡。

132. *Mencius*, 7A2. As translated in Legge. 孟子曰：「莫非命也，順受其正。是故知命者，不立乎巖牆之下。盡其道而死者，正命也。桎梏死者，非正命也。」

133. *Mencius*, 7B12. Translation adapted from Legge. 孟子曰：「不信仁賢，則國空虛。無禮義，則上下亂。無政事，則財用不足。」

The man of virtue serves his prince contemplates simply the leading him in the right path, and directing his mind to benevolence.[134] Therefore, Mencius strongly advises King Hsiang of Liang that he should institute a government whose action shall be benevolent This will cause all the officers in the kingdom to wish to stand in his court, and all the farmers to wish to plough in his fields, and all the merchants, both travelling and stationary, to wish to store their goods in his market-places, and all travelling strangers to wish to make their tours on his roads, and all throughout the kingdom who feel aggrieved by their rulers to wish to come and complain to him.[135]

Human Unity, Filial Piety, and Moral Education

In time of war, for Mencius human unity by benevolent government is the most powerful weapon rather than Earth's advantageous terrain and Heaven's favorable weather. Mencius states:

> Heaven's favorable weather is less important than Earth's advantageous terrain, and Earth's advantageous terrain is less important than human unity. There is a city, with an inner wall of three li in circumference, and an outer wall of seven. The enemies surround and attack it, but they are not able to take it. Now, to surround and attack it, there must have been vouchsafed to them by Heaven the opportunity of time, and in such case their not taking it is because opportunities of time vouchsafed by Heaven are not equal to advantages of situation afforded by the Earth. There is a city, whose walls are distinguished for their height, and whose moats are distinguished for their depth, where the arms of its defenders, offensive and defensive, are distinguished for their strength and sharpness, and the stores of rice and other grain are very large. Yet it is obliged to be given up and abandoned. This is because advantages of situation afforded by the Earth are not equal to the union arising from the accord of Men ... When the being assisted by many reaches its highest point, the whole kingdom becomes obedient to the prince. When one to whom the whole kingdom is prepared to be obedient, attacks those from whom their own relations revolt, what must be the

---

134. *Mencius*, 6B8, 君子之事君也，務引其君以當道，志於仁而已。

135. *Mencius*, 1A7, 蓋亦反其本矣。今王發政施仁，使天下仕者皆欲立於王之朝，耕者皆欲耕於王之野，商賈皆欲藏於王之市，行旅皆欲出於王之塗，天下之欲疾其君者皆欲赴愬於王。其若是，孰能禦之？

result? Therefore, the true ruler will prefer not to fight; but if he does fight, he must overcome.[136]

For Mencius, the major source of power for overcoming war is not military but human unity formed by benevolent government. Mencius explained to King Hui of Liang why a benevolent government can overcome powerful countries in the military dimension like Qin and Chu in relation to moral education of filial piety and self-cultivation.[137] According to him, if the king delivers benevolent government to the people, being sparing in the use of punishments and fines, and making the taxes and levies light, so causing that the fields to be ploughed deep, and the weeding of them carefully attended to, and that the strong-bodied, during their days of leisure, shall cultivate their filial piety, fraternal respectfulness, sincerity, and truthfulness, serving thereby, at home, their fathers and elder brothers, and, abroad, their elders and superiors, the king will then have a people who can be employed, with sticks which they have prepared, to oppose the strong armor and sharp weapons of the troops of Qin and Chu. It is because the rulers of those States rob their people of their time that they cannot plough and weed their fields to support their parents. Their parents suffer from cold and hunger. Brothers, wives, and children are separated and scattered abroad. Mencius points out those rulers drive their people into pit-falls, or drown them. According to him, "a man can have no greater crimes than to disown his parents and relatives, and the relations of sovereign and minister, superiors and inferiors."[138] As he considers the richest fruit of benevolence to be the service of one's parents, the essence of benevolence is filial piety.[139] Hence, he argues if only everyone loved his parents and treated his elders with

---

136. *Mencius*, 2B1. Translation adapted from Lau and Legge. 孟子曰：「天時不如地利，地利不如人和。三里之城，七里之郭，環而攻之而不勝。夫環而攻之，必有得天時者矣；然而不勝者，是天時不如地利也。城非不高也，池非不深也，兵革非不堅利也，米粟非不多也；委而去之，是地利不如人和也。故曰：域民不以封疆之界，固國不以山谿之險，威天下不以兵革之利。得道者多助，失道者寡助。寡助之至，親戚畔之；多助之至，天下順之。以天下之所順，攻親戚之所畔；故君子有不戰，戰必勝矣。」

137. *Mencius*, 1A5. 孟子對曰：「地方百里而可以王。王如施仁政於民，省刑罰，薄稅斂，深耕易耨。壯者以暇日修其孝悌忠信，入以事其父兄，出以事其長上，可使制梃以撻秦楚之堅甲利兵矣。彼奪其民時，使不得耕耨以養其父母，父母凍餓，兄弟妻子離散。彼陷溺其民，王往而征之，夫誰與王敵？故曰：『仁者無敵。』王請勿疑！」

138. *Mencius*, 7A34. As translated in Legge. 人莫大焉亡親戚、君臣、上下。

139. *Mencius*, 4A27. 仁之實，事親是也

Xue (學) and Moral Learning

deference, the Empire would be at peace.[140] For him, the Way lies at hand. It is because filial affection for parents as the working of benevolence and respect for elders as the working of righteousness are an intuitive ability and knowledge possessed by men without having been acquired by learning and without the exercise of thought.[141] For him, those feelings are universal under heaven. Yet, those feelings do not guarantee the automatic practice of filial piety. Mencius shows that filial piety as the service of parents can be properly practiced in support of self-cultivation since it is the root of all others as follows:

> Of services, which is the greatest? The service of parents is the greatest. Of charges, which is the greatest? The charge of one's self is the greatest. That those who do not fail to keep themselves are able to serve their parents is what I have heard. But I have never heard of any, who, having failed to keep themselves, were able notwithstanding to serve their parents. There are many services, but the service of parents is the root of all others. There are many charges, but the charge of one's self is the root of all others.[142]

This could be applied to Mencius' moral education between father and son. Mencius states that "the trouble with people is that they are too eager to assume the role of teacher."[143] This indicates the danger of moral teaching without self-cultivation. Mencius points out even the man of virtue might lose his temper in teaching his children, so the ancients exchanged sons, and one taught the son of another to avoid offending between father and son.[144] This shows how important filial piety is in his formation of moral self. Therefore, Mencius strongly asserts that reforming economic, social, and educational systems should be undertaken in

---

140. *Mencius*, 4A11. 孟子曰：「道在爾而求諸遠，事在易而求之難。人人親其親、長其長而天下平。」

141. *Mencius*, 7A15. 孟子曰：「人之所不學而能者，其良能也；所不慮而知者，其良知也。孩提之童，無不知愛其親者；及其長也，無不知敬其兄也。親親，仁也；敬長，義也。無他，達之天下也。」

142. *Mencius*, 4A19. As translated in Legge. 孟子曰：「事孰為大？事親為大；守孰為大？守身為大。不失其身而能事其親者，吾聞之矣；失其身而能事其親者，吾未之聞也。孰不為事？事親，事之本也；孰不為守？守身，守之本也。」

143. *Mencius*, 4A23. As translated in Legge. 孟子曰：「人之患在好為人師。」

144. *Mencius*, 4A18. 公孫丑曰：「君子之不教子，何也？」 孟子曰：「勢不行也。教者必以正；以正不行，繼之以怒；繼之以怒，則反夷矣。『夫子教我以正，夫子未出於正也。』則是父子相夷也。父子相夷，則惡矣。古者易子而教之。父子之間不責善。責善則離，離則不祥莫大焉。」

the perspective of filial piety.[145] For Mencius the first step along the Kingly way is to make the people support their parents when alive or mourn of them when dead, and the filial and fraternal duties should be taught in schools. According to Mencius, there is taxation levied in cloth, in grain, and in labor. The man of virtue employs one to the full while relaxing the other two since if two are employed to the full, there would be death from starvation amongst the people, and if all three are so employed, father will be separated from son.[146] Following the matter of taxation, Mencius stresses the importance of establishing educational institutions in order to enhance human relationships as the purpose of moral education since good government does not lay hold of the people so much as good moral education as follows:

> Establish Xiang, Xu, Xue, and Xiao, all those educational institutions, for the purpose of education. The name Xiang indicates nourishing as its object; Xiao, indicates teaching; and Xu indicates archery. By the Xia dynasty the name Xiao was used; by the Yin, that of Xu; and by the Zhou, that of Xiang. As to the Xue, they belonged to the three dynasties, and by that name. The object of them all is to illustrate the human relations. When those are thus illustrated by superiors, kindly feeling will prevail among the inferior people below.[147]

Mencius claims that good government is feared by the people and the people's wealth, while good moral education is loved by them and gets their hearts.[148] So when a prince seeks by his goodness to nourish men, he will be able to subdue the whole kingdom since if they are well fed, warmly clad, and comfortably lodged, without being taught at the same time, they become almost like the beasts.[149] Hence, the sage Shun appointed Xie to be the Minister of Education, to teach the relations of humanity: how, between father and son, there should be affection;

---

145. *Mencius*, 1A3.

146. *Mencius*, 7B27. 孟子曰：「有布縷之征，粟米之征，力役之征。君子用其一，緩其二。用其二而民有殍，用其三而父子離。」

147. *Mencius*, 3A3. Translation adapted from Lau and Legge. 「設為庠序學校以教之：庠者，養也；校者，教也；序者，射也。夏曰校，殷曰序，周曰庠，學則三代共之，皆所以明人倫也。人倫明於上，小民親於下。有王者起，必來取法，是為王者師也。」

148. *Mencius*, 7A14. 孟子曰：「善政，不如善教之得民也。善政民畏之，善教民愛之；善政得民財，善教得民心。」

149. *Mencius*, 4B16. 孟子曰：「以善服人者，未有能服人者也；以善養人，然後能服天下。天下不心服而王者，未之有也。」

between sovereign and minister, righteousness; between husband and wife, attention to their separate functions; between old and young, a proper order; and between friends, fidelity.[150]

Environment and Asceticism

Mencius, even more than Confucius, deals at length with the matter of the natural environment for moral education, and not only human nature.[151] Why did Mencius pay attention to improving people's living conditions? Ironically, this can be explained in relation to his theory of human nature. As Kao Tzu said:

> Human nature is like water whirling round in a corner. Open a passage for it to the east, and it will flow to the east; open a passage for it to the west, and it will flow to the west. Human nature

---

150. *Mencius*, 3A4. As translated in Legge. 人之有道也，飽食、煖衣、逸居而無教，則近於禽獸。聖人有憂之，使契為司徒，教以人倫：父子有親，君臣有義，夫婦有別，長幼有序，朋友有信。放勳曰：『勞之來之，匡之直之，輔之翼之，使自得之，又從而振德之。』聖人之憂民如此，而暇耕乎？

151. Tu offers Confucian self-cultivation as the highest purpose of human life, as opposed to the Legalist approach to man as an instrument of the state. Particularly, he expounds the innate moral qualities in the aspect of the Mencian perception of moral self-development. He acknowledges that Mencius is acutely aware of the influences of environment in the formation of moral self; "It is not difficult to show that he recognizes that economic conditions, political situations, and social relations have a profound impact on a person's ethical life. Furthermore, he insists that improvements be made in those crucial areas of the environment before realistic programs of moral education can be implemented." However, he argues, for Mencius, there is more important something than environment in moral education; "this something is neither learned nor acquired; it is a given reality, endowed by Heaven as the defining characteristic of being human." Mencius' strategy of presenting his position on the matter is best shown in his exchanges with Kao Tzu who takes a naturalist position. For Mencius, four germinations such as humanity, righteousness, propriety, and wisdom are not drilled into us from outside. These are inborn and can be lost, but are always recoverable if one wills to preserve it. Hence, according to Tu, Mencius insists the way of learning is none other than finding the lost mind (6A11). In other words, for Mencius moral education is ultimately the problem of mind rather than environment. Tu proves human nature is more important than environment in Mencius' moral education, but his explanation that instinctual demands such as appetites for food and sex can be solved by "a holistic way" in order to be human is still ambiguous. Weiming Tu, *Humanity and Self-Cultivation: Essays in Confucian Thought* (Boston: Cheng & Tsui Co, 1998), 58, 59, 64, 66.

is indifferent to good and evil, just as the water is indifferent to the east and west.[152]

Kao Tzu considers human nature neutral. In contrary to his understanding of human nature, Mencius asserts the tendency of human nature is good just as there is no water that does not flow downwards:

> It certainly is the case, said Mencius, that water does not show any preference for either east or west, but does it show the same indifference to high and low? Human nature is good just as water seeks low ground. There is no man who is not good; there is no water that does not flow downwards. Now in the case of water, by splashing it one can make it shoot up higher than one's forehead, and by forcing it one can make it stay on a hill. How can that be the nature of water? It is the circumstances being what they are. That man can be made bad shows that his nature is no different from that of water in this respect.[153]

According to circumstances, water could be changed to flow upwards, but it is not the nature of water. Likewise, that man can be made bad is because human nature is affected by circumstances, not Heaven. For example, Mencius shows that the children of the people are most of them good in good years whereas in bad years the most of them abandon themselves to evil. He stresses that the abandonment does not derive from "any difference of their natural powers conferred by Heaven that they are thus different" but "the circumstances through which they allow their minds to be ensnared and drowned in evil."[154] In this context, Mencius states that "A man's environment transforms his air just as the food he eats changes his body."[155] Therefore, Mencius explains the importance of economic environments in the formation of the moral self by comparing scholars and ordinary people; "Only scholars can have a constant without a certain livelihood. The people, on the other hand, will

---

152. *Mencius*, 6A2. 性猶湍水也，決諸東方則東流，決諸西方則西流。

153. *Mencius*, 6A2. As translated in Legge. 告子曰：「性猶湍水也，決諸東方則東流，決諸西方則西流。人性之無分於善不善也，猶水之無分於東西也。」孟子曰：「水信無分於東西。無分於上下乎？人性之善也，猶水之就下也。人無有不善，水無有不下。今夫水，搏而躍之，可使過顙；激而行之，可使在山。是豈水之性哉？其勢則然也。人之可使為不善，其性亦猶是也。」

154. *Mencius*, 6A7. As translated in Legge. 孟子曰：「富歲，子弟多賴；凶歲，子弟多暴，非天之降才爾殊也，其所以陷溺其心者然也。

155. *Mencius*, 7A36. Translation adapted from Lau. 居移氣，養移體，大哉居乎！

not have constant hearts if they have not a certain livelihood. And if they have not constant hearts, there is nothing which they will not do, in the way of self-abandonment, of moral deflection, of depravity, and of wild license."[156] Mencius explains that for ordinary people it is challenging to secure time for studying about ritual propriety and righteousness if they do not properly support their parents, wives, and children as follows:

> When they thus have been involved in crime, to follow them up and punish them—this is to entrap the people. How can such a thing as entrapping the people be done under the rule of a benevolent man? Therefore an intelligent ruler will regulate the livelihood of the people, so as to make sure that, for those above them, they shall have sufficient wherewith to serve their parents, and, for those below them, sufficient wherewith to support their wives and children; that in good years they shall always be abundantly satisfied, and that in bad years they shall escape the danger of perishing. After this he may urge them, and they will proceed to what is good, for in this case the people will follow after it with ease. Now, the livelihood of the people is so regulated, that, above, they have not sufficient wherewith to serve their parents, and, below, they have not sufficient wherewith to support their wives and children. Notwithstanding good years, their lives are continually embittered, and, in bad years, they do not escape perishing. In such circumstances they only try to save themselves from death, and are afraid they will not succeed. What time can they spare for studying about ritual propriety and righteousness?[157]

Hence, Mencius makes an emphasis on the importance of moral education for filial and fraternal duties on the basis on economic reformation as follows:

> If your Majesty wishes to effect this regulation of the livelihood of the people, why not turn to that which is the essential step to it? Let mulberry-trees be planted about the homesteads with their five mu, and persons of fifty years may be clothed with silk. In keeping fowls, pigs, dogs, and swine, let not their times

---

156. *Mencius*, 1A7. Translation adapted from Legge. 無恆產而有恆心者，惟士為能。若民，則無恆產，因無恆心。苟無恆心，放辟，邪侈，無不為已。

157. *Mencius*, 1A7. Translation adapted from Legge. 及陷於罪，然後從而刑之，是罔民也。焉有仁人在位，罔民而可為也？是故明君制民之產，必使仰足以事父母，俯足以畜妻子，樂歲終身飽，凶年免於死亡。然後驅而之善，故民之從之也輕。今也制民之產，仰不足以事父母，俯不足以畜妻子，樂歲終身苦，凶年不免於死亡。此惟救死而恐不贍，奚暇治禮義哉？

of breeding be neglected, and persons of seventy years may eat flesh. Let there not be taken away the time that is proper for the cultivation of the farm with its hundred *mu*, and the family of eight mouths that is supported by it shall not suffer from hunger. Let careful attention be paid to education in schools, the inculcation in it especially of the filial and fraternal duties, and grey-haired men will not be seen upon the roads, carrying burdens on their backs or on their heads. It never has been that the ruler of a State where such results were seen, the old wearing silk and eating flesh, and the black-haired people suffering neither from hunger nor cold, did not attain to the royal dignity.[158]

In other words, according to Mencius' classification, only scholars can have a constant character without a certain livelihood. That which the man of virtue follows as his nature is not added to when he holds sway over the Empire, nor is it detracted from when he is reduced to straitened circumstances since that which the man of virtue follows as his nature, that is to say, benevolence, rightness, ritual propriety, and wisdom, is rooted in his heart.[159] In this context, he shows he who is equipped with every virtue cannot be led astray even by a wicked world.[160] It is because the happiness the man of virtue seeks is different from ordinary people:

> There are three things the man of virtue delights in, and being ruler over the Empire is not amongst them. His parents are alive and his brothers are well. This is the first delight. Above, he is not ashamed to face Heaven; below, he is not ashamed to face man. This is the second delight. He has the good fortune of having the most talented pupils in the Empire. This is the third delight.[161]

The business of scholars is, as Mencius claims, to set their mind on high principles such as benevolence and righteousness in order to

---

158. *Mencius*, 1A7. As translated in Legge. 王欲行之，則盍反其本矣。五畝之宅，樹之以桑，五十者可以衣帛矣；雞豚狗彘之畜，無失其時，七十者可以食肉矣；百畝之田，勿奪其時，八口之家可以無飢矣；謹庠序之教，申之以孝悌之義，頒白者不負戴於道路矣。老者衣帛食肉，黎民不飢不寒，然而不王者，未之有也。

159. *Mencius*, 7A21. 君子所性，雖大行不加焉，雖窮居不損焉，分定故也。君子所性，仁義禮智根於心。其生色也，睟然見於面，盎於背，施於四體，四體不言而喻。」

160. *Mencius*, 7B10. 周于德者，邪世不能亂。

161. *Mencius*, 7A20. Translation adapted from Lau. 孟子曰：君子有三樂，而王天下不與存焉。父母俱存，兄弟無故，一樂也。仰不愧於天，俯不怍於人，二樂也。得天下英才而教育之，三樂也。

be moral. For the scholars, to put a single innocent person to death is contrary to benevolence and to take what one has not a right to is contrary to righteousness.[162] For the man of virtue, in other words, desire for eating and sex is not true happiness. In contrast, the people will not have constant hearts if they do not have a certain livelihood, so that they will lose their morality. Thus, he argues, to punish them after they have fallen foul of the law is not proper since the cause of crime is due to the governor's misrule. After taking action for solving the livelihood of the people, they can have time for studying about propriety and righteousness and be educated about filial and fraternal duties in schools in order to be virtuous.[163] Interestingly, Mencius also stresses the influence the educational environment in making a ruler virtuous. This is not an economic dimension like moral education for ordinary people. He shows that it is necessary for a king to be surrounded by virtuous people to be himself virtuous, by drawing upon the parable of learning languages. Mencius supposes that there is a great officer of Chu here, who wishes his son to learn the speech of Qi. He thought that it is not enough solely to employ a man of Qi as his tutor to the speech of Qi if there are a multitude of men of Chu continually shouting out about him. It is impossible for him to learn it in this environment even though his father beat him every day.[164] Likewise, if a king is surrounded by virtuous scholars, he will be naturally virtuous.[165]

162. *Mencius*, 7A33. 仁義而已矣。殺一無罪，非仁也；非其有而取之，非義也。

163. *Mencius*, 7A23. 孟子曰：「易其田疇，薄其稅斂，民可使富也。食之以時，用之以禮，財不可勝用也。民非水火不生活，昏暮叩人之門戶，求水火，無弗與者，至足矣。聖人治天下，使有菽粟如水火。菽粟如水火，而民焉有不仁者乎？」

164. *Mencius*, 3B6. As translated in Legge. 孟子謂戴不勝曰：「子欲子之王之善與？我明告子。有楚大夫於此，欲其子之齊語也，則使齊人傳諸？使楚人傳諸？」曰：「使齊人傳之。」曰：「一齊人傳之，眾楚人咻之，雖日撻而求其齊也，不可得矣；引而置之莊嶽之間數年，雖日撻而求其楚，亦不可得矣。」

165. *Mencius*, 3B6. As translated in Legge. "You supposed that Xue Ju Zhou was a scholar of virtue, and you have got him placed in attendance on the king. Suppose that all in attendance on the king, old and young, high and low, were Xue Ju Zhous, whom would the king have to do evil with? And suppose that all in attendance on the king, old and young, high and low, are not Xue Ju Zhous, whom will the king gave to do good with? What can one Xue Ju Zhou do alone for the king of Song?" 孟子謂戴不勝曰：「子欲子之王之善與？我明告子。有楚大夫於此，欲其子之齊語也，則使楚人傳諸？使楚人傳諸？」曰：「使齊人傳之。」曰：「一齊人傳之，眾楚人咻之，雖日撻而求其齊也，不可得矣；引而置之莊嶽之間數年，雖日撻而求其楚，亦不可得矣。子謂薛居州，善士也。使之居於王所。在於王所者，長

At this point, it is high time to reconsider Mencius' anti-asceticism asserted by Norden in the context of relations between the environment and moral learning in Mencius' moral education.[166] Mencius acknowledges the king can not only obtain happiness from the natural environment[167] but also might seek money and sex in achieving happiness:

> You may be fond of money, but what is it to you so long as you share this fondness with the people? The king said, "I have an infirmity; I am fond of sex." The reply was, formerly, King Tai was fond of sex, and loved his wife. It is said in the *Book of Poetry*, "Gu Gong Tan Fu, came in the morning, galloping his horse, by the banks of the western waters, as far as the foot of Qi hill, along with the lady of Jiang; They came and together chose the site for their settlement." At that time, there were neither girls pining for a husband nor men without a wife. You may be fond of women, but what is it to you so long as you share this fondness with the people?[168]

幼卑尊，皆薛居州也，王誰與為不善？在王所者，長幼卑尊，皆非薛居州也，王誰與為善？一薛居州，獨如宋王何？」

166. Norden presents a deeper understanding of Mencius' self-reflection in the dimension of self-cultivation. Mencius acknowledges the importance of environmental factors related to people's basic material needs. Norden calls it "passive cultivation." However, Mencius seems more interested in the influence of environment on adults than he does in its influence on children in spite of the importance of environmental factors. Mencius himself, according to Norden, does not seem to stress the importance of childhood itself as a unique, irreplaceable opportunity for ensuring the growth and continued existence of our sprouts. Hence, Norden focuses on Mencius' self-reflection as inner-directed of self-cultivation. Norden claims that "Mengzi is not an ascetic: he states that the enjoyment of music, ritual hunting (1B1), wealth, and sex (1B5) are all legitimate, so long as they are done in an ethical manner." Bryan W. Van Norden, *Virtue Ethics and Consequentialism in Early Chinese philosophy* (Cambridge: Cambridge University Press, 2007), 231.

167. *Mencius*, 1A2. 孟子見梁惠王，王立於沼上，顧鴻鴈麋鹿，曰：「賢者亦樂此乎？」 孟子對曰：「賢者而後樂此，不賢者雖有此，不樂也。《詩》云：『經始靈臺，經之營之，庶民攻之，不日成之。經始勿亟，庶民子來。王在靈囿，麀鹿攸伏，麀鹿濯濯，白鳥鶴鶴。王在靈沼，於牣魚躍。』文王以民力為臺為沼。而民歡樂之，謂其臺曰靈臺，謂其沼曰靈沼，樂其有麋鹿魚鱉。古之人與民偕樂，故能樂也。《湯誓》曰：『時日害喪？予及女偕亡。』民欲與之偕亡，雖有臺池鳥獸，豈能獨樂哉？」

168. *Mencius*, 1B5. As translated in Legge. 王如好貨，與百姓同之，於王何有？王曰：「寡人有疾，寡人好色。」 對曰：「昔者大王好色，愛厥妃。《詩》云：『古公亶甫，來朝走馬，率西水滸，至于岐下。爰及姜女，聿來胥宇。』當是時也，內無怨女，外無曠夫。王如好色，與百姓同之，於王何有？」

Xue (學) and Moral Learning

In this dialogue, what Mencius wants to say is that the king needs to share such pleasures with the people together; "The people will delight in the joy of him who delights in their joy, and will worry over the troubles of him who worries over their troubles. He who delights and worries on account of the Empire is certain to become a true King."[169] For example, in terms of sex, he shows "that male and female should dwell together is the greatest of human relations" in the dimension of filial piety. The king ought to recognize the desire of young people for marriage by reflecting his sexual desire.[170] His anti-asceticism can be only justified in the perspective of the relation between a king and their people. Ultimately, he stresses a moderate living in dealing only with life style of the king in the evidence of the ancient sovereigns:

> Descending along with the current, and forgetting to return, is what I call yielding to it. Pressing up against it, and forgetting to return, is what I call urging their way against it. Pursuing the chase without satiety is what I call being wild. Delighting in wine without satiety is what I call being lost. The ancient sovereigns had no pleasures to which they gave themselves as on the flowing stream; no doings which might be so characterized as wild and lost. It is for you, my prince, to pursue your course.[171]

In particular, he warns against indulging in food and drinking in the process of learning doctrine of the ancients.[172] In this context, he advises a true follower who loves his prince ought to restrain his prince's faults since he spent his youth in learning the principle of right government.[173] It is because such pleasures by the prince could lead to calamities to his kingdom.[174] Therefore, Mencius shows that "a ruler who is endowed with talents and virtue will be gravely complaisant and economical, showing a respectful politeness to his ministers, and taking from the people only

---

169. *Mencius*, 1B4. As translated in Lau. 樂民之樂者，民亦樂其樂；憂民之憂者，民亦憂其憂。樂以天下，憂以天下，然而不王者，未之有也。

170. *Mencius*, 5A2. 男女居室，人之大倫也。

171. *Mencius*, 1B4. As translated in Legge. 從流下而忘反謂之流，從流上而忘反謂之連，從獸無厭謂之荒，樂酒無厭謂之亡。先王無流連之樂，荒亡之行。惟君所行也。... 其詩曰：『畜君何尤？』畜君者，好君也。

172. *Mencius*, 4A25. 孟子謂樂正子曰：「子之從於子敖來，徒餔啜也。我不意子學古之道，而以餔啜也。」

173. *Mencius*, 1B9. 夫人幼而學之，壯而欲行之。

174. *Mencius*, 2A4. 孔子曰：『為此詩者，其知道乎！能治其國家，誰敢侮之？』今國家閒暇，及是時般樂怠敖，是自求禍也。禍福無不自己求之者。

in accordance with regulated limits."[175] For Mencius, the right ruler is complaisant and economical since the respectful do not despise others and the economical do not plunder others.[176] Hence, he presents the best way to cultivate the mind is to make the desires few.[177] In other words, he states that "Do not do what you would not do; do not desire what you would not desire."[178]

Imitation, Tradition, and Heaven

Along with educational environment, Mencius lays great emphasis on imitating sages as the object of moral learning as follows:

> A sage is the teacher of a hundred generations—this is true of Bo Yi and Hui of Liu Xia. Therefore, when men now bear the character of Bo Yi, the corrupt become pure, and the weak acquire determination. When they hear the character of Hui of Liu Xia, the mean become generous, and the niggardly become liberal. Those two made themselves distinguished a hundred generations ago, and after a hundred generations, those who hear of them, are all aroused in this manner. Could such effects be produced by them, if they had not been sages? And how much more did they affect those who were in contiguity with them, and felt their inspiring influence![179]

Sages have an ability to make people virtuous. Given that Mencius hugely paid attention to the matter of how to make a ruler economical and benevolent, it is noticeable that Bo Yi and Hui of Liu Xia make people's character pure and generous. According to Mencius, this can be only realized by sages. For him, sages must be the teacher of a hundred generations, so it is necessary to study them to take after their characters. Yet,

---

175. *Mencius*, 3A3. 是故賢君必恭儉禮下，取於民有制。

176. *Mencius*, 4A16. 孟子曰：「恭者不侮人，儉者不奪人。侮奪人之君，惟恐不順焉，惡得為恭儉？恭儉豈可以聲音笑貌為哉？」

177. *Mencius*, 7B35. 孟子曰：「養心莫善於寡欲。其為人也寡欲，雖有不存焉者，寡矣；其為人也多欲，雖有存焉者，寡矣。」

178. *Mencius*, 7A17. As translated in Lau. 孟子曰：「無為其所不為，無欲其所不欲，如此而已矣。」

179. *Mencius*, 7B15. As translated in Legge. 孟子曰：「聖人，百世之師也，伯夷、柳下惠是也。故聞伯夷之風者，頑夫廉，懦夫有立志；聞柳下惠之風者，薄夫敦，鄙夫寬。奮乎百世之上。百世之下，聞者莫不興起也。非聖人而能若是乎，而況於親炙之者乎？」

it seems to be difficult to follow their way since their principles are lofty. Nevertheless, Mencius would not lower such standards to cause learners to consider them attainable, just as a great artificer does not, for the sake of a stupid workman, alter or do away with the marking-line. He expects those who are able will follow such principles if he keeps standing exactly in the middle of the path.[180] If so, how can one encounter such sages? He shows studying their poems and books as specific methods for becoming acquainted with sages of antiquity is one of the best ways. Mencius said to Wan Zhang as follows:

> The scholar whose virtue is most distinguished in a village shall make friends of all the virtuous scholars in the village. The scholar whose virtue is most distinguished throughout a State shall make friends of all the virtuous scholars of that State. The scholar whose virtue is most distinguished throughout the kingdom shall make friends of all the virtuous scholars of the kingdom. When a scholar feels that his friendship with all the virtuous scholars of the kingdom is not sufficient to satisfy him, he proceeds to ascend to consider the men of antiquity. He repeats their poems, and reads their books, and as he does not know what they were as men, to ascertain this, he considers their history. This is to ascend and make friends of the men of antiquity.[181]

According to Mencius, the method of imitating others' good characters is conducted even by sages in order to do good works.[182] For example, when any one told Zi Lu that he had a fault, he rejoiced. When Yu heard good words, he bowed to the speaker. The great Shun had a still greater delight in what was good. He regarded virtue as the common property of himself and others, giving up his own way to follow that of others, and delighting to learn from others how to practice what was good. The most

---

180. *Mencius*, 7A41. 公孫丑曰：「道則高矣，美矣，宜若登天然，似不可及也。何不使彼為可幾及而日孳孳也？」 孟子曰：「大匠不為拙工改廢繩墨，羿不為拙射變其彀率。君子引而不發，躍如也。中道而立，能者從之。」

181. *Mencius*, 5B8. As translated in Legge. 孟子謂萬章曰：「一鄉之善士，斯友一鄉之善士；一國之善士，斯友一國之善士；天下之善士，斯友天下之善士。以友天下之善士為未足，又尚論古之人。頌其詩，讀其書，不知其人，可乎？是以論其世也。是尚友也。」

182. *Mencius*, 2A8. 孟子曰：「子路，人告之以有過則喜。禹聞善言則拜。大舜有大焉，善與人同。舍己從人，樂取於人以為善。自耕、稼、陶、漁以至為帝，無非取於人者。取諸人以為善，是與人為善者也。故君子莫大乎與人為善。」

important thing is that he was continually learning from others until he became emperor. The purpose of imitating is to practice virtue together.

For Mencius, imitating sages means studying tradition since they are the examples of good tradition. He places immense emphasis on the importance of laying the foundation of the tradition since it will be continued by his successors and then they may attain to royal dignity.[183] He points out such virtuous deeds do not guarantee good results. Contrary to human will in dealing with practicing benevolent government, Mencius focuses on the authority of Heaven who alone can grant success in reigning over the whole country. According to him, when a man goes forward, there is something which urges him on; when he halts, there is something which holds him back.[184] But to advance a man or to stop his advance is truly beyond the power of other men. What is this power? For Mencius, this power beyond human will is clearly Heaven. In this context, he praises Confucius whose actions were timely; "Bo Yi among the sages was the pure one; Yi Yin was the one most inclined to take office; Hui of Liu Xia was the accommodating one; and Confucius was the sage whose actions were timely. Confucius was the one who gathered together all that was good."[185] The limit of human will is explained as follows:

> To gather together all that is good is similar to open with bells and conclude with jade tubes. To open with bells is to begin in an orderly fashion; to conclude with jade tubes is to end in an orderly fashion. To begin in an orderly fashion pertains to wisdom while to end in an orderly fashion pertains to sageness. Wisdom is like skill, shall I say, while sageness is like strength. It is like shooting from beyond a hundred paces. It is due to your strength that the arrow reaches the target, but it is not due to your strength that it hits the mark.[186]

---

183. *Mencius*, 1B14. 「苟為善，後世子孫必有王者矣。君子創業垂統，為可繼也。若夫成功，則天也。君如彼何哉？彊為善而已矣。」

184. *Mencius*, 1B16. 曰：「行或使之，止或尼之。行止，非人所能也。吾之不遇魯侯，天也。」

185. *Mencius*, 5B1. Translation adapted from Lau. 孟子曰：「伯夷，聖之清者也；伊尹，聖之任者也；柳下惠，聖之和者也；孔子，聖之時者也。孔子之謂集大成。」

186. *Mencius*, 5B1. Translation adapted from Lau. 集大成也者，金聲而玉振之也。金聲也者，始條理也；玉振之也者，終條理也。始條理者，智之事也；終條理者，聖之事也。智，譬則巧也；聖，譬則力也。由射於百步之外也，其至，爾力也；其中，非爾力也。

Xue (學) *and Moral Learning*

As Mencius states that "it is due to your strength that the arrow reaches the target, but it is not due to your strength that it hits the mark," he points out the limit of sageness by virtue. The power of hitting the mark beyond human will comes from Heaven. This indicates the importance of time according to Heaven. Thus, Confucius would follow order by Heaven in securing office.[187] If so, how can we recognize the order of Heaven? Does Heaven speak? According to Mencius, Heaven did not speak about it when Yao presented Shun to Heaven. Yet, he is convinced that Heaven accepted him since the people accepted Shun when Yao presented him to the people.[188] Mencius asserts that the order of Heaven is revealed through personal conduct and conduct of affairs as follows:

> He caused him to preside over the sacrifices, and all the spirits were well pleased with them; thus Heaven accepted him. He caused him to preside over the conduct of affairs, and affairs were well administered, so that the people reposed under him; thus the people accepted him. Heaven gave the throne to him. The people gave it to him. Therefore I said, "The sovereign cannot give the throne to another. Shun assisted Yao in the government for twenty and eight years—this was more than man could have done, and was from Heaven. After the death of Yao, when the three years' mourning was completed, Shun withdrew from the son of Yao to the south of South river. The princes of the kingdom, however, repairing to court, went not to the son of Yao, but they went to Shun. Litigants went not to the son of Yao, but they went to Shun. Singers sang not the son of Yao, but they sang Shun. Therefore I said, Heaven gave him the throne." It was after these things that he went to the Middle Kingdom, and occupied the seat of the Son of Heaven. If he had, before these things, taken up his residence in the palace of Yao, and had applied pressure to the son of Yao, it would have been an act of usurpation, and not the gift of Heaven. This sentiment is expressed in the words of The Great Declaration: "Heaven sees according as my people see; Heaven hears according as my people hear."[189]

---

187. *Mencius*, 5A8. 孔子曰：『有命。』孔子進以禮，退以義。Lau translates *ming* (命) as "decree" while Legge as being "ordered by Heaven."

188. *Mencius*, 5A5. 昔者堯薦舜於天而天受之，暴之於民而民受之，故曰：天不言，以行與事示之而已矣。

189. *Mencius*, 5A5. As translated in Legge. 曰：「使之主祭而百神享之，是天受；使之主事而事治，百姓安之，是民受之也。天與之，人與之，故曰：天子不能以天下與人。舜相堯二十有八載，非人之所能為也，天也。堯崩，三年

As Heaven sees and hears through people's eyes and ears, kings ought to pay attention to people even in commencing war. Mencius suggests king Wu and Wen as good examples; "If the people of Yan will be pleased with your taking possession of it, then do so. Among the ancients there was one who acted on this principle, namely king Wu. If the people of Yan will not be pleased with your taking possession of it, then do not do so. Among the ancients there was one who acted on this principle, namely king Wen."[190] For Mencius, securing the heart of people is a touchstone for confirming the order of Heaven. Therefore, he advises it is still important to try one's best to do good. For instance, Mencius regards king Wen as the founder of the tradition. When he ruled over Qi, tillers of land were taxed one part in nine; descendants of officials received hereditary emoluments; there was inspection but no levy at border stations and market-places; fish-traps were open for all to use; punishment did not extend to the wife and children of an offender.[191] In particular, when he put benevolent measures into effect, he always gave first consideration to old men without wives, old women without husbands, old people without children, and young children without fathers since these four classes are the most destitute and have no one to turn to for help. In these aspects, he was a truly benevolent king. Nevertheless, he did not succeed in extending his influence over the whole Empire when he died at the age of a hundred. It was only after his work was carried on by king Wu and the Duke of Zhou, that influence greatly prevailed.[192] Given that Confucius significantly respected the Duke of Zhou, king Wen's virtuous achievement played a pivotal role in establishing such good tradition.

Shun and King Wen are, as can be seen above, presented as the proper role models of a sage. Why did Mencius deal with them at the

---

之喪畢，舜避堯之子於南河之南。天下諸侯朝覲者，不之堯之子而之舜；訟獄者，不之堯之子而之舜；謳歌者，不謳歌堯之子而謳歌舜，故曰天也。夫然後之中國，踐天子位焉。而居堯之宮，逼堯之子，是篡也，非天與也。《太誓》曰：『天視自我民視，天聽自我民聽』，此之謂也。」

190. *Mencius*, 1B10. As translated in Legge. 孟子對曰：「取之而燕民悅，則取之。古之人有行之者，武王是也。取之而燕民不悅，則勿取。古之人有行之者，文王是也。」

191. *Mencius*, 1B5. 王曰：「王政可得聞與？」對曰：「昔者文王之治岐也，耕者九一，仕者世祿，關市譏而不征，澤梁無禁，罪人不孥。老而無妻曰鰥。老而無夫曰寡。老而無子曰獨。幼而無父曰孤。此四者，天下之窮民而無告者。文王發政施仁，必先斯四者。《詩》云：『哿矣富人，哀此煢獨。』」

192. *Mencius*, 2A1. 且以文王之德，百年而後崩，猶未洽於天下；武王、周公繼之，然後大行。

same level in spite of different backgrounds and timelines? According to Mencius, "Shun was an Eastern barbarian; he was born in Zhu Feng, moved to Fu Xia, and died in Ming Tiao. King Wen was a Western barbarian; he was born in Zhou by mount Qi and died in Bi Ying. Their native places were over a thousand *li* apart, and there were a thousand years between them. Yet when they had their way in the Central Kingdoms, their actions matched like the two halves of a tally. The standards of the two sages, one earlier and one later, were identical."[193] In other words, their principles are no different. In this context, he always cited Yao and Shun as his authorities as well as king Wen when explaining about the goodness of human nature.[194] For Mencius, the purpose of study is to go back and set forth in brief what is essential.[195] That is the Way of the former kings. Just as to raise a thing high, one must begin from the top of a mound or a hill and to dig to a great depth, one must commence in the low ground of a stream or a marsh, the wise proceed according to "the Way of the former kings" in the exercise of government. Mencius warns that "when those above have no principles and those below have no laws, when courtiers have no faith in the way and craftsmen have no faith in measures, when the man of virtue offend against what is right and common people risk punishment, then it is good fortune indeed if a state survives."[196] He highlights the importance of imitating the Way of Yao and Shun as the Way of the former kings as follows:

> The power of vision of Li Lou, and skill of hand of Gong Shu, without the compass and square, could not form squares and circles. The acute ear of the music-master Kuang, without the pitch-tubes, could not determine correctly the five notes. The Way of Yao and Shun, without a benevolent government, could not secure the tranquil order of the kingdom. There are now princes who have benevolent hearts and a reputation for benevolence, while yet the people do not receive any benefits from them, nor

---

193. *Mencius*, 4B1. As translated in Legge. 孟子曰：「舜生於諸馮，遷於負夏，卒於鳴條，東夷之人也。文王生於岐周，卒於畢郢，西夷之人也。地之相去也，千有餘里；世之相後也，千有餘歲。得志行乎中國，若合符節。先聖後聖，其揆一也。」

194. *Mencius*, 3A1. 孟子道性善，言必稱堯舜。

195. *Mencius*, 4B15. 孟子曰：「博學而詳說之，將以反說約也。」

196. *Mencius*, 4A1. As translated in Lau. 故曰，為高必因丘陵，為下必因川澤。為政不因先王之道，可謂智乎？是以惟仁者宜在高位。不仁而在高位，是播其惡於眾也。上無道揆也。下無法守也，朝不信道，工不信度，君子犯義，小人犯刑，國之所存者幸也。

will they leave any example to future ages—all because they do not put into practice the Way of the ancient kings.[197]

Why did Mencius explain the Way of Yao and Shun in relation to implementing the benevolent government? In order to understand it, it is necessary to examine how he defined the relation between benevolence and the Way. According to him, benevolence is the distinguishing characteristic of man. As embodied in man's conduct, he calls it the Way.[198] For him, benevolence and the Way are intertwined. In this context, Mencius said a destroyer of the people would not have been tolerated in the times of Yao and Shun since to employ an uninstructed people in war may be said to be destroying the people.[199] This indicates benevolence and righteousness were deeply embedded in the nature of Yao and Shun.[200] In particular, Mencius extols Shun's achievements in relation to human nature. According to him, as the waters, flowing out of their channels, inundated the Middle Kingdom in the time of Yao, the people had no place where they could settle themselves. In order to improve this situation, Shun employed Yu to repel the waters.[201] By leading the flood water into the seas through cutting channels for it in the ground, Yu made the ground habitable. How did Yu can manage water? Mencius explains it as follows:

> All who speak about human nature have in fact only their phenomena to reason from, and the value of a phenomenon is in its being natural. What I dislike in your wise men is their boring out their conclusions. If those wise men would only act as Yu did when he conveyed away the waters, there would be nothing to dislike in their wisdom. The manner in which Yu conveyed away the waters was by doing what gave him no trouble. If your wise men would also do that which gave them no trouble, their knowledge would also be great. There is heaven so high; there

197. *Mencius*, 4A1. 孟子曰：「離婁之明，公輸子之巧，不以規矩，不能成方員；師曠之聰，不以六律，不能正五音；堯舜之道，不以仁政，不能平治天下。今有仁心仁聞而民不被其澤，不可法於後世者，不行先王之道也。

198. *Mencius*, 7B16. 孟子曰：「仁也者，人也。合而言之，道也。」

199. *Mencius*, 6B8, 孟子曰：「不教民而用之，謂之殃民。殃民者，不容於堯舜之世。」

200. *Mencius*, 7A30. 堯舜，性之也

201. *Mencius*, 3B9. 孟子曰：「予豈好辯哉？予不得已也。天下之生久矣，一治一亂。當堯之時，水逆行，氾濫於中國，蛇龍居之，民無所定。下者為巢，上者為營窟。《書》曰：『洚水警余。』洚水者，洪水也。使禹治之，禹掘地而注之海，驅蛇龍而放之菹。水由地中行，江、淮、河、漢是也。險阻既遠，鳥獸之害人者消，然後人得平土而居之。

are the stars so distant. If we have investigated their phenomena, we may, while sitting in our places, go back to the solstice of a thousand years ago.[202]

Yu solved the matter of flood by following the natural tendency of water in dealing with water. Hence, Mencius said floods are detested by the benevolent man since inundating waters are against the nature of waters.[203] For Mencius, the inversion of order against the nature of things is not benevolent. Along with managing flood, furthermore, Mencius presents Shun as the example of filial piety. It is because for Shun filial piety is much more important than sex, riches, and honors as follows:

> The possession of beauty is what men desire, and Shun had for his wives the two daughters of Yao, but this was not sufficient to remove his sorrow. Riches are what men desire, and the kingdom was the rich property of Shun, but this was not sufficient to remove his sorrow. Honors are what men desire, and Shun had the dignity of being sovereign, but this was not sufficient to remove his sorrow. The reason why being the object of men's delight, with the possession of beauty, riches, and honors was not sufficient to remove his sorrow, was that it could be removed only by his getting his parents to be in accord with him. The desire of the child is towards his father and mother. When he becomes conscious of the attractions of beauty, his desire is towards young and beautiful women. When he comes to have a wife and children, his desire is towards them. When he obtains office, his desire is towards his sovereign—if he cannot get the regard of his sovereign, he burns within. But the man of great filial piety, to the end of his life, has his desire towards his parents. In Shun I have seen an example of a son who, even at the age of fifty, yearned for his parents.[204]

---

202. *Mencius*, 4B26. 孟子曰：「天下之言性也，則故而已矣。故者以利為本。所惡於智者，為其鑿也。如智者若禹之行水也，則無惡於智矣。禹之行水也，行其所無事也。如智者亦行其所無事，則智亦大矣。天之高也，星辰之遠也，苟求其故，千歲之日至，可坐而致也。」

203. *Mencius*, 6B11. 孟子曰：「子過矣。禹之治水，水之道也。是故禹以四海為壑，今吾子以鄰國為壑。水逆行，謂之洚水。洚水者，洪水也，仁人之所惡也。吾子過矣。」

204. *Mencius*, 5A1. As translated in Legge. 好色，人之所欲，妻帝之二女，而不足以解憂；富，人之所欲，富有天下，而不足以解憂；貴，人之所欲，貴為天子，而不足以解憂。人悅之、好色、富貴，無足以解憂者，惟順於父母，可以解憂。人少，則慕父母；知好色，則慕少艾；有妻子，則慕妻子；仕則慕君，不得於君則熱中。大孝終身慕父母。五十而慕者，予於大舜見之矣。

Regardless of getting older, Shun sought to get the hearts of his parents. According to Mencius, Shun alone was able to look upon the fact that the Empire, being greatly delighted, was turning to him, as of no more consequence than trash.[205] He considered that if one could not get the hearts of his parents he could not be considered a man, and that if he could not get to an entire accord with his parents, he could not be considered a son. Thus, Shun did everything that was possible to serve his parents, and succeeded, in the end, in pleasing his father Gu Sou. When Gu Sou was brought to find that delight, the whole kingdom was transformed. When Gu Sou was brought to find that delight, all fathers and sons in the kingdom were established in their respective duties. Mencius calls this great filial piety. In other words, for Shun the source of changing the whole kingdom was not military power but filial piety. In spite of Yao and Shun's great achievements, Mencius warns against deification of them. He explicitly states "Yao and Shun were just the same as other men."[206]

In terms of imitating sages, for Mencius the most important sage is Confucius. According to Mencius, Bo Yi, Yi Yin, and Confucius were all sages of antiquity, but they should not be placed in the same rank. There never was another Confucius. Thus, Mencius states that "what I wish to do is to learn to be like Confucius."[207] Why did Mencius focus on studying Confucius? From the perspective of Mencius, the Way of Confucius is inextricably linked to previous sages such as Yao, Shun, Yi Yin, and Wen as follows:

> From Yao and Shun down to Tang were 500 years and more. As to Yu and Gao Yao, they saw those earliest sages, and so knew their doctrines, while Tang heard their doctrines at second hand but knew them well. From Tang to king Wen were 500 years and more. As to Yi Yin, and Lai Zhu, they saw Tang and knew his doctrines, while king Wen heard them as transmitted, and

---

205. *Mencius*, 4A28. 孟子曰：「天下大悅而將歸己。視天下悅而歸己，猶草芥也。惟舜為然。不得乎親，不可以為人；不順乎親，不可以為子。舜盡事親之道而瞽瞍厎豫，瞽瞍厎豫而天下化，瞽瞍厎豫而天下之為父子者定，此之謂大孝。」

206. *Mencius*, 4B32. 孟子曰：「何以異於人哉？堯舜與人同耳。」

207. *Mencius*, 2A2. 曰：「伯夷、伊尹何如？」曰：「不同道。非其君不事，非其民不使；治則進，亂則退，伯夷也。何事非君，何使非民；治亦進，亂亦進，伊尹也。可以仕則仕，可以止則止，可以久則久，可以速則速，孔子也。皆古聖人也，吾未能有行焉；乃所願，則學孔子也。」「伯夷、伊尹於孔子，若是班乎？」曰：「否。自有生民以來，未有孔子也。」

so knew them. From king Wen to Confucius were 500 years and more. As to Tai Gong Wang and San Yi Sheng, they saw Wen, and so knew his doctrines, while Confucius heard them as transmitted, and so knew them. From Confucius downwards until now, there are only 100 years and somewhat more. The distance in time from the sage is so far from being remote, and so very near at hand was the sage's residence. In these circumstances, is there no one to transmit his doctrines? Is there no one to do so?[208]

This passage above shows there are two modes in terms of delivering the Way. Yu, Gao Yao, Yi Yin, Lai Zhu, Tai Gong Wang, and San Yi Sheng were handed over through personal contacts with sages, while Tang, Wen, and Confucius knew such doctrines by hearing what was passed down. In this context, Mencius states that "The influence of a sovereign sage terminates in the fifth generation. The influence of a mere sage does the same. Although I could not be a disciple of Confucius himself, I have endeavored to cultivate my virtue by means of others who were."[209] Given that Mencius points out that there is no one to transmit Confucius' doctrines at his time, this indicates that his doctrines were succeeded by Mencius. Thus, Mencius was convinced that he can only bring peace to the Empire as follows:

> That was one time, and this is another. It is a rule that a true royal sovereign should arise in the course of five hundred years, and that during that time there should be men illustrious in their generation. From the commencement of the Zhou dynasty till now, more than seven hundred years have elapsed. Judging numerically, the date is past. Examining the character of the present time, we might expect the rise of such individuals in it. But Heaven does not yet wish that the kingdom should enjoy tranquility and good order. If it wished this, who is there besides me to bring it about? How should I be otherwise than dissatisfied?[210]

---

208. *Mencius*, 7B38. As translated in Legge. 孟子曰：「由堯舜至於湯，五百有餘歲，若禹、皋陶，則見而知之；若湯，則聞而知之。由湯至於文王，五百有餘歲，若伊尹、萊朱則見而知之；若文王，則聞而知之。由文王至於孔子，五百有餘歲，若太公望、散宜生，則見而知之；若孔子，則聞而知之。由孔子而來至於今，百有餘歲，去聖人之世，若此其未遠也；近聖人之居，若此其甚也，然而無有乎爾，則亦無有乎爾。」

209. *Mencius*, 4B22. As translated in Legge. 孟子曰：「君子之澤五世而斬，小人之澤五世而斬。予未得為孔子徒也，予私淑諸人也。」

210. *Mencius*, 2B13. As translated in Legge. 曰：「彼一時，此一時也。五百年必有王者興，其間必有名世者。由周而來，七百有餘歲矣。以其數則過矣，以

His confidence for administration derives from Confucius. According to Mencius, if Confucius were to become ruler over a hundred *li* square, he would have been capable of winning the homage of the feudal lords and taking possession of the Empire.[211] In order to obtain the throne, he would not have committed one act of unrighteousness, or put to death one innocent person. Confucius focused on practicing the Way. However, the reality he confronted was stern. He never completed in any State a residence of three years because he had a clear standard in taking office; "Confucius took office when he saw that the practice of his doctrines was likely; he took office when his reception was proper; he took office when he was supported by the State. In the case of his relation to Qi Huan, he took office, seeing that the practice of his doctrines was likely. With the duke Ling of Wei he took office, because his reception was proper. With the duke Xiao of Wei he took office, because he was maintained by the State."[212] From the perspective of Mencius, Confucius seems to be a sage. However, Mencius describes Confucius as an imperfect man like Yao and Shun. Mencius said as follows:

> Oh! what words are these? Formerly Zi Gong asked Confucius, saying, "Master, are you a Sage?" Confucius answered him, "A Sage is what I cannot rise to. I study without satiety, and teach without being tired." Zi Gong said, "You study without satiety—that shows your wisdom. You teach without being tired—that shows your benevolence. Benevolent and wise—Master, you are a Sage." Now, since Confucius would not allow himself to be regarded as a Sage, what words were those?[213]

Even Mencius himself declines to be called a sage like Confucius. For Mencius, the important aspect of Confucius is that he kept studying and teaching as the modes of wisdom and benevolence.

其時考之則可矣。夫天，未欲平治天下也；如欲平治天下，當今之世，舍我其誰也？吾何為不豫哉？」

211. *Mencius*, 2A2. 曰：「有。得百里之地而君之，皆能以朝諸侯有天下。行一不義、殺一不辜而得天下，皆不為也。是則同。」

212. *Mencius*, 5B4. As translated in Legge. 曰：「為之兆也。兆足以行矣，而不行，而後去，是以未嘗有所終三年淹也。孔子有見行可之仕，有際可之仕，有公養之仕也。於季桓子，見行可之仕也；於衛靈公，際可之仕也；於衛孝公，公養之仕也。」

213. *Mencius*, 2A2. As translated in Legge. 曰：「惡！是何言也？昔者子貢、問於孔子曰：『夫子聖矣乎？』孔子曰：『聖則吾不能，我學不厭而教不倦也。』子貢曰：『學不厭，智也；教不倦，仁也。仁且智，夫子既聖矣！』夫聖，孔子不居，是何言也？」

In this section, I showed that Mencius emphasizes that a king needs to become the man of virtue to realize benevolent government where filial piety is a core value. Mencius claimed to reform economic, social, and educational systems for supporting filial piety. Just as Confucius highlighted the importance of practice, Mencius stressed continually imitating from the Way of sages such as Yao, Shun, and Confucius.

AUGUSTINE'S MORAL LEARNING

Divine Illumination: Christ as the Interior Teacher

Just as Confucius and Mencius treated virtue as a means for achieving happiness, Augustine deals with happiness and virtue throughout his writings. In his early writing *De Moribus Ecclesiae Catholicae*, he claims that "we all wish to live happily"[214] as a "eudaemonist"[215] like Greco-Roman philosophers such as Epicureans, Stoics, and Skeptics. That happiness is the product of virtue was a universal assumption in the ancient world where the soul cannot achieve whatever its perfection might be without virtue as the excellence of the soul.[216] With the classical traditions Augustine accepts that human happiness is the result of virtue, further, that what constitutes the nature of our happiness can be understood by rational argument.[217] According to Augustine, if we intend to live happily, we must possess our supreme good. It is because "no one is happy without the supreme good, which is discerned and acquired in the truth that we call wisdom."[218] He shows two conditions of this supreme good as follows:

> Therefore, man's supreme good is not inferior to man ... For if happiness is the possession of a good than which there is none greater, and this is what we call the supreme good, how can a person be said to be happy who has not yet attained his supreme good? Or how can it be called the supreme good if there

---

214. *mor.* 1.3.4. trans. Richard Stothert in *Nicene and Post-Nicene Fathers*, vol. 4 (New York: Christian Literature Publishing Co., 1887). Hereafter I use this translation.

215. John M. Rist, *Augustine: Ancient Thought Baptized* (Cambridge: Cambridge University Press, 1997), 49.

216. Ryan N. S. Topping, *St. Augustine* (London: Contimuum, 2010), 32.

217. Topping, *St. Augustine*, 31.

218. *lib. arb.* 2.9.26. trans. Thomas Williams (Cambridge: Hackett Publishing Company, 1993). Hereafter I use this translation.

is something better that he can attain? Such being the case, it follows that one cannot lose it against his will, for no one can be confident of a good he knows can be snatched from him even though he wishes to keep and cherish it.[219]

For Augustine, the two conditions this supreme good are that "nothing is better than it" and "it cannot be lost against one's will." According to him, human beings are composed of body and soul.[220] He argues that "man's supreme good is not the supreme good of the body alone, but the supreme good of the soul."[221] For him, an important question is about what makes soul perfect. He deals with the attainment of virtue in connection with soul rather than body in that "virtue perfects the soul."[222] Presenting that "soul must pursue something else in order that virtue may arise within itself," he insists that this something else is God rather than a wise man who can be taken from us against our will.[223] Hence, he stresses that if we reach God, we live not only well but also happily.[224] For him, happiness is "the enjoyment of man's supreme good."[225] While for Confucius and Mencius the Way (*dao* 道) is truth to lead to happiness, for Augustine God is the supreme good. One way of comparing the two is to indicate that both traditions envisage the moral life as a path or journey of formation shaped by the quest for the truth. For Augustine seeking happiness is the matter of finding God who is the "immaterial, the unchanging, all-loving good."[226] Given that for Augustine the aim of a happy life is to know God and its process is intellectual enquiry,[227] the purpose of moral education is to assist the learner to develop a love of intellectual enquiry, through which man progressively enlarges his understanding of real existence, introducing order into the apparent chaos of human experience, and seeing the flux of the temporal world against a secure background of unchanging truth.[228] At this point, the question

219. *mor.* 1.3.5.
220. *mor.* 1.4.6.
221. *mor.* 1.5.8.
222. *mor.* 1.6.9.
223. *mor.* 1.6.10.
224. *mor.* 1.6.10.
225. *mor.* 1.3.5.
226. Topping, *St. Augustine*, 43
227. George Howie, *Educational Theory and Practice in St Augustine* (London: Routledge & K. Paul, 1969), 42.
228. Howie, *Educational Theory and Practice in St Augustine*, 41.

of how man knows such divine ideas may be the most important and the most difficult problem in Augustine's moral learning.[229] For this task, it is necessary to look at Augustine's early writings after his conversion to survey his epistemology as the starting point of the formation of his moral self. In the *Confessions*, Augustine talks about certainty in his mind in the moment of conversion as follows:

> I was saying these things and weeping in the most bitter contrition of my heart, when I heard the voice as of a boy or girl, I know not which, coming from a neighboring house, chanting, and often repeating, "Take up and read; take up and read."... I grasped, opened, and in silence read that paragraph on which my eyes first fell—"Not in rioting and drunkenness, not in chambering and wantonness, not in strife and envying; but put on the Lord Jesus Christ, and make not provision for the flesh, to fulfil the lusts thereof." (Rom 13:13-14) No further would I read, nor did I need; for instantly, as the sentence ended—by a light, as it were, of security infused into my mind—all the gloom of doubt vanished away.[230]

Why did Augustine think of the matter of certainty in connection with sexual lust after reading the verse in 386? This is derived from his past life in relation to skepticism.[231] Moving from Thagaste to Carthago to learn rhetoric in 371, Augustine not only became deeply interested in philosophy as loving wisdom by reading Cicero's *Hortensius*, but also fell in the errors of the Manichaeans.[232] His growing dissatisfaction with Manichaeism in Rome at the beginning of his stay in Italy, whose dogmatic dualism he had embraced as an eighteen-year-old in 372, made him a temporary skeptic in about 383 or 384, at a particularly insecure and unstable period of his life.[233] During this period, he found himself increasingly attracted to the skeptical position taken by the Academics, the followers of Arcesilaus and the New Academy, who, as he writes in his *Confessions*, "held that everything is a matter of doubt and asserted that

---

229. Nash, *The Light of the Mind: St. Augustine's Theory of Knowledge* (Lexington: University Press of Kentucky, 1969), 77.

230. *conf.* 8.12.29. trans. R. S. Pine-Coffin (London: Penguin Group, 1961). Hereafter I use this translation.

231. Brown, *Augustine of Hippo*, 109.

232. *conf.* 3.4.7.

233. *conf.* 5.7.12.

we can know nothing for certain."[234] What Augustine knew of ancient skepticism, including the debate between Arcesilaus and the Stoic Zeno of Citium, he seems to have learned from Cicero's *Academica*. A year or two later he encountered Platonism in Milan, and then he converted to Christianity. In the aftermath of his conversion, he wrote his earlier works such as *Contra Academicos, De beata vita, De ordine*, and *Solioquia* at a villa in Cassiciacum near Milan. Here Augustine stayed from the autumn of 386 until Lent in 387 in the company of his mother (Monica), his son (Adeodatus), his brother (Navigius), two cousins (Lastidianus and Rusticus), two pupils (Licentius and Trygetius), and a friend (Alypius). In spite of performing some manual labor, for the group the main interest of each day centered in study and philosophical discussions. Shaping dialogues on the model of Plato and Cicero, these discussions were recorded by a stenographer, and Augustine then revised the notes.[235] Above all, it is noticeable that the first of the programmatic series of these writings is *Contra Academicos* in 386. This work is a criticism of skeptical positions and defense of the attainability of knowledge by laying the foundations of the theory of cognitive certainty. Even though he seems never to have become a skeptic himself, skepticism remained as a threat for much of his life, so that he felt he needed to respond to. Augustine's *Against the Academicians*, which is directed at Cicero's *Academica*, is his principal response to skeptical arguments of New Academy for defending the possibility of knowledge. Like Cicero's Academic books, it is written in dialogue form where Augustine, two pupils, and a friend took part in philosophical discussion, enquiry, and reflection. Like Hellenistic philosophers such as Epicureanism, Stoicism, and Skepticism, Augustine considers the aim of moral education the happy life as the result of virtue. In this context, Augustine's *Against the Academicians* starts from the matter of certainty by dealing with wisdom in connection with happiness. He claims the sage alone is happy since the sage alone has secure knowledge of truths like the Stoic view. In this premise, he raises a question about whether wisdom consists in finding truth or in seeking it. He points out that Academic wisdom is a skeptical strategy, and does not entail knowledge of something called wisdom.[236] In contrast, he proves the possibility of knowl-

---

234. *conf.* 5.10.19.

235. Eavid E. Roberts, "The Earliest Writings," in *A Companion to the Study of St. Augustine*, ed. Roy W. Battenhouse (New York: Oxford University Press, 1955), 94.

236. *c. Acad.* 3.4.9. trans. Peter King (Cambridge: Hackett publishing Company, 1995). Hereafter I use this translation.

edge through logical truths, pure appearance-claims, and mathematical truths. Hence, his principal objection to the Academics is directed at the claim attributed to them that one may be wise and attain happiness in the quest for truth, even if there is no possibility of its attainment.[237] Truth is reached through authority by means of belief and through reason by means of understanding.[238]

More importantly, Augustine's *De magistro* in 389, written in dialogue form between Augustine and his natural son, Adeodatus, is inextricably linked to the matter of moral learning. It offers his theory of illumination to explain how moral knowledge is acquired by means of a philosophically improved Christianized version of Plato's theory of recollection. Through Cicero, he must have been aware of it, according to which learning is just the process of making manifest to ourselves this latent knowledge since before our birth we have knowledge of the Forms from a direct communion with them.[239] In the process of exploring the truth, Augustine advises we can derive anything even from profane sources, for truth belongs to God regardless wherever truth may be found.[240] For example, we do not need to abandon music owing to the superstition of the heathen, since we may lay hold upon spiritual things by investigating about harps and other instruments.[241] In this context, Augustine claims that Plato is to be held as excelling other philosophers in moral, natural, and rational philosophies.[242] In particular, logic as rational philosophy discriminating between the true and the false shows the excellence of Plato's philosophy in that Plato "distinguished those things which are conceived by the mind from those which are perceived by the senses, neither taking away from the senses anything to which they are competent, nor attributing to them anything beyond their competency." This was contrary to Stoics and Epicureans who "ascribed to the bodily senses that expertness in disputation which they so ardently

---

237. *c. Acad.* 1.3.7.

238. *c. Acad.* 3.20.19.

239. Gareth B. Matthews, "Knowledge and illumination," in *The Cambridge Companion to Augustine*, ed. Eleonore Stump and Norman Kretzmann (Cambridge: Cambridge University Press, 2001), 180.

240. *doc. Chr.* 2.18.28. trans. James Shaw in *Nicene and Post-Nicene Fathers*, vol. 2 (New York: Christian Literature Publishing Co., 1887). Hereafter I use this translation.

241. *doc. Chr.* 2.18.28.

242. *civ. Dei.* 8.4. trans. R. W. Dyson (Cambridge: Cambridge University Press, 2007). Hereafter I use this translation.

love, called by them dialectic, asserting that from the senses the mind conceives the notions (ἔννοιαι) of those things which they explicate by definition."[243] In this context, his *De magistro* is directed at Plato's *Meno* where Socrates explains how virtue is acquired by introducing positive ideas such as the immortality of the soul and the theory of knowledge as recollection (ἀνάμνησις). For Plato, moral learning is innate and the soul's recollection.[244] The theory is vividly illustrated by Socrates asking a slave boy questions about geometry. At first the boy gives the wrong answer; when this is pointed out to him, he is puzzled, but by asking questions Socrates is able to help him to reach the true answer. This is intended to show that, as the boy was not told the answer, he could only have reached the truth by recollecting what he had already known but forgotten. This, as Plato concludes, is an internal process as recollection.[245] In this dialogue, Socrates regards himself as a midwife rather than a teacher, aiding with the birth of knowledge that was already there in the student. For Augustine, like Socrates and Plato, moral learning has an internal aspect as follows:

> When we deal with things that we perceive by the mind, namely by the intellect and reason, we're speaking of things that we look upon immediately in the inner light of Truth, in virtue of which the so-called inner man is illuminated and rejoices ... He's taught not by my words but by the things themselves made manifest within when God discloses them.[246]

In moral learning, Augustine emphasizes divine illumination of Truth by the inner Teacher rather than language by external teachers. According to him, "words have force only to the extent that they remind us to look for things."[247] In spite of the function of reminding, according to him, words as instruments of teaching are inadequate in that words are only a sign and things not signifying anything cannot be signs.[248] There-

---

243. *civ. Dei.* 8.7.
244. Plato, *Meno*, 82b-85b.
245. Ibid., 98a3-5.
246. *mag.* 12.40. trans. Peter King (Cambridge: Hackett Publishing Company, 1995). Hereafter I use this translation.
247. *mag.* 11.36.
248. *mag.* 7.19.

fore, knowledge of words is made complete once the things are known.[249] He claims that:

> We have to admit that we learn words we didn't know only after their significance has been perceived, and this happens not by hearing the mere sounds uttered but by knowing the things signified ... when words are spoken we either know what they signify or we don't; if we know, then it's reminding rather than learning; but if we don't know, it isn't even reminding, though perhaps we recollect that we should inquire.[250]

In this context, Augustine thinks that "someone who presents what I want to know to my eyes, or to any of my bodily senses, or even to my mind itself, does teach me something."[251] As he states that "we don't consult a speaker who makes sounds outside us, but the Truth that presides within over the mind itself" with regard to "each of the things we understand." He identifies Christ as the Teacher operating within us;[252] Our real teacher is "He Who is said to dwell in the inner man, does teach: Christ—that is, the unchangeable power and everlasting wisdom of God."[253] For Augustine, Christ as the interior teacher, who is the Word of God illuminating the human soul is our true teacher as follows:

> Thus, in the gospel He speaks through the flesh; and this sounded outwardly in the ears of men, that it might be believed and sought inwardly, and that it might be found in the eternal Truth, where the good and only Master teaches all His disciples. There, O Lord, I hear Your voice, the voice of one speaking unto me, since He speaks unto us who teaches us. But He that teaches us not, although He speaks, speaks not to us. Moreover, who teaches us, unless it be the immutable Truth? For even when we are admonished through a changeable creature, we are led to the Truth immutable.[254]

By the light of Christ or the light of God mind is able to distinguish the objects of intellectual vision. Augustine insists that our minds have direct access to the eternal truth of reason in that the mind is illuminated

---

249. *mag.* 11.36.
250. *mag.* 11.36.
251. *mag.* 11.36.
252. *mag.* 11.38.
253. *mag.* 11.38.
254. *conf.* 11.8.10.

with knowledge by the inner Teacher; "When the teachers have explained by means of words all the disciplines they profess to teach, even the disciplines of virtue and of wisdom, then those who are called students consider within themselves whether truths have been stated. They do so by looking upon the inner Truth, according to their abilities."[255] In this way no external human teacher can teach.[256]

Particularly, Augustine's idea of divine illumination is intensively discussed in the dimension of proof of the existence of God in book 2 of *De libero arbitrio*.[257] Before proving God's existence, he deals with belief as a preliminary matter, for "understanding" is impossible with it. On the basis of Isaiah's saying "Unless you believe, you will not understand," he claims that at first we ought to believe before we desire to understand the great and divine things.[258] According to him, above all, it is Jesus' teaching:

> At first our Lord himself by his words and deeds urged those whom he had called to salvation to believe in him. But later, when he spoke of the gift that he was going to give to those who believed, he did not say, "This is eternal life, that they may believe," but "This is eternal life, that they may know you, the true God, and him whom you have sent, Jesus Christ." And he said to those who already believe, "Seek, and you will find."

255. *mag.* 14.45.

256. "There is widespread disagreement as to exactly what Augustine might have meant by his theory of learning, in which Christ, the truth, teaches within. The precise interpretation of Augustine's doctrine of illumination has been the subject of centuries of debate. How is this kind of learning process which Augustine outlines—a process by which the word of God illumines the soul—to be understood? The major schools of thought on this subject have been: the *ontologistic* version, which regards the immediate presence of the divine light, the continuity between the mind of man and the mind of God, as primary in the act of learning; the *ideogenetic* version, which regards the activity of the word of God, mysteriously producing ideas in the human mind, as primary in the learning process; and, finally, what we might call the *normative* version, which understands the metaphor of illumination to refer to the way in which the divine light provides an ultimate standard of certainty by which knowledge is evaluated, rather than describing an inner, psychological process through which the act of learning occurs. This last approach—which has been subscribed to by such Augustinian scholars as Gilson, Jolivet, Bourke, Howie, Copleston and TeSelle—has been very popular, largely because it provides a convenient means for accommodating both Augustinian and Thomist approaches to knowledge." David Chidester, "The Symbolism of Leaning in St. Augustine," *Harvard Theological Review* 76, no. 1 (1983), 73.

257. Charles Taylor, *Sources of the Self: The Making of the Modern Identity* (Cambridge: Cambridge University Press, 1989), 132,

258. *lib. arb.* 2.2.6.

Xue (學) and Moral Learning

For something that is believed but not known has not yet been found, and no one becomes ready to find God unless he first believes what he will afterwards know.[259]

Hence, Augustine advises we ought to "diligently obey the Lord's command" in seeking, for "he himself will show us what we seek at his urging."[260] This indicates that a sense of purpose and direction is prerequisite for the successful outcome of moral learning in that it cannot be carried forward on the basis of skepticism.[261]

And then, Augustine attempts to show the role of reason by proving existence, life, and understanding of himself as undeniable truth, for "whatever understands must certainly also exist and be alive."[262] Just as a stone exists and an animal is alive, but a stone is alive or an animal understands, human beings who have all three qualities are superior to something that lacks any of them.[263] According to him, "a nature that has existence but not life or understanding, like an inanimate body, is inferior to a nature that has both existence and life but not understanding, like the souls of animals; and such a thing is in turn inferior to something that has all three, like the rational mind of a human being."[264] Life has "inner sense" and "bodily senses" such as sight, hearing, smell, taste, and touch. According to Augustine, inner sense is higher than bodily senses, for it judges bodily senses.[265] However, inner sense is not reason itself, which animals do not have.[266] It is lower than reason and is present both in human beings and in animals.[267] By reason human beings understand these things and recognize that they are so.[268] Reason judges material objects, the bodily senses, and the inner sense.[269] Thus, Augustine calls it "an agent of reason" in that "it takes whatever it comes into contact with

---

259. *lib. arb.* 2.2.6.
260. *lib. arb.* 2.2.6.
261. Howie, *Educational Theory and Practice in St Augustine*, 52.
262. *lib. arb.* 2.3.7.
263. *lib. arb.* 2.3.7.
264. *lib. arb.* 2.6.14.
265. *lib. arb.* 2.3.8.
266. *lib. arb.* 2.3.8.
267. *lib. arb.* 2.5.12.
268. *lib. arb.* 2.3.8.
269. *lib. arb.* 2.6.13.

and presents that to reason so that reason can delimit the things that are perceived and grasp them by knowledge and not merely by sense."[270]

Furthermore, Augustine claims that there is anything in human nature more exalted than reason in the evidence of mathematics. According to him, numbers are not perceived by the bodily senses when each number is named on the basis of how many times it contains one:

> For example, if it contains one twice, it is called 'two', if three times, 'three', and if ten times, 'ten'. For any numbers at all, its name will be the number of times that it contains one. But anyone who thinks correctly will surely find that one cannot be perceived by the bodily senses.[271]

This indicates that Augustine rejects the possibility of an empirical basis for mathematics.[272] Observing that "this order is fixed, secure, and unchangeable for all numbers," he raises questions about where to learn that this order extends to all of them and how to see "this indisputable truth about number, which extends through infinitely many numbers."[273] Concerning these questions, Augustine shows that "we see it by an inner light of which the bodily sense knows nothing."[274] Hence, he demonstrates "for those inquirers to whom God has given the ability, whose judgment is not clouded by stubbornness, these and many other such examples suffice to show that the order and truth of numbers has nothing to do with the senses of the body, but that it does exist, complete and immutable, and can be seen in common by everyone who uses reason."[275] His argument for proof of the existence of God is the matter of how to ascend to God by intellect which is illuminated by God.

The notion of an interior teacher is a pivotal theme running even through his later writings such as *De doctrina Christiana*, *Confessions*, and *De civitate Dei*.[276] Nevertheless, scholars usually look first at early works such as *De magistro* to interpret Augustine's account of learning by

---

270. *lib. arb.* 2.3.9.
271. *lib. arb.* 2.8.22.
272. Nash, *The Light of the Mind: St. Augustine's Theory of Knowledge*, 78.
273. *lib. arb.* 2.8.23.
274. *lib. arb.* 2.8.23. "in luce interior conspicitur, quam corporis sensus ignorat"
275. *lib. arb.* 2.8.24.
276. T. Brian Mooney and Mark Nowacki (eds.), *Understanding Teaching and Leaning: Classic Texts on Education by Augustine, Aquinas, Newman and Mill* (Exeter: Imprint Academic, 2011), 65.

illumination. As a result, later works have been neglected in the discussion of illumination.[277] Schumacher points out that such scholarly tendency to read Augustine's early writings on illumination could lose "reference to the theological context he later elucidates in works like *De Trinitate*."[278] What is the theological context of illumination in *De Trinitate*? This matter is inextricably linked to the purpose of *De Trinitate*. For Augustine, one of main aims in writing *De Trinitate* is to "convince his readers that salvation and spiritual growth are connected with knowing themselves as images of the Triune God."[279] In other words, Augustine's moral learning is based on his doctrine of the image of God in that human beings were created in the image of the Trinity according to Genesis 1.26. His moral learning theory is closely linked to creation.[280] For Augustine, the image of God is not just an image of the one God but of the Trinity.[281] He found the image of Trinity in the incorporeal soul around his baptism by escaping the Manichaean inference.[282] In *De Genesi ad litteram libri dudecim*, Augustine writes on his account of the possibility of the interaction of God and the human soul in connection with creation as follows:

> But the light itself is something else, the light by which the soul is enlightened in order truly to understand and observe all things either in itself or in this light. For this light is now God himself, while the soul is a creature, even though a rational and intelligent one made to his image.[283]

This indicates that the aim of divine illumination is to enlighten the soul. For Augustine, as Miles defines, "the soul is not primarily a separated entity for whom the problem is the formation of relationships with other souls, with the natural environment, and with God; Augustine's

277. Lydia Schumacher, *Divine Illumination: the History and Future of Augustine's Theory of Knowledge* (Chichester: Wiley-Blackwell, 2011), 25.

278. Schumacher, *Divine Illumination*, 26.

279. Mary T. Clark, "De Trinitate," in *the Cambridge Companion to Augustine*, ed. Eleonore Stump and Norman Kretzmann (Cambridge: Cambridge University Press, 2001), 91.

280. Chidester, "The Symbolism of Learning in St. Augustine," 74.

281. Roland Teske, "Augustine's philosophy of memory," in *The Cambridge Companion to Augustine*, ed. Eleonore Stump and Norman Kretzmann (Cambridge: Cambridge University Press, 2001), 155.

282. Teske, "Augustine's philosophy of memory," 155.

283. *Gn. litt. imp.* 12.31.59. trans. Matthew O'Connell in *a Translation for the 21st Century*, vol. 13 (New York: New City Press, 2002). Hereafter I use this translation.

soul is primarily a partially centered energy, initially barely distinguishable from its cosmic, physical, and spiritual environment, which comes to be cumulatively distinguished and defined by the objects of its attention and affection."[284] Particularly, Augustine deals with the matter of memory in the perspective of the human soul of the three Persons in the one God in *De Trinitate*.[285] He expounds the theological context of memory, understanding, and will as three aspects of the mind in the dimension of the Persons of the Trinity as follows:

> Since, then, these three, memory, understanding, will, are not three lives, but one life; nor three minds, but one mind; it follows certainly that neither are they three substances, but one substance. Since memory, which is called life, and mind, and substance, is so called in respect to itself; but it is called memory, relatively to something ... But they are three, in that wherein they are mutually referred to each other; and if they were not equal, and this not only each to each, but also each to all, they certainly could not mutually contain each other; for not only is each contained by each, but also all by each. For I remember that I have memory and understanding, and will; and I understand that I understand, and will, and remember; and I will that I will, and remember, and understand; and I remember together my whole memory, and understanding, and will. For that of my memory which I do not remember, is not in my memory; and nothing is so much in the memory as memory itself. Therefore I remember the whole memory.[286]

Like the Persons of the Trinity which is distinguished as one God, Augustine explains the relation among memory, understanding, and will; "while all are mutually comprehended by each, and as wholes, each as a whole is equal to each as a whole, and each as a whole at the same time to all as wholes; and these three are one, one life, one mind, one essence."[287]

---

284. Margaret Miles, "Vision: The Eye of the Body and the Eye of the Mind in Saint Augustine's "De trinitate" and "Confessions,"" *The Journal of Religion* 63, no. 2 (1983), 129.

285. Teske, "Augustine's philosophy of memory," 155.

286. *Trin.* 10.11.18. trans. Arthur West Haddan in *Nicene and Post-Nicene Fathers*, vol. 3 (New York: Christian Literature Publishing Co., 1887). Hereafter I use this translation.

287. *Trin.* 10.11.18. cf. Jong Sung Rhee, *Augustine's Doctrine of the Trinity* (Seoul: Korea Institute of Advanced Christian Studies, 2001), 277.

Friendship in Christ: Ambrose, Monica, Monastery

Through reflection on his own experiences of education as a pupil Augustine realised the limit of external teachers in the methodology of moral learning. In the *Confessions*, he states that he hated to be forced to learn in spite of having "no love of learning" in his childhood.[288] For him, "external compulsion alone was not a suitable motivation for a student to learn a subject for which a specific inclination was lacking and that there must be other factors that direct the desire to learn."[289] However, given that Augustine was always to be found in the company of others in the beginning of the outset of his life, the impacts of external teachers in his life cannot be entirely neglected. Topping argues Augustine's moral education can improve individuals but not societies as follows:

> The first reason why education cannot advance society, which we have already seen, is that with the birth of Christ there is in principle no further revelation that humanity awaits. The second reason for this limit is, more directly, because of our lack of moral virtue, which is manifest in both private and public life. I take up virtue in individuals first.[290]

In Augustine's view, progress is limited because both our knowledge and our virtue are limited. In the dimension of an eschatological goal, social progress primarily in intellectual terms, secondarily in moral terms, and not at all in material terms. Hence, Topping insists, as Wetzel and O'Donovan argue, that Augustine's pedagogy is best understood against the horizon of his evolution on the possibilities of human perfectibility, and in particular the limits of virtue which "can be encouraged but not guaranteed."[291] In *Christianity and the Secular*, Markus replies about criticism that his interpretation of Augustine's view on the limits and functions of public authority comes perilously close to making Augustine a "precursor of modern secular liberalism" and to casting the debate in terms of a "modern individualist liberalism" by emphasizing the eschatological character of Augustine's views.[292] In contrast with Markus, Oliver

---

288. *conf.* 1.12.19.

289. Leonardo Franchi, "Healing the Wounds: St. Augustine, Catechesis, and Religious Education Today," *The Official Journal of the Religious Education Association* 106, no. 3 (2011), 307.

290. Topping, *St. Augustine*, 86.

291. Ibid., 90, 94.

292. Robert A. Markus, *Christianity and the Secular* (Notre Dame: University of

O'Donovan offers a less affirming and engaging place for the secular within the economy of God than Markus's interpretation does. John Howard Yoder, Stanley Hauerwas, and John Milbank reject the notion that the secular has positive attributes.

For example, several mentors of various backgrounds and personalities such as Ambrose, Monica, and some close friends influenced him at different periods of his life.[293] The early parts of the *Confessions* refer frequently to his need to be with others, it was part of his nature and, looking back on this period, Augustine was able to be realistic about its dangers but also about its graces:

> By means of my inner sense I coordinated my sensible impressions, and in my little thoughts about little things I delighted in truth. I was unwilling to be deceived, I had a lively memory, I was being trained in the use of words, I was comforted by friendship, and I shrank form pain, groveling and ignorance.[294]

It is noteworthy that he mentions the role of 'friendship' in moral learning. Friendship plays a central role in Augustine's moral learning. He thought that in this world two things are essential: life and friendship. God created people to exist and be alive. Mere life is not enough: if a human being is to be a real person then there must be friendship. For him, friendship is essential in life.[295] Augustine states:

> Particularly when I am worn out by the upsets of the world, I cast myself without reservation on the love of those who are especially close to me. I know I can safely entrust my thoughts and considerations to those who are aflame with Christian love and have become faithful friends to me. For I am entrusting them not to another human, but to God in Whom they dwell and by Whom they are who they are.[296]

Notre Dame, 2006), 51.

293. Edward L. Smither, *Augustine as Mentor: A Model for Preparing Spiritual Leaders* (Nashville: B & H Academic, 2008), 92.

294. *conf.* 1.20.31.

295. *s.* 16.1. trans. John E. Rotelle (New York: New City Press, 1997). Hereafter I use this translation.

296. *ep.* 73.3. trans. Roland Teske (New York: New City Press, 2001). Hereafter I use this translation.

It is because all who God have desire for loving neighbor.[297] Above all, friendship is inextricably connected with searching for truth; "I am delighted because I see that your mind is drawing near to it [wisdom] and is ablaze with the desire to attain it. From it, of course, there also flows true friendship that is not to be judged by temporal advantages but it to be valued as gratuitous love. For no one can be truly a friend unless he is first a friend of the truth, and if that is not done gratuitously it cannot be done at all."[298] Contrary to friends who make us perverted by their flattery, true friends correct our faults by seeking the truth.[299] In this context, for Augustine the encounter with Bishop Ambrose of Milan through his preaching was significant moment:

> And to Milan I came, unto Ambrose the bishop, known to the whole world as among the best of men, Your devout servant; whose eloquent discourse did at that time strenuously dispense unto Your people the flour of Your wheat, the gladness of Your oil, and the sober intoxication of Your wine. To him was I unknowingly led by You, that by him I might knowingly be led to You.[300]

Given that Ambrose was described by Augustine as "one of the best of men," "a devout worshipper of God," and a "man of God," his holy life profoundly impacted on Augustine. In particular, Ambrose's educational background made him one of the most notable bishops of this time. Prior to becoming bishop of Milan, he had been its governor. He had been well educated in Rome as he prepared for a career in civil service. He was not only familiar with the texts that orators were expected to know, but with philosophical and contemporary texts since he was fluent in both Greek and Latin. Scholars have noted in his extant sermons ample evidence of his broad reading including Greek sources such as the Platonist Plotinus, Eastern Christian writers, and Philo of Alexandria as well as Latin ones such as Virgil and Seneca.[301] Hence, he understood his encounter with Ambrose as "a sign of divine grace" in that Ambrose played an important role in helping him overcome Manichean deceptions by his teaching

---

297. *vera rel.* 87. trans. Edmund Hill in *a Translation for the 21st Century*, vol. 8 (New York: New City Press, 2005). Hereafter I use this translation.

298. *ep.* 155.

299. *conf.* 9.8.18.

300. *conf.* 5.14.24.

301. Paul R. Kolbet, *Augustine and the Cure of Souls* (Notre Dame: University of Notre Dame Press, 2010), 74.

of salvation.[302] Augustine was deeply touched by Ambrose's intellectual preaching as follows:

> For although I took no trouble to learn what he spoke, but only to hear how he spoke (for that empty care alone remained to me, despairing of a way accessible for man to You), yet, together with the words which I prized, there came into my mind also the things about which I was careless; for I could not separate them. And while I opened my heart to admit how skillfully he spoke, there also entered with it, but gradually, and how truly he spoke! For first, these things also had begun to appear to me to be defensible; and the Catholic faith, for which I had fancied nothing could be said against the attacks of the Manicheans, I now conceived might be maintained without presumption.[303]

Augustine acknowledges that he was interested in how Ambrose speaks by assessing his "rhetorical craft" rather than what he speaks in his initial trips to hear Ambrose's preaching.[304] "Despite his initial motives Augustine became attracted to Ambrose who was not only kind but also demonstrated that it was possible for someone to be both an intellectual and a Christian."[305] Furthermore, Ambrose's allegorical approach changed Augustine's attitude to the Scriptures. It is noteworthy that Augustine was once disappointed about expounding the Holy Scripture due to being swollen with "pride"[306] just after reading Cicero's *Hortensius* when nineteen years old as follows:

---

302. Franchi, "Healing the Wounds: St. Augustine, Catechesis, and Religious Education Today," 307.

303. *conf.* 5.14.25.

304. Kolbet, *Augustine and the Cure of Souls*, 73.

305. Smither, *Augustine as Mentor*, 106.

306. Herdt deals with the matter of virtue's acquisition in Augustine's moral learning in relation to Aristotle, Aquinas, Erasmus and so on in order to solve the false dichotomy between virtue that comes by imitation within a community that teaches putting on virtue, and God's transforming grace that makes us new creatures. Herdt argues that Augustine entirely condemned pagan virtue, calling its root pride, in contrast to Aquinas who rightly rehabilitates Aristotle's pagan account by accenting virtue's semblances and circumscribing the vice of hypocrisy and Erasmus who sustains the best features of the Augustinian account of the imitation of Christ as gradual habituation in Christian virtue but marries this with a characteristically humanist generosity toward pagan virtue. Furthermore, she points out how so many of our modern tendencies are rooted in hyper-Augustinian errors as well as post-Luther and post-Bunyan. In this context, she attempts to redress Christian militancy against pagan virtue and re-appropriate mimesis as central to any account of Christian virtue by

I resolved, therefore, to direct my mind to the Holy Scriptures, that I might see what they were. And behold, I perceive something not comprehended by the proud, not disclosed to children, but lowly as you approach, sublime as you advance, and veiled in mysteries; and I was not of the number of those who could enter into it, or bend my neck to follow its steps. For not as when now I speak did I feel when I tuned towards those Scriptures, but they appeared to me to be unworthy to be compared with the dignity of Tully; for my inflated pride shunned their style, nor could the sharpness of my wit pierce their inner meaning. Yet, truly, were they such as would develop in little ones; but I scorned to be a little one, and, swollen with pride, I looked upon myself as a great one.[307]

Such disappointment made Augustine fall into the errors of the Manicheans.[308] Augustine commenced to overcome the attacks of the Manicheans by hearing Ambrose's appealing interpretation of the Scriptures. As a result, he began listening to Ambrose's sermons for their content more than their eloquent packaging. Even though Augustine had little personal contact with Ambrose, they seemed to enjoy a sense of intimacy at a distance through the form or language of preaching in that the sermon became a quasi-dialogue although Ambrose was the only one speaking.[309] The relation between Ambrose and Augustine needs to be comprehended as friendship in Christ. When Ambrose stood to preach the Scripture, unveiling through skilled interpretation the inspiring content of their meaning in a form that was eloquent and even entertaining, this medium was a familiar language that Augustine the rhetor could connect with on a profound level.[310] Augustine assimilated Ambrose's teaching, the sermon served as a catalyst for Augustine's ongoing commitment to seeking truth, a pursuit that often included dialogue with others.[311] In this aspect, Ambrose should, as Smither claims, be credited with helping Augustine go from a rhetor to a preacher.[312]

---

criticizing features of particularly post-Augustine's legacy. Jennifer A. Herdt, *Putting on Virtue: The Legacy of the Splendid Vices* (Chicago: The University of Chicago Press, 2008), 13, 71. cf. *conf*. 3.3.5.

307. *conf*. 3.5.9.
308. *conf*. 3.6.10.
309. Smither, *Augustine as Mentor*, 106.
310. Ibid., 106.
311. Ibid., 107.
312. Ibid., 107.

His mother Monica had a special friendship with Augustine. Their "intense bonding" stems from Monica's moral teachings.[313] She was most often depicted in the *Confessions* as a woman of prayer and tears. When Augustine fell into the errors of the Manicheans, Monica earnestly requested a bishop to guide him "shedding copious tears." Yet, the bishop rejected her entreaty. Instead, he said "Go your way, and God bless you, for it is not possible that the son of these tears should perish."[314] She accepted it as "a voice from heaven."[315] Even though she was uneducated and simple, she resolutely dealt with Augustine becoming a Manichean by expelling him from her home as follows:

> And You sent Your hand from above, and drew my soul out of that profound darkness, when my mother, Your faithful one, wept to you on my behalf more than mothers are wont to weep the bodily death of their children. For she saw that I was dead by that faith and spirit which she had from You, and You heard her, O Lord. You heard her, and despised not her tears, when, pouring down, they watered the earth under her eyes in every place where she prayed; yea, You heard her. For whence was that dream with which You consoled her, so that she permitted me to live with her, and to have my meals at the same table in the house, which she had begun to avoid, hating and detesting the blasphemies of my error?[316]

Though Monica's program of moral education was informally conducted at home, her example of virtue, prayer, and devotion to the church ultimately contributed not only to Augustine's conversion to faith in Christ but also to his philosophy of training new believers, particularly in his manual *De Catechizandis Rudibus*.[317]

Along with Ambrose and Monica, friends also play a central role in Augustine's moral learning. Not all friends made constructive contributions. Due to his friends Augustine used to be led in wrong directions in his youth. For example, in spite of Monica's advice on not committing obscene acts, Augustine took pleasure in such vices not only for the enjoyment of what he did, but also for the applause he won by his friends

---

313. Richard B. Miller, "Evil, Friendship, and Iconic Realism in Augustine's Confessions," *Harvard Theological Review* 104, no. 4 (2011), 401.
314. *conf.* 3.12.21.
315. *conf.* 3.12.21.
316. *conf.* 3.11.19.
317. Smither, *Augustine as Mentor*, 98-99.

in his adolescence.[318] Why did he commit such crimes? According to his own analysis, the causes of committing sin are due to the desire of gaining and the fear of losing material things belong to the lowest order,[319] for such things seem to be "attractive and have beauty, although they are paltry trifles in comparison with the worth of God's blessed treasures."[320] His problem in youth was abandoning those higher and better things to obtain the lowest order of good.[321] Therefore, he gave in more and more to vice simply in order not to be despised by his companions. When he had not sinned enough among his companions, he used to pretend that he had done things he had not done at all, because he "was afraid that innocence would be taken for cowardice and chastity for weakness."[322] Even during Augustine's youth, friends influenced him to steal pears from a tree. They intensified his desire to commit robbery through "a lustiness of iniquity."[323] For Augustine, such companions were not true friends as they led him to sinful ways:

> These were the companions with whom I walked the streets of Babylon. I wallowed in its mire as if it were made of spices and precious ointments, and to fix me all the faster in the very depths of sin the unseen enemy trod me underfoot and enticed me to himself, because I was an easy prey for his seductions.[324]

Before conversion to Christianity, he planned to establish a common household with a group of his friends in the basis of friendship in order to "live a life of peace" away from the crowd. According to him, "the plan was to arrange this life of leisure by pooling our possessions and using such money as we had between us to create a common fund. In the spirit of sincere friendship none of us would claim this or that as his/her own, but all would be thrown together and the whole would belong to each and to all."[325] For Augustine, friendship seemed to be one solace in human society filled with misunderstanding and calamities.[326] However,

318. *conf.* 2.3.7.
319. *conf.* 2.3.11.
320. *conf.* 2.3.11.
321. *conf.* 2.5.10.
322. *conf.* 2.3.7.
323. *conf.* 2.4.9.
324. *conf.* 2.3.8.
325. *conf.* 6.14.24.
326. *civ. Dei.* 19.8.

all their arrangements speedily collapsed, for they worried whether their wives would agree the plan. As a result, Augustine trod the wide, well-beaten tracks of the world, and thought jostled thought in his heart again.[327] After his conversion to faith in Jesus Christ in adulthood, however, his aim of friendship was transformed. For Augustine, the world is no longer pure material and true reality is only comprehended when we know of the transcendent God. In order to seek God he invited a diverse group of friends such as Alypius, Nebridius, and Evodius to friendship in the monastic community.[328] By bringing together such a community, he attempted to pursue the happy life. They became friends in Christ. For Augustine community and friendship are necessary elements for moral learning.[329] When Augustine retired to Cassiciacum in September 386 in the aftermath of his conversion, he gathered his friends to focus on spiritual understanding by entering upon a life of creative leisure. As he was released from the profession of rhetoric, it seemed to be possible:

> Praising you and full of joy I set out for the house in the country with all my friends and relations. Once we were there I began at last to serve you with my pen. The books I wrote are evidence of this, although the old air can still be sensed in them, as though I were still panting from my exertions in the school of pride. In them are recorded the discussions I held with my friends who were with me and my deliberations with myself when I was alone in your presence.[330]

And then when he returned to Tagaste where he attempted to "organize his community, to found the personal relations within it upon a permanent code of behavior, to be responsible for the measure of authority over them. As a result, the group of like-minded slow and subtle stages, to resemble a monastery, with Augustine as a spiritual father."[331] After arriving at Hippo he looked for somewhere to found a monastery "devoted to the reading of the Scriptures" and invited others who were not already his friends.[332] For him, all Christian people are friends in Christ.[333] At

---

327. *conf.* 6.14.24.
328. *conf.* 8.6.13.
329. Smither, *Augustine as Mentor*, 100.
330. *conf.* 9.4.7.
331. Brown, *Augustine of Hippo*, 129.
332. Ibid., 129.
333. "This monastery was still recruited from among Augustine's past friends. Evodius and Alypius were there. Inevitably, however, a permanent institution, such

Hippo, Augustine put his heart and soul into the monastery in order to foster moral learning. "Augustine was never to live alone in Hippo. As a priest, he would return from his duties to preside over the Monastery in the Garden. Later, when fully occupied as a bishop, he would envy the monks their regular life of prayer, reading and manual labor."[334] Particularly, immersion in the Scriptures would have equipped Augustine and his followers more fully for an active life in the African church.[335] The monastery instituted, inspired, and directed by Augustine became a pivotal development in the life of the church of Africa during the last decade of the fourth century and the first quarter of the fifth century.[336] As his monastery became a "seminary" in the true sense of the word, it came to form an influential group within African church.[337]

This section shows that in moral learning Augustine emphasized the development of a love of intellectual enquiry for God as man's supreme good against the flux of the temporal world, contrary to Confucius and Mencius who stressed filial piety as the essence of the Way in achieving benevolent government. For Augustine, divine illumination and friendship in Christ are critical methods of moral learning.

SUMMARY

In this chapter, I dealt with Confucius, Mencius, and Augustine's moral learning in internal, communitarian, and transcendental aspects. In terms of Confucius' moral learning, he stressed the study of virtue (德) as a means of solving political turmoil in the dimension of self-cultivation because it leads to benevolent government by fostering the man of virtue. For him, moral learning is beyond individual dimensions. He designated Heaven (天) as a significant object of moral learning since it produces

---

as a monastery, would attract younger men, whose tastes, culture and past history did not resemble that of Augustine and his friends. Such a man was Possidius—a straightforward and pertinacious disciple. It is paradoxical that Possidius should have written the only contemporary biography of Augustine; and that he should have chosen to present his complex hero largely in terms of the tranquil, uncomplicated life that he had created for others." Ibid., 136.

334. Ibid., 136.
335. Ibid., 130.
336. Pierce Beaver, "The Rise of Monasticism in the Church of Africa," *Church History* 6, no 4 (1937), 350.
337. Brown, *Augustine of Hippo*, 137.

virtue in relation to human nature. In addition, he offered Zhou dynasty as the ideal model of antiquity for an object of moral learning instead of exploring extraordinary things, feats of strength, disorder, spiritual beings, and death. Just as Augustine presented liberal disciplines in his moral learning, Confucius offered 'Six Disciplines' (六藝) which was arts conducted in the Zhou dynasty such as ritual propriety (禮), music (樂), archery (射), chariot-riding (御), calligraphy (書), and computation (數). In relation to ritual propriety, Confucius stressed loyalty (忠) and reciprocity (恕) in the *Book of Poetry*. It is because he thought tradition and imitating good teachers are the best methods for the practice of virtue. Given that for Confucius the aim of moral learning is to cultivate moral self, he asserted the importance of practicing filial piety (孝) and fraternal submission (弟) as a method of moral learning. In aspiring to moral learning he laid emphasis on overcoming sexual desire and poverty through will (志).

Like Confucius, for Mencius becoming the man of virtue is inextricably linked to establishing benevolent government since the purpose of a ruler is to protect his people in supporting God. According to Mencius, kings ought to pay attention to people even in commencing war because Heaven sees and hears through people's eyes and ears. Considering political chaos raised by war in his time, for Mencius human unity by benevolent government is the most powerful weapon. Mencius regards filial piety as a core of benevolent government, so he enthusiastically insisted on reform of economic, social, and educational systems as a means of supporting filial piety. In other words, he thought moral learning of filial piety could be possible on the basis of economic and social supports for ordinary people. In contrast to Norden's argument, I stressed the importance of asceticism in Mencius' moral learning for the superior. Norden's anti-asceticism could be only justified in the relation between a king and their people. Ultimately, Mencius stresses moderate living in dealing only with the life style of the king as demonstrated by the ancient sovereigns. He suggested imitating the Way of Yao, Shun, and Confucius as a method of moral learning. Just as Confucius highlighted the importance of practice, Mencius stressed continually learning from sages. For him, the purpose of imitating sages is to practice virtue together.

Like Confucius and Mencius Augustine sought happiness by securing truth. For Confucius and Mencius happiness depends on whether one attains the Way. For Augustine happiness is the enjoyment of God as man's supreme good. The purpose of moral learning is to develop a love of intellectual enquiry against the flux of the temporal world. I offered divine illumination as the first step of moral learning to cover the matter of certainty by dealing with wisdom in connection with happiness in Augustine's earlier and later writings. For Augustine, moral learning is internal. In moral learning, Augustine highlights divine illumination of Truth by the inner Teacher rather than language by external teachers. According to him, our minds have direct access to the eternal truth of reason in that the mind is illuminated with knowledge by the inner Teacher since by the light of Christ or the light of God mind is able to distinguish the objects of intellectual vision. The notion of an interior teacher is a pivotal theme running even through his later writings. Augustine's moral learning is based on his doctrine of the image of God in that human beings were created to the image of the Trinity according to Genesis 1.26. For Augustine, the image of God is not just an image of the one God but of the Trinity. He explained it in relation to memory, understanding, and will. Along with divine illumination, Augustine presented the value of friendship in Christ in moral learning in the dimension of community. This indicates that Augustine did not entirely ignore the intervention of other persons, worship, community, and language even though he emphasized divine illumination. Augustine's moral learning is communitarian as well as internal. Not all his friends made constructive contributions to his moral learning. Ambrose and Monica significantly contributed to his conversion and after his conversion to faith in Jesus Christ in adulthood he shared friendship with Alypius, Nebridius, and Evodius in order to seek to God in the monastic community.

3

Si (思) and Contemplation

INTRODUCTION

JUST AS CONFUCIUS, MENCIUS, Augustine's moral learning were discussed in internal, communitarian, and transcendental aspects in the previous chapter, Confucius and Mencius' self-reflection (*si* 思) and Augustine's contemplation are also related to such dimensions. In this chapter I first explore Confucius' self-reflection in relation to his moral learning. And then I investigate Mencius' account of self-reflection. This deals with how Mencius' self-reflection is interconnected with Heaven and virtues such as benevolence, righteousness, ritual propriety, and wisdom embedded in human nature, habitual self-reflection, and how suffering contributes to fostering the man of virtue in connection with patience. Finally, I expound Augustine's account of contemplation as a binding of the mind to God by purifying our mind. This includes that contemplation as a step of ascension, Augustine's contemplative experience at Ostia, and the Scripture as the object of contemplation by focusing on divine wisdom as knowledge of God.

CONFUCIUS' SELF-REFLECTION

Limit of Self-Reflection

In order to achieve peaceful and flourishing society Confucius envisioned that people have to develop their own virtue.[1] This asked them

---

1. Ivanhoe, *Confucian Moral Self Cultivation* (Indianapolis: Hackett Publishing Company, 2000), 2.

Si (思) and Contemplation

to reflect deeply upon what they studied. In other words, Confucius expounded self-reflection in relation to study; "Study without reflection is a waste. Self-reflection without study is in peril."[2] This indicates that study and self-reflection are complementary. In particular, he states that "if a man takes no thought about what is distant, he will find sorrow near at hand."[3] Furthermore, he presented nine things the man of virtue thinks as follows:

> The man of virtue has nine things which are subjects with him of thoughtful consideration. In regard to the use of his eyes, he is anxious to see clearly. In regard to the use of his ears, he is anxious to hear distinctly. In regard to his countenance, he is anxious that it should be benign. In regard to his demeanor, he is anxious that it should be respectful. In regard to his speech, he is anxious that it should be sincere. In regard to his doing of business, he is anxious that it should be reverently careful. In regard to what he doubts about, he is anxious to question others. When he is angry, he thinks of the difficulties (his anger may involve him in). When he sees gain to be got, he thinks of righteousness.[4]

This indicates that Confucius dealt with self-reflection in the dimension of how to live as the man of virtue. However, there are the dangers of two misunderstandings of Confucius' self-reflection. The one is, as Ivanhoe argues, that for Confucius self-reflection never means abstract and theoretical cogitation. It is not ratiocination, in the sense of a logical process of deduction or demonstration that leads one to conclusions.[5] Chiefly it indicates to keep one's attention engaged with something, often a goal or ideal which one intends to achieve. Of course, Confucius took this sense of the word to direct people's attention toward moral goals and ideals, but the notion of focusing one's attention upon and longing for some desired person or object may well derived from an older, more general, usage. At the same time, si does appear to include relating such goals and ideals to one's attitudes and particular situation and hence includes

---

2. *Analects*, 2.15. Translation adapted from Dawson and Ivanhoe. 子曰：「學而不思則罔，思而不學則殆。」

3. *Analects*, 15.12. As translated in Legge. 子曰：「人無遠慮，必有近憂。」

4. *Analects*, 16.10. Translation adapted from Legge. 孔子曰：「君子有九思：視思明，聽思聰，色思溫，貌思恭，言思忠，事思敬，疑思問，忿思難，見得思義。」

5. Ivanhoe, *Confucian Moral Self Cultivation*, 2.

a certain level of practical reasoning.[6] The other is about how much Confucius deals with self-reflection. It is necessary to recognize that self-reflection is rarely mentioned in *Analects*. In terms of the relation between self-reflection and study, on the basis of his experience Confucius clearly insists that study is more important than self-reflection; "I once did not eat all day and did not sleep all night in order to think, but there was no benefit. It would have been better to study."[7] Even he advised that it is enough to think twice when he heard Ji Wen Zi thought three times before acting.[8] Compared to Mencius, for Confucius self-reflection is not important for the formation of moral self.

MENCIUS' SELF-REFLECTION

Human Nature, Sage, and Heaven

Occasionally, Mencius mentions the value of external teachers. For example, he presents five ways in which the man of virtue effects his teaching:

> There are some on whom his influence descends like seasonable rain. There are some whose virtue he perfects, and some of whose talents he assists the development. There are some whose inquiries he answers. There are some who privately cultivate and correct themselves. These five ways are the methods in which the man of virtue affects his teaching.[9]

However, Mencius fundamentally points out the limit of external teaching in the formation of moral self;[10] "A carpenter or a carriage-

---

6. Ivanhoe, *Confucian Moral Self Cultivation*, 3.

7. *Analects*, 15.31. As translated in Dawson. 子曰：「吾嘗終日不食，終夜不寢，以思，無益，不如學也。」

8. *Analects*, 5.20. 季文子三思而後行。子聞之，曰：「再，斯可矣。」

9. *Mencius*, 7A40. As translated in Legge. 孟子曰：「君子之所以教者五：有如時雨化之者，有成德者，有達財者，有答問者，有私淑艾者。此五者，君子之所以教也。」

10. Nivison proposes the importance of human nature in Confucian formation of moral self. For early Chinese kings, how a king could acquire virtue was an important issue since it was regarded as power or charisma by which early Chinese kings rule without needing to resort to force or violence. Nivison points out that one cannot perform a genuinely virtuous act, unless one is virtuous already. He calls this "the paradox of virtue", and argues that it is central to understanding the development of early Chinese philosophy. In contrast to Mozi who takes an extreme "voluntarist" position and Aristotle who held that one can become a more virtuous person by

maker may give a man the circle and square, but cannot make him skillful in the use of them."[11] Why did Mencius devalue it? In order to response this question, it is necessary to consider why he insisted that "the great man is the one who does not lose his child's-heart."[12] In this context, his method for the formation of moral self is based on seeking for the lost mind like benevolence and righteousness as follows:

> Benevolence is man's mind, and righteousness is man's path. How lamentable is it to neglect the path and not pursue it, to lose this mind and not know to seek it again! When men's fowls and dogs are lost, they know to seek for them again, but they lose their mind, and do not know to seek for it. The great end of learning is nothing else but to seek for the lost mind.[13]

When people lose their properties, they immediately try to retake them contrary to losing benevolence and righteousness.[14] Why does

---

performing virtuous actions without the appropriate virtuous motivations, Mencius solves the paradox by insisting that all humans already are virtuous, so we all can perform genuinely virtuous actions with his view of human nature and the "four sprouts." For Mencius, hence, the teacher's task is skillfully calling one's attention to one's moral sprouts, and coaching one in nurturing them since the student of morality does have to be moral already. Nivison argues that Mencius shows that not only how moral education is possible, but also moral education seems to be unnecessary. On the other hand, Nivision points out simply cultivating potentially moral-making capacities is not going to be sufficient to make one a moral person. Even if one has the given set of sprouts that Mencius supposes, one must also identify the right objects of the moral-making attitudes of sympathy, affection, dutifulness, courteousness, etc. And this identification must come from outside the process of cultivation itself. Mencius makes an emphasis on cultivating heart-mind which can lead one just to the right things. However, Nivision does not offer specific methods for cultivating heart-mind in his attention to moral education. Nivison, *The Ways of Confucianism*, 6, 32, 41, 43.

11. *Mencius*, 7B5. As translated in Legge. 孟子曰：「梓匠輪輿能與人規矩，不能使人巧。」

12. *Mencius*, 4B12. 孟子曰：「大人者，不失其赤子之心者也。」

13. *Mencius*, 6A11. As translated in Legge. 孟子曰：「仁，人心也；義，人路也。舍其路而弗由，放其心而不知求，哀哉！人有雞犬放，則知求之；有放心，而不知求。學問之道無他，求其放心而已矣。」

14. Shun offers the role of self-reflecting in the formation of moral self. For Mencius the human heart/mind has certain predispositions such as *jen, yi, li,* and *chih* as already in human beings. Being ethical or unethical is a matter of preserving or losing something in one's heart/mind. Hence, Mencius, according to Shun, regards "learning as a matter of seeking the lost heart/mind." Being a great person is just not losing predispositions in the heart/mind. In seeking predispositions, Shun focuses on self-reflection in the dimension of self-cultivation. He argues that for Mencius ethical failure is related to a lack of self-reflection. Kwong-loi Shun, *Mencius and Early Chinese*

happen such miserable situation? With regard to this problem, Mencius laments that people do not know how to cultivate their self in the dimension of controlling the desire of their body even though they know how to cultivate trees. In particular, he points out that "their want of reflection is extreme."[15] This shows how important self-reflection is in retaking the lost mind. According to Mencius, self-reflection, human nature, and Heaven are interconnected in recovering virtues.[16] Through

---

Thought (Stanford: Stanford University, 1997), 136.

15. *Mencius*, 6A13. As translated in Legge. 孟子曰：「拱把之桐梓，人苟欲生之，皆知所以養之者。至於身，而不知所以養之者，豈愛身不若桐梓哉？弗思甚也。」

16. According to Ivanhoe, Mencius saw himself as a follower and defender of Confucius but, in fact, in the face of new intellectual competitors, transformed the teachings of Confucius. Wang Yangming, on the other hand, borrowed freely and knowingly from Buddhism, even though Buddhist thought affected him in ways he did not see. Mencius based his claims about morality on his anthropology, while Wang based his moral claims on his metaphysical theory. In terms of self-cultivation, according to Ivanhoe, the key difference is that Mencius holds a "development model" whereas Wang uses a "discovery model." Essentially, this means that Mencius thought of self-cultivation as a process of development, while Wang looked upon the task of self-cultivation as reaching completion upon the happy discovery that one is already perfect and always has been. At first, Ivanhoe deals with the thought of Confucius to explain why Mencius ought to expound human nature for self-cultivation. Ivanhoe claims that at the heart of Confucius' conception of the good life as the Way (道) "is a model of a harmonious and happy family, one whose different members each contribute to the welfare and flourishing of the whole, according to their role-specific obligations." Ivanhoe believes that Confucius was a traditionalist who held that there was only one way to live and that this Way had been discovered and put into practice by certain sage-kings in the past. However, by Mencius' time, many competitors like the Mohists rejected Confucius' appeal to tradition and his conception of the golden age. In this context, Mencius preserved Confucius' traditionalism but grounded it in a new and persuasive vision of human nature and its relation to society. For example, according to Ivanhoe, Mencius accepts Confucius' traditionalist account of this while adding a novel account of why those particular characteristics thought to have been exhibited by the sage-kings were excellences. At bottom, Mencius seeks to base his account of moral justification in a theory of human nature. Mencius argues "that the ancient traditions, ideals, and values that Kongzi cherished were ... the perfect expression of what we by nature truly are." Ivanhoe argues Mencius goes even further in his development of Confucius' ideas by introducing a form of moral intuitionism into the foundations of the Confucian tradition. Ivanhoe suggests that a key part of Mencius' originality in the Western sense lies in his fusion of virtue ethics and the notion of an innate moral sense. Ivanhoe describes Confucius as a traditionalist holding an undeveloped form of virtue ethics, and Mencius as a virtue ethicist adhering to moral intuitionism and ethical naturalism. On the other hand, Wang is described the one who holds a form of moral intuitionism but drops Confucius and Mencius' virtue ethics. Hence, Ivanhoe presents the thought of Confucius and Mencius is more

self-reflection one can retake benevolence embedded in his nature since this process leads to knowing Heaven. For him, the way to serve Heaven is to preserve one's mental constitution, and nourish one's nature. Hence, he states that "when neither a premature death nor long life causes a man any double-mindedness, but he waits in the cultivation of his personal character for whatever issue; this is the way in which he establishes his Heaven-ordained being."[17] In other words, he stresses the importance of effort in realizing virtues. For example, Mencius thinks the way the mouth is disposed towards tastes, the eye towards colors, the ear towards sounds, the nose towards smells, and the four limbs towards ease is human nature, yet securing them depends on the Decree. In contrast, the way benevolence pertains to the relation between father and son, the observance of righteousness to the relation between sovereign and minister, the ritual propriety to the relation between guest and host, wisdom to the good and wise man, the sage to the way of Heaven, is the Decree, but its realization depends on human nature. That is why man of virtue does not ascribe it to Decree but does his best to actualize it by following human nature.[18] This indicates self-reflection is a way of self-cultivation; "The man of virtue steeps himself in the Way because he wishes to find it in himself. When he finds it in himself, he will be at ease in it; when he is at ease in it, he can draw deeply upon it; when he can draw deeply upon it, he finds its source wherever he turns. That is why the man of virtue wishes to find the Way in himself."[19] His self-cultivation through self-reflection is based on his human nature theory. Of course, at his time, not everyone agreed with his opinion. For example, Kao Tzu who insists "Man's nature is neither good nor bad" argued that to make morality out of human nature is like making cups and bowls out of the willow since

---

contributable to the revival of virtue ethics than that of Wang. Philip J. Ivanhoe, *Ethics in the Confucian Tradition: The Thought of Mengzi and Wang Yangming*, 2nd ed (Indianapolis: Hackett, 2002), 1, 4, 12, 11, 12, 107, 109.

17 *Mencius*, 7A1. As translated in Legge. 孟子曰：「盡其心者，知其性也。知其性，則知天矣。存其心，養其性，所以事天也。殀壽不貳，修身以俟之，所以立命也。」

18. *Mencius*, 7B24. 孟子曰：「口之於味也，目之於色也，耳之於聲也，鼻之於臭也，四肢之於安佚也，性也，有命焉，君子不謂性也。仁之於父子也，義之於君臣也，禮之於賓主也，智之於賢者也，聖人之於天道也，命也，有性焉，君子不謂命也。」

19. *Mencius*, 4B14. Translation adapted from Legge. 孟子曰：「君子深造之以道，欲其自得之也。自得之，則居之安；居之安，則資之深；資之深，則取之左右逢其原，故君子欲其自得之也。」

human nature is like the willow.[20] Regarding his argument, Mencius replied that "If you must do violence and injury to the willow in order to make cups and bowls with it, on your principles you must in the same way do violence and injury to humanity in order to fashion from it benevolence and righteousness!"[21] Thus, he warned Kao Tzu's theory would lead all men on to reckon benevolence and righteousness to be calamities. Along with Kao Tzu, at his time, some asserted the nature of some is good, and the nature of others is bad. According to them, it was that under such a sovereign as Yao there yet appeared Xiang; that with such a father as Gu Sou there yet appeared Shun; and that with Zhou for their sovereign, and the son of their elder brother besides, there were found Qi, the viscount of Wei, and the prince Bi Gan.[22] Against such assertions, Mencius demonstrates why human nature is good as follows:

> As far as what is genuinely in him is concerned, a man is capable of becoming good. That is what I mean by good. As for his becoming bad, that is not the fault of his native endowment. The heart of compassion is possessed by all men alike; likewise the heart of shame, the heart of respect, and the heart of right and wrong. The heart of compassion pertains to benevolence, the heart of shame to righteousness, the heart of respect to propriety, and the heart of right and wrong to wisdom. Benevolence, righteousness, propriety, and wisdom are not infused into us from the outside; they are in us originally. And a different view is simply owing to want of reflection. Hence it is said, "Seek and you will find them. Neglect and you will lose them." There are cases where one man is twice, five times or countless times better than another man, but this is only because there are people who fail to make the best of their native endowment. It is said in the Book of Poetry, "Heaven in producing mankind, Gave them their various faculties and relations with their specific laws. These are the invariable rules of nature for all to hold, and all love this admirable virtue." Confucius said, "The maker of this ode knew indeed the principle of our nature!" We may thus see that every faculty and relation must have its law, and since there

---

20. *Mencius*, 6A6. 告子曰：『性無善無不善也。』

21. *Mencius*, 6A1. As translated in Legge. 孟子曰：「子能順杞柳之性而以為桮棬乎？將戕賊杞柳而後以為桮棬也？如將戕賊杞柳而以為桮棬，則亦將戕賊人以為仁義與？率天下之人而禍仁義者，必子之言夫！」

22. *Mencius*, 6A6. 或曰：『有性善，有性不善；是故以堯為君而有象，以瞽瞍為父而有舜；以紂為兄之子且以為君，而有微子啟、王子比干。』

are invariable rules for all to hold, they consequently love this admirable virtue.[23]

The reason why there are cases where one man is twice, five times or countless times better than another man or becoming bad is not the fault of his native endowment. It is because there are people who fail to make the best of their native endowment. According to Mencius, human nature is good in that a man is capable of becoming good as far as what is genuinely in him is concerned. For example, Mencius explains why no man is devoid of a heart sensitive to the suffering of others is this as follows:

> Suppose a man were, all of a sudden, to see a young child on the verge of falling into a well. He would certainly be moved to compassion, not because he wanted to get in the good graces of the parents, nor because he wished to win the praise of his fellow villagers or friends, nor yet because he disliked the cry of the child. From this it can be seen that whoever is devoid of the heart of compassion is not human, whoever is devoid of the heart of shame is not human, whoever is devoid of the heart of courtesy and modesty is not human and whoever is devoid of the heart of right and wrong is not human.[24]

On the basis of empathy at seeing a child falling into a well, Mencius states:

> The heart of compassion is the germ of benevolence; the heart of shame, of righteousness; the heart of courtesy and modesty, of propriety; the heart of right and wrong, of wisdom. Man has these four germs just as he has four limbs. For a man possessing these four germs to deny his own potentialities is for him to cripple himself; for him to deny the potentialities of his prince

---

23. *Mencius*, 6A6. As translated in Lau. 孟子曰：「乃若其情，則可以為善矣，乃所謂善也。若夫為不善，非才之罪也。惻隱之心，人皆有之；羞惡之心，人皆有之；恭敬之心，人皆有之；是非之心，人皆有之。惻隱之心，仁也；羞惡之心，義也；恭敬之心，禮也；是非之心，智也。仁義禮智，非由外鑠我也，我固有之也，弗思耳矣。故曰：『求則得之，舍則失之。』或相倍蓰而無算者，不能盡其才者也。《詩》曰：『天生蒸民，有物有則。民之秉夷，好是懿德。』孔子曰：『為此詩者，其知道乎！故有物必有則，民之秉夷也，故好是懿德。』」

24. *Mencius*, 2A6. As translated in Lau. 孟子曰：「人皆有不忍人之心。先王有不忍人之心，斯有不忍人之政矣。以不忍人之心，行不忍人之政，治天下可運之掌上。所以謂人皆有不忍人之心者，今人乍見孺子將入於井，皆有怵惕惻隱之心。非所以內交於孺子之父母也，非所以要譽於鄉黨朋友也，非惡其聲而然也。由是觀之，無惻隱之心，非人也；無羞惡之心，非人也；無辭讓之心，非人也；無是非之心，非人也。」

is for him to cripple his prince. If a man is able to develop all these four germs that he possesses, it will be like a fire starting up or a spring coming through. When these are fully developed, he can tend the whole realm within the Four Seas, but if he fails to develop them, he will not be able even to serve his parents.[25]

Thus, he emphasizes the importance of self-reflection in order to find virtues in our mind originally such as benevolence, righteousness, ritual propriety, and wisdom. Theses virtues are not infused from outside and universal to all people as he notes that "the heart of compassion is the germ of benevolence; the heart of shame, of righteousness; the heart of courtesy and modesty, of propriety; the heart of right and wrong, of wisdom."[26] It is natural for people to love these virtues. If one seeks them through self-reflection, he can easily find them since he already has them in his mind:

25. *Mencius*, 2A6. As translated in Lau. 惻隱之心，仁之端也；羞惡之心，義之端也；辭讓之心，禮之端也；是非之心，智之端也。人之有是四端也，猶其有四體也。有是四端而自謂不能者，自賊者也；謂其君不能者，賊其君者也。凡有四端於我者，知皆擴而充之矣，若火之始然，泉之始達。苟能充之，足以保四海；苟不充之，不足以事父母。

26. Nuyen offers the importance of innatism in Mencius' moral education by comparing with that of Aquinas. Nuyen presents the key epistemological claim that combines elements of innatism and empiricism as the similarity between Mencius and Aquinas. Just as Aquinas speaks of the "seeds of knowledge" implanted in us by God, which presumably include the seeds of moral knowledge, Mencius speaks of the "four sprouts" that are naturally embedded in a person's heart-mind (*xin*). However, while Aquinas takes these seeds to be general concepts and principles, Mencius takes them to be the psychological beginnings of the virtues. With the four "sprouts" embedded in oneself, a person can discover moral knowledge unaided, as if being taught "interiorly" by God. Hence, Mencius stresses the importance of "interior" learning, of seeking within oneself, over being taught by others. In speaking of self-cultivation, Mencius means not just the cultivation of the self but also the cultivation by the self. The cultivation of the self by the self is the more natural process. Thus, Mencius, according to Nuyen, sees much less a need for exterior teaching than Aquinas who advocates the doctrine of original sin and Xunzi who believes that human nature is bad. As Mencius' "agricultural metaphor" shows the importance of self-cultivation, "teaching is more like guiding, encouraging, and setting examples" rather than the act of intervention. External teaching is only required when a person fails to cultivate the sprouts. Still, Mencius believes that the sprouts that nature has placed in the human heart-mind are all good and strong and will naturally grow properly, given the right cultivation. In spite of the emphasis of innatism, Nuyen argues Mencius attaches greater importance to active life than contemplative life in moral education since the ultimate aim of education is social harmony. In order to achieve it, rulers themselves should be morally educated in order to govern effectively. Nuyen, 'Can Morality Be Taught? Aquinas and Mencius on Moral Education,' 108, 109, 111.

When we get by our seeking and lose by our neglecting—in that case seeking is of use to getting, and the things sought for are those which are in ourselves. When the seeking is according to the proper course, and the getting is only as appointed—in that case the seeking is of no use to getting, and the things sought are without ourselves.[27]

In this context, Mencius stresses there are no differences between sages and people in finding such virtues in mind. For him, sages are those who only apprehended before me that of which my mind approves along with other men.[28] According to him, all men are capable of becoming a Yao or a Shun.[29] In this process, the important thing is to make an effort. The cause of failure is simply due to not making the effort. Given that the Way of Yao and Shun was simply that of filial piety and fraternal duty, one can be a Yao just by wearing the clothes of Yao, repeating the words of Yao, and doing the actions of Yao. In other words, the Way is like a wide road, so it is not at all difficult to find. The trouble with people is simply that they do not seek for it. The weakness of will is the main reason of failure in retaking the lost mind.

Human Relationship, Weakness of Will, and Habit

For Mencius the man of virtue is not a unique being but the one who preserves such virtues in his heart as follows:

> The man of virtue differs from other men in that he retains his heart. The man of virtue retains his heart by means of benevolence and ritual propriety. The benevolent man loves others. The man of ritual propriety shows respect to others. He who loves others is constantly loved by them. He who respects others is constantly respected by them. Here is a man, who treats me in a perverse and unreasonable manner. The man of virtue in such a case will turn round upon himself, "I must have been wanting in

27. *Mencius*, 7A3. As translated by Legge. 孟子曰：「求則得之，舍則失之，是求有益於得也，求在我者也。求之有道，得之有命，是求無益於得也，求在外者也。」

28. *Mencius*, 6A7. 聖人先得我心之所同然耳。

29. *Mencius*, 6B2. 曹交問曰：「人皆可以為堯舜，有諸？」 孟子曰：「然。」... 亦為之而已矣。有人於此，力不能勝一匹雛，則為無力人矣；今日舉百鈞，則為有力人矣。然則舉烏獲之任，是亦為烏獲而已矣。夫人豈以不勝為患哉？弗為耳。... 堯舜之道，孝弟而已矣。子服堯之服，誦堯之言，行堯之行，是堯而已矣 ；子服桀之服，誦桀之言，行桀之行，是桀而已矣。」

benevolence; I must have been wanting in ritual propriety; how else could such a thing happen to me? When, looking into himself, he finds that he has benevolent and propriety, and yet this outrageous treatment continues, then the man of virtue will say to himself, "I must have failed to do my best for him." He turns round upon himself, and proceeds to do his utmost, but still the perversity and unreasonableness of the other are repeated. On this the man of virtue says, "This is a man utterly lost indeed! Since he conducts himself so, what is there to choose between him and an animal? Why should I go to contend with an animal?" Thus it is that the man of virtue has a life-long anxiety and not one morning's calamity. As to what is matter of anxiety to him, that indeed be has. He says, "Shun was a man, and I also am a man. But Shun set an example for the Empire worthy of being handed down to posterity, yet here am I, just an ordinary man. That is something worth worrying about. And in what way is he anxious about it? Just that he may be like Shun: then only will he stop. As to what the man of virtue would feel to be a calamity, there is no such thing. He does nothing which is not according to propriety. If there should befall him one morning's calamity, the man of virtue does not account it a calamity."[30]

Here, self-reflection not only is internal but also concerns human relationships. The man of virtue who treats others in benevolence and ritual propriety might face a man whose behavior is in a perverse and unreasonable manner. Before regarding him as a man like an animal, at first the man of virtue examines himself through self-reflection in order to inspect whether he is benevolent and courteous:

> If a man love others, and no responsive attachment is shown to him, let him turn inwards and examine his own benevolence. If he is trying to rule others, and his government is unsuccessful, let him turn inwards and examine his wisdom. If he treats others politely, and they do not return his politeness, let him

---

30. *Mencius*, 4B28. Translation adapted from Lau. 孟子曰：「君子所以異於人者，以其存心也。君子以仁存心，以禮存心。仁者愛人，有禮者敬人。愛人者人恆愛之，敬人者人恆敬之。有人於此，其待我以橫逆，則君子必自反也：我必不仁也，必無禮也，此物奚宜至哉？其自反而仁矣，自反而有禮矣，其橫逆由是也，君子必自反也：我必不忠。自反而忠矣，其橫逆由是也，君子曰：『此亦妄人也已矣。如此則與禽獸奚擇哉？於禽獸又何難焉？』是故君子有終身之憂，無一朝之患也。乃若所憂則有之：舜人也，我亦人也。舜為法於天下，可傳於後世，我由未免為鄉人也，是則可憂也。憂之如何？如舜而已矣。若夫君子所患則亡矣。非仁無為也，非禮無行也。如有一朝之患，則君子不患矣。」

turn inwards and examine his own respect. When we do not, by what we do, realize what we desire, we must turn inwards, and examine ourselves in every point. When a man's person is correct, the whole kingdom will turn to him with recognition and submission.[31]

This is the process of self-reflection. Hence, Mencius notes that "all things are already complete in us. There is no greater delight than to be conscious of sincerity on self-reflection. If one acts with a vigorous effort at the law of reciprocity, when he seeks for the realization of benevolence, nothing can be closer than his approximation to it."[32] Furthermore, Mencius argues such difficulty raised in spite of his benevolent and courteous behavior cannot make the man of virtue anxious in the process of self-reflection. Rather, the man of virtue has perennial worries such as how to imitate Shun while he has no unexpected vexations. He asserts one can overcome anxiety by imitating Shun. For the man of virtue, the important thing is just to live according to benevolence and propriety which are already embedded in his mind.

Nevertheless, to put into practice benevolence, as Mencius points out, often seems to be hard due to the weakness of will. For instance, when the king Xuan of Qi saw an ox going to consecrate a bell with its blood, he could not bear its frightened appearance, as if it were an innocent person going to the place of death. Instead, he ordered to change it into a sheep. Regarding it, Mencius assessed his conduct was an artifice of benevolence and his heart seen in this is sufficient to carry you to the royal sway.[33] This indicates that the king already has benevolence in his heart. However, even though his kindness is sufficient to reach to animals, no benefits are extended from it to the people. Just as the feather is

---

31. *Mencius*, 4A4. As translated in Legge. 孟子曰：「愛人不親反其仁，治人不治反其智，禮人不答反其敬。行有不得者，皆反求諸己，其身正而天下歸之。《詩》云：『永言配命，自求多福。』」

32. *Mencius*, 7A4. As translated in Legge. 孟子曰：「萬物皆備於我矣。反身而誠，樂莫大焉。強恕而行，求仁莫近焉。」

33. *Mencius*, 1A7, 「無以，則王乎？」曰：「德何如，則可以王矣？」曰：「保民而王，莫之能禦也。」... 曰：「臣聞之胡齕曰，王坐於堂上，有牽牛而過堂下者，王見之，曰：『牛何之？』對曰：『將以釁鐘。』王曰：『舍之！吾不忍其觳觫，若無罪而就死地。』對曰：『然則廢釁鐘與？』曰：『何可廢也？以羊易之！』不識有諸？」曰：「有之。」曰：「是心足以王矣。百姓皆以王為愛也，臣固知王之不忍也。」... 曰：「無傷也，是乃仁術也，見牛未見羊也。君子之於禽獸也，見其生，不忍見其死；聞其聲，不忍食其肉。是以君子遠庖廚也。」

not lifted because strength is not used, it is because he does not employ kindness for protecting and loving his people, not because you are not able to do it. Extending benevolence is easy like breaking off a branch from a tree. In this context, Mencius states that "treat with the reverence due to age the elders in your own family, so that the elders in the families of others shall be similarly treated; treat with the kindness due to youth the young in your own family, so that the young in the families of others shall be similarly treated—do this, and the kingdom may be made to go round in your palm."[34] This implies that he is greatly interested in the methods of extending virtues. Hence, Mencius explains benevolence and righteousness in the dimension of extending what one already has as follows:

> All men have some things which they cannot bear; extend that feeling to what they can bear, and benevolence will be the result. All men have some things which they will not do; extend that feeling to the things which they do, and righteousness will be the result. If a man can give full development to the feeling which makes him shrink from injuring others, his benevolence will be more than can be called into practice. If he can give full development to the feeling which refuses to break through, or jump over, a wall, his righteousness will be more than can be called into practice. If he can give full development to the real feeling of dislike with which he receives the salutation, "Thou," "Thou," he will act righteously in all places and circumstances.[35]

This passage demonstrates that benevolence and righteousness are the result of extending the feeling of what cannot bear and awareness of what should not do respectively. [36] For Mencius, these feelings are

---

34. *Mencius*, 1A7, 「今恩足以及禽獸, 而功不至於百姓者, 獨何與？然則一羽之不舉, 為不用力焉；輿薪之不見, 為不用明焉, 百姓之不見保, 為不用恩焉。故王之不王, 不為也, 非不能也。」 曰：「不為者與不能者之形何以異？」 曰：「挾太山以超北海, 語人曰『我不能』, 是誠不能也。為長者折枝, 語人曰『我不能』, 是不為也, 非不能也。故王之不王, 非挾太山以超北海之類也；王之不王, 是折枝之類也。老吾老, 以及人之老；幼吾幼, 以及人之幼。天下可運於掌」

35. *Mencius*, 7B31. As translated in Legge. 孟子曰：「人皆有所不忍, 達之於其所忍, 仁也；人皆有所不為, 達之於其所為, 義也。人能充無欲害人之心, 而仁不可勝用也；人能充無穿踰之心, 而義不可勝用也。人能充無受爾汝之實, 無所往而不為義也。」

36. Liu proposes and defends a human-nature-based moral sensibility theory by combining Hume's theory of sympathy and Mencius' way of moral self-cultivation. According to Liu, Mencius' idea that humans innately incline to compassion, which

already embedded in heart, so one can extend to others by fully developing them. Hence, he highlights the importance of preserving what one already has as follows:

> The trees of the Niu mountain were once beautiful. Being situated, however, in the borders of a large State, they were hewn down with axes and bills—and could they retain their beauty? Still through the activity of the vegetative life day and night, and the nourishing influence of the rain and dew, they were not without buds and sprouts springing forth, but then came the cattle and goats and browsed upon them. To these things is owing the bare and stripped appearance of the mountain, and when people now see it, they think it was never finely wooded. But is this the nature of the mountain? And so also of what properly belongs to man; shall it be said that the mind of any man was without benevolence and righteousness? The way in which a man loses his proper goodness of mind is like the way in which the trees are denuded by axes and bills. Hewn down day after day, can it—the mind—retain its beauty? But there is a development of its life day and night, and in the calm air of the morning, just between night and day, the mind feels in a degree those desires and aversions which are proper to humanity, but the feeling is not strong, and it is fettered and destroyed by what takes place

---

develops through cultivation into the virtue of humanity (仁) resembles Hume's discussions of sympathy and humanity. In spite of this similarity, Liu points out Hume failed to elaborate on three important theses: Humanity is the unity of the virtues; in order to move from sympathy to humanity, self-cultivation is absolutely necessary; and sympathy is the ground of all characteristically human feelings. Hence, Liu thinks Mencius' philosophy helpfully complements Hume's picture in that Mencius gives more explicit discussion of how humanity underlies and unifies the other virtues, how humanity is cultivated, and how sympathy is the essential human feeling which gives rise to all other characteristically human feelings. For Mencius, *ren* is different from the Christian concept of love, *agape* which is rooted in the transcendent idea of God. Rather, *Ren* which is rooted in the constitution of the mind starts from a family setting. In particular, Liu expounds about how Mencius' *ren* can be actualized through self-cultivation. According to Liu, for Mencius "self-cultivation aims at two things: (a) to protect and nurture the characteristically human dispositions and tendencies; (b) to limit and regulate material desires and to conquer those that are harmful. Mencius claims that all human beings to some degree possess the characteristically human tendencies and dispositions." In order to achieve these goals, Mencius offers extending (*tui*, 推) and self-reflecting. Additionally, Liu proposes an interpretation of Mencius' internalism in connection with motivation, human nature, and moral recognition, which, Liu argues, brings new insight to the ongoing internalism/externalism debate. Xiusheng Liu, *Mencius, Hume and the Foundations of Ethics* (Hampshire: Ashgate, 2003), 11, 49, 67, 68, 165.

during the day. This fettering taking place again and again, the restorative influence of the night is not sufficient to preserve the proper goodness of the mind; and when this proves insufficient for that purpose, the nature becomes not much different from that of the irrational animals, and when people now see it, they think that it never had those powers which I assert. But does this condition represent the feelings proper to humanity? Therefore, if it receives its proper nourishment, there is nothing which will not grow. If it loses its proper nourishment, there is nothing which will not decay away. Confucius said, "Hold it fast, and it remains with you. Let it go, and you lose it. Its outgoing and incoming cannot be defined as to time or place." It is the mind of which this is said![37]

It is noticeable that Mencius thought the way in which a man loses his proper goodness of mind is similar to the way in which the trees are denuded by axes and bills. This shows not only the relation between self-cultivation and environment but also how important habit is in the process of self-reflection for preserving goodness in heart.[38] In other words, it is necessary to provide continuous nourishment to grow goodness in heart. According to Mencius, "the hungry think any food sweet, and the thirsty think the same of any drink, and thus they do not get the right taste of what they eat and drink. The hunger and thirst, in fact, injure their palate. And is it only the mouth and belly which are injured by hunger and thirst? Men's minds are also injured by them. If a man can prevent the evils of hunger and thirst from being any evils to his mind, he need not have any sorrow about not being equal to other men."[39] Hence, he states that "there are the footpaths along the hills; if suddenly they

---

37. *Mencius*, 6A8. As translated in Legge. 孟子曰：「牛山之木嘗美矣，以其郊於大國也，斧斤伐之，可以為美乎？是其日夜之所息，雨露之所潤，非無萌蘖之生焉，牛羊又從而牧之，是以若彼濯濯也。人見其濯濯也，以為未嘗有材焉，此豈山之性也哉？雖存乎人者，豈無仁義之心哉？其所以放其良心者，亦猶斧斤之於木也，旦旦而伐之，可以為美乎？其日夜之所息，平旦之氣，其好惡與人相近也者幾希，則其旦晝之所為，有梏亡之矣。梏之反覆，則其夜氣不足以存；夜氣不足以存，則其違禽獸不遠矣。人見其禽獸也，而以為未嘗有才焉者，是豈人之情也哉？故苟得其養，無物不長；苟失其養，無物不消。孔子曰：『操則存，舍則亡；出入無時，莫知其鄉。』惟心之謂與？」

38. Prasenjit Duara, *The Crisis of Global Modernity: Asian Traditions and a Sustainable Future* (Cambridge: Cambridge University, 2015), 2.

39. *Mencius*, 7A27. As translated in Legge. 孟子曰：「飢者甘食，渴者甘飲，是未得飲食之正也，飢渴害之也。豈惟口腹有飢渴之害？人心亦皆有害。人能無以飢渴之害為心害，則不及人不為憂矣。」

be used, they become roads; and if, as suddenly they are not used, the wild grass fills them up. Now, the wild grass fills up your mind."[40] For example, Mencius presents how to nourish courage in our mind through habit based on repetition as follows:

> Mencius told him, "I understand words. I am skillful in nourishing my vast, flowing passion-nature." Chou pursued, "I venture to ask what you mean by your vast, flowing passion-nature!" The reply was, "It is difficult to describe it. This is the passion-nature: It is exceedingly great, and exceedingly strong. Being nourished by rectitude, and sustaining no injury, it fills up all between heaven and earth. This is the passion-nature: It is the mate and assistant of righteousness and reason. Without it, man is in a state of starvation. It is produced by the accumulation of righteous deeds; it is not to be obtained by incidental acts of righteousness. If the mind does not feel complacency in the conduct, the nature becomes starved."[41]

The passion-nature which is can be regarded as courage cannot be obtained by incidental acts of righteousness but can be produced by the accumulation of righteous deeds in support of rectitude and no injury to mind. What kinds of injury does Mencius concern about? He suggests supposing that there was a man who was grieved that his growing corn was not longer, and so he pulled it up.[42] Having done this, he returned home, looking very stupid, and said to his people, "I am tired today. I have been helping the corn to grow long." His son ran to look at it, and found the corn all withered. Pulling out his corn symbolizes incidental acts. This just injures the passion-nature. Likewise, Mencius offers the importance of habit in nourishing benevolence; "The case of one of the present princes wishing to become sovereign is like the having to seek for mugwort three years old, to cure a seven years' sickness. If it has not been

---

40. *Mencius*, 7B21. As translated in Legge. 孟子謂高子曰：「山徑之蹊閒，介然用之而成路。為閒不用，則茅塞之矣。今茅塞子之心矣。」

41. *Mencius*, 2A2. 曰：「我知言，我善養吾浩然之氣。」 「敢問何謂浩然之氣？」 曰：「難言也。其為氣也，至大至剛，以直養而無害，則塞于天地之閒。其為氣也，配義與道；無是，餒也。是集義所生者，非義襲而取之也。行有不慊於心，則餒矣。」

42. *Mencius*, 2A2. As translated in Legge. 我故曰，告子未嘗知義，以其外之也。必有事焉而勿正，心勿忘，勿助長也。無若宋人然：宋人有閔其苗之不長而揠之者，芒芒然歸。謂其人曰：『今日病矣，予助苗長矣。』 其子趨而往視之，苗則槁矣。天下之不助苗長者寡矣。以為無益而舍之者，不耘苗者也；助之長者，揠苗者也。非徒無益，而又害之。

kept in store, the patient may all his life not get it. If one does not aim steadfastly at benevolence, one will suffer worry and disgrace all one's life and end in the snare of death."[43] Why did he stress to aim steadfastly at benevolence? According to him, even though one plays chess which is a small art, one ought to give one's whole mind to it in order to master it. He suggests supposing two men are taught by the best chess-player in all the kingdom.[44] The one gives to the subject his whole mind and bends to it all his will, doing nothing but listening to him. The other, although he seems to be listening to him, has his whole mind running on a swan which he thinks is approaching, and wishes to bend his bow, adjust the string to the arrow, and shoot it. Mencius expects he does not come up to him although he is learning along with the other. Mencius insists that this is not due to the difference of intelligence. In other words, habitual self-reflection is the pivotal point in seeking for the lost mind. It is because "the student who has set his mind on the doctrines of the sage does not advance to them but by completing one lesson after another."[45] This is like digging a well since to dig the well to a depth of seventy-two cubits, and stop without reaching the spring is just an abandoned well.[46] To be sure, Mencius warns the peril of habit without self-reflection; "To act without understanding, and to do so habitually without examination, pursuing the proper path all the life without knowing its nature—this is the way of multitudes."[47]

43. *Mencius*, 4A9. As translated in Legge. 猶七年之病求三年之艾也。苟為不畜，終身不得。苟不志於仁，終身憂辱，以陷於死亡。

44. *Mencius*, 6A9. 孟子曰：「無或乎王之不智也，雖有天下易生之物也，一日暴之，十日寒之，未有能生者也。吾見亦罕矣，吾退而寒之者至矣，吾如有萌焉何哉？今夫弈之為數，小數也；不專心致志，則不得也。弈秋，通國之善弈者也。使弈秋誨二人弈，其一人專心致志，惟弈秋之為聽。一人雖聽之，一心以為有鴻鵠將至，思援弓繳而射之，雖與之俱學，弗若之矣。為是其智弗若與？曰非然也。」

45. *Mencius*, 7A24. 君子之志於道也，不成章不達。

46. *Mencius*, 7A29. 孟子曰：「有為者辟若掘井，掘井九軔而不及泉，猶為棄井也。」

47. *Mencius*, 7A5. As translated in Legge. 孟子曰：「行之而不著焉，習矣而不察焉，終身由之而不知其道者，眾也。」

Suffering, Patience, and Man of Virtue

Above all, Mencius presents that the habitual self-reflection could enhance the man of virtue's faith on the Way.[48] When the Way disappears from the kingdom, the man of virtue does not hesitate to sacrifice his life in order to protect it.[49] In other words, the courageous minister cultivated by self-reflection does not afraid of losing his head.[50] For Mencius, the man of virtue is the one who preserves righteousness even in suffering as follows:

> I like fish, and I also like bear's paws. If I cannot have the two together, I will let the fish go, and take the bear's paws. So, I like life, and I also like righteousness. If I cannot keep the two together, I will let life go, and choose righteousness. I like life indeed, but there is that which I like more than life, and therefore, I will not seek to possess it by any improper ways. I dislike death indeed, but there is that which I dislike more than death, and therefore there are occasions when I will not avoid suffering. If among the things which man likes there were nothing which he liked more than life, why should he not use every means by which he could preserve it? If among the things which man dislikes there were nothing which he disliked more than death, why should he not do everything by which he could avoid suffering? There are cases when men by a certain course might preserve life, and they do not employ it; when by certain things they might avoid suffering, and they will not do them. Therefore, men have that which they like more than life, and that which they dislike more than death. They are not men of distinguished talents and virtue only who have this mental nature. All men have it; what belongs to such men is simply that they do not lose it.[51]

---

48. *Mencius*, 6B12. 孟子曰：「君子不亮，惡乎執？」

49. *Mencius*, 7A42. 孟子曰：「天下有道，以道殉身；天下無道，以身殉道。未聞以道殉乎人者也。」

50. *Mencius*, 5B7. 志士不忘在溝壑，勇士不忘喪其元。

51. *Mencius*, 6A10. As translated in Legge. 孟子曰：「魚，我所欲也；熊掌，亦我所欲也，二者不可得兼，舍魚而取熊掌者也。生，亦我所欲也；義，亦我所欲也，二者不可得兼，舍生而取義者也。生亦我所欲，所欲有甚於生者，故不為苟得也；死亦我所惡，所惡有甚於死者，故患有所不辟也。如使人之所欲莫甚於生，則凡可以得生者，何不用也？使人之所惡莫甚於死者，則凡可以辟患者，何不為也？由是則生而有不用也，由是則可以辟患而有不為也。是故所欲有甚於生者，所惡有甚於死者，非獨賢者有是心也，人皆有之，賢者能勿喪耳。

Even though all men have righteousness most of them lose it in suffering. Why does this situation take place? According to Mencius, those who follow that part of themselves which is great are great men; those who follow that part which is little are little men. He claims that some parts of the body are noble, and some ignoble; some great, and some small. The great must not be injured for the small, nor the noble for the ignoble. For Mencius, the small part of body is the senses of hearing and seeing. It is because they do not contribute one's self-reflection, and are obscured by external things. When one thing comes into contact with another, as a matter of course it leads it away. Hence, Mencius warns a man who only eats and drinks will be counted mean by others since he nourishes what is little to the neglect of what is great.[52] In contrast, Mencius presents that the organ of the mind bestowed by Heaven can conduct self-reflection, by which it gets the right view of things. It is noteworthy that Mencius describes mind in relation with Heaven. According to him, there are honors such as benevolence, righteousness, conscientiousness, truthfulness bestowed by Heaven, and there are honors such as the position of a Ducal Minister bestowed by man. Contrary to his time, the men of antiquity cultivated their nobility of Heaven, and the nobility of man came to them in its train.[53] They sought honors bestowed by Heaven first since the honors which men confer are not true honors. Given that all men have in themselves that which is truly honorable, it is not difficult to find honors bestowed by Heaven.[54] In this context, Mencius stresses the necessity of self-reflection. For him, the method of being great and honor man is to make one's stand on mind in the first instance instead of the senses of hearing and seeing.[55]

52. *Mencius*, 6A14. 孟子曰：「人之於身也，兼所愛。兼所愛，則兼所養也。無尺寸之膚不愛焉，則無尺寸之膚不養也。所以考其善不善者，豈有他哉？於己取之而已矣。體有貴賤，有小大。無以小害大，無以賤害貴。養其小者為小人，養其大者為大人。今有場師，舍其梧檟，養其樲棘，則為賤場師焉。養其一指而失其肩背，而不知也，則為狼疾人也。飲食之人，則人賤之矣，為其養小以失大也。飲食之人無有失也，則口腹豈適為尺寸之膚哉？」

53. *Mencius*, 6A16. 孟子曰：「有天爵者，有人爵者。仁義忠信，樂善不倦，此天爵也；公卿大夫，此人爵也。古之人修其天爵，而人爵從之。

54. *Mencius*, 6A16. 孟子曰：「欲貴者，人之同心也。人人有貴於己者，弗思耳。人之所貴者，非良貴也。

55. *Mencius*, 6A15. 公都子問曰：「鈞是人也，或為大人，或為小人，何也？」孟子曰：「從其大體為大人，從其小體為小人。」曰：「鈞是人也，或從其大體，或從其小體，何也？」曰：「耳目之官不思，而蔽於物，物交物，則引之而已矣。心之官則思，思則得之，不思則不得也。此天之所與我者，先立乎其大者，則其小者弗能奪也。此為大人而已矣。」

Particularly, Mencius makes an emphasis on the importance of patience in the process of self-reflection in relation with benevolence in order to overcome suffering. Just as the five types of grain are the best of plants, yet if they are not ripe they are worse than the wild varieties, the value of benevolence depends entirely on its being brought to maturity.[56] Furthermore, he presents that benevolence overcomes cruelty just as water overcome fire, so it is impossible to put out a cartload of burning firewood with a cupful of water.[57] In the process of practicing benevolence against cruelty, self-reflection needs to be patiently conducted. Mencius shows how helpful suffering is for fostering the man of virtue as follows:

> Shun rose from the fields. Fu Yue was called to office from the midst of his building frames; Jiao Ge from his fish and salt; Guan Yi Wu from the hands of the prison officer; Sun Shu Ao from his hiding by the sea-shore; and Bai Li Xi from the market. Thus, when Heaven is about to confer a great office on any man, it first exercises his mind with suffering, and his sinews and bones with toil. It exposes his body to hunger, and subjects him to extreme poverty. It confounds his undertakings. By all these methods it stimulates his mind, hardens his nature, and supplies his incompetence. As a rule, men can mend his ways only after he has made mistakes. They are distressed in mind and perplexed in their thoughts, and then they arise to vigorous reformation. When things have been evidenced in men's looks, and set forth in their words, then they understand them. If a prince has not about his court families attached to the laws and worthy counsellors, and if abroad there are not hostile States or other external calamities, his kingdom will generally come to ruin. From these things we see how life springs from sorrow and calamity, and death from ease and pleasure.[58]

---

56. *Mencius*, 6A19. 孟子曰：「五穀者，種之美者也；苟為不熟，不如荑稗。夫仁亦在乎熟之而已矣。」

57. *Mencius*, 6A18. 孟子曰：「仁之勝不仁也，猶水勝火。今之為仁者，猶以一杯水，救一車薪之火也；不熄，則謂之水不勝火，此又與於不仁之甚者也。亦終必亡而已矣。」

58. *Mencius*, 6B15. As translated in Legge. 孟子曰：「舜發於畎畝之中，傅說舉於版築之閒，膠鬲舉於魚鹽之中，管夷吾舉於士，孫叔敖舉於海，百里奚舉於市。故天將降大任於是人也，必先苦其心志，勞其筋骨，餓其體膚，空乏其身，行拂亂其所為，所以動心忍性，曾益其所不能。人恆過，然後能改；困於心，衡於慮，而後作；徵於色，發於聲，而後喻。入則無法家拂士，出則無敵國外患者，國恆亡。然後知生於憂患而死於安樂也。」

Heaven first exercises one's mind with sufferings such as poverty when it is going to confer a great office on any man. The suffering including physical difficulties makes his character patient and improves his ability. In particular, that one can reform his thought after being frustrated in mind indicates the critical role of self-reflection. For Mencius, such suffering is an essential course for the man of virtue. According to Mencius, "men who are possessed of intelligent virtue and prudence in affairs will generally be found to have been in sickness and sufferings. They are the friendless minister and concubine's son, who keep their hearts under a sense of peril, and use deep precautions against calamity. On this account they become distinguished for their intelligence."[59] In other words, the man of virtue is different from ordinary people. The man of virtue can be content even in suffering and does not lose righteousness in poverty since he attends to his own virtue in solitude.[60] When he advances to dignity, he makes whole kingdom virtuous not by leaving the proper path. In this context, ordinary people cannot be expected to understand the behavior of the man of virtue.[61] Suffering makes the man of virtue more virtuous.

AUGUSTINE'S CONTEMPLATION

Contemplative Ascension

In antiquity, "that God should exist outside the physical cosmos" and "that the soul might come to perceive ultimate reality through spiritual reflection and recover its roots beyond space and time" were challenging conceptions.[62] With regard to this matter, Augustine shows about how to see God as follows:

> Since, therefore, we must enjoy to the full that truth which lives unchangeably, and since, within it, God the Trinity, the author and creator of everything, takes thought for the things that he has created, our minds must be purified so that they are able to

---

59. *Mencius*, 7A18. As translated in Legge. 孟子曰：「人之有德慧術知者，恆存乎疢疾。獨孤臣孽子，其操心也危，其慮患也深，故達。」

60. *Mencius*, 7A9. 曰：「尊德樂義，則可以囂囂矣。故士窮不失義，達不離道。窮不失義，故士得己焉；達不離道，故民不失望焉。古之人，得志，澤加於民；不得志，脩身見於世。窮則獨善其身，達則兼善天下。」

61. *Mencius*, 6B6. As translated in Legge. 君子之所為，眾人固不識也。

62. John Peter Kenny, *Contemplation and Classical Christianity: A Study in Augustine* (Oxford: Oxford University Press, 2014), vi.

perceive that light and then hold fast to it. Let us consider this process of cleansing as a trek, or a voyage, to our homeland; though progress towards the one who is ever present is not made through space, but through the cultivation of pure desires and virtuous habits.[63]

As a way of purifying our minds, Augustine makes an emphasis on cultivating "pure desires and virtuous habits." For him contemplation of things unseen as immediate knowledge of a transcendent God discovered within the soul plays an important role in the formation of moral self.[64] As he states that "you made us for yourself and our hearts find no peace until they rest in you," soul's hungers and thirsts can be found real satisfaction only in God.[65] He regards contemplation of God as the supreme good (*Summum Bonum*).[66] The rubric under which Augustine above all comprehends the mind's transformative engagement with God is contemplation (*contemplatio*), and to understand what he means by knowledge of God, we must take the significance of contemplation in his thought.[67] It is because his contemplation was not formed just by abstract consideration. It stemmed from his life. In a very real sense, he continually faced relationship between action and contemplation as he struggled to reconcile his early and continuing preference for the contemplative life with the many duties surrounding his priesthood, and later, his episcopacy.[68] In the absence of his enforced ordination and subsequent role as ecclesiastical leader, Augustine would seek the peace of a monastic community modeled on his Cassiciacum experience, but a growing sense of responsibility to the temporal needs of his congregation contributed to a balancing of contemplation and action in Augustine's writings and life.[69]

---

63. *doc. Chr.* 1.10. cf. *Trin.* 1.8.17.

64. John Peter Kenney, *The Mysticism of Saint Augustine: Rereading the Confessions* (London: Routledge, 2005), ix.

65. *conf.* 1.1.

66. *Trin.* 1.13.31.

67. A. N. Williams, "Contemplation: Knowledge of God in Augustine's *De Trinitate*," in *Knowing the Triune God: The Work of the Spirit in the Practice of the Church*, ed. James J. Buckley & David S. Yeago (Cambridge: William B. Eerdmans Publishing Company, 2001), 137.

68. N. Joseph Torchia, "Contemplation and Action," in *Augustine through the Ages: An Encyclopedia*, ed. Allan D. Fitzgerald (Cambridge: Wm. B. Eerdmans Publishing Company, 1999), 235.

69. Torchia, "Contemplation and Action," 235.

Particularly, the matter of essence of contemplation has been a heated issue in the discussion of Augustine's contemplation. Butler, who regards Augustine as the prince of mystics,[70] deals with his contemplation under the rubric of mysticism.[71] He claims that the beginnings of his conversion to Christianity derive from the fact that in 385 some books of the Neo-Platonists came into his hands and greatly impressed him, so that from that time onward he accepted the main principles of the neo-Platonic philosophy, and his whole intellectual outlook, his mysticism included, was colored by it to the end.[72] In this aspect, he explains Augustine's contemplation in a process of purification in that "the indispensable condition of contemplation is such a purification of the soul as will render it fit for the ascent to the contemplation of God: a purification which is the result of a long process of self-denial and self-conquest, of mortification and the practice of virtue."[73] Burnaby insists upon Augustine's view of contemplation as the task of all Christians, not only those who have reached extraordinary heights in prayer.[74] Nash views reason in Augustine's thought as the contemplation of the truth.[75] Stalnaker regards Augustine's contemplation as just one of three main types of prayer.[76] For him, prayer consists of petitionary, confessional, and contemplation. However, for Augustine contemplation, as Williams demonstrates, is not an advanced form of prayer.[77] According to Williams, contemplation is clearly not construed as a form of wordless prayer practiced by the spiritually adept. Williams demonstrates that such modern associations of contemplation with advanced forms of prayer led to missing significant aspect of contemplation. He stresses that for Augustine contemplation is equated with wisdom and he uses wisdom to denote knowledge of God;[78] "contemplation of eternal things ... is ascribed to wisdom ... wisdom

---

70. Dom Cuthbert Butler, *Western Mysticism: The Teachings of SS Augustine, Gregory, and Bernard on Contemplation and the Contemplative life: Neglected Chapters in the History of Religion* (London: Constable, 1922), 24.

71. Ibid., 26.

72. Ibid., 23.

73. Ibid., 36.

74. John Burnaby, *Amor Dei: A Study of the Religion of St. Augustine* (London: Hodder & Stoughton, 1991), 61, 64.

75. Nash, *The Light of the Mind*, 64

76. Stalnaker, *Overcoming Our Evil*, 227.

77. Williams, "Contemplation: Knowledge of God in Augustine's *De Trinitate*," 137.

78. Ibid., 138.

belongs to contemplation."[79] This wisdom is about eternal things, not knowledge of temporal matter. Augustine's wisdom corresponds to knowledge of God. He understands contemplation in the dimension of a binding of the mind to God.[80]

Augustine's understanding of contemplation is based on his depiction of human nature as a substantial unity of soul and body, the inner and outer aspects of the person, respectively.[81] For Augustine, purification is prerequisite in order to have knowledge of God. Augustine's initial deliberations on contemplation reveal an emphasis on the importance of individual effort in purifying the soul and attuning the mind to God.[82] It is because man's supreme good is not the supreme good of the body alone, but the supreme good of the soul.[83] As Augustine demonstrates that "order is what leads us to God," he emphasizes the importance of orderly progression from one step to the next step.[84] In *De quantitte animae*, the sequence of these steps sets out.[85] The first degree of the soul is animation (*animatio*). The activity of the soul as the vegetative stage is directed towards the nutrition, growth and reproduction of the body; "The soul by its presence gives life to this mortal and earthy body; it brings the body together into a unity and keeps it in unity; it prevents the body from breaking up and wasting away; it regulates the proper distribution of nourishment throughout the parts of the body, giving each its due share; it preserves the apt arrangement and proportion of the body, not only to delight the eye but to grow and generate. But, these powers are easily seen to be the common possession of men and plants. For, we say of them, too, that they live; we see and acknowledge that every one of them in its own way is preserved and nourished, grow and germinates."[86]

---

79. *Trin.* 12. 22.

80. Williams, "Contemplation: Knowledge of God in Augustine's *De Trinitate*," 138.

81. Torchia, "Contemplation and Action," 233; Phillip Cary, *Augustine's Invention of the Inner Self: the Legacy of a Christian Platonist* (Oxford: Oxford University Press, 2000), 10.

82. Torchia, "Contemplation and Action," 234.

83. *mor.* 1.5.7.

84. *ord.* 1.9.27. trans. Silvano Borruso (Indiana: St. Augustine's Press, 2007). Hereafter I use this translation.

85. *quant.* 33.70-76. trans. John J. McMahon in the Fathers of the Church, vol. 4 (Washington: The Catholic University of America Press, 1947); Howie, *Educational Theory and Practice in St Augustine*, 136-137.

86. *quant.* 33.70.

The second degree of the soul is sense perception (*sensus*). The soul applies itself to the sense of touch, through which it feels and distinguishes hot and cold, rough and smooth, hard and soft, light and heavy. Then it distinguishes between unnumbered differences of taste and smell and sound and shapes, by tasting, smelling, hearing and seeing. Then it distinguishes between unnumbered differences of taste and smell and sound, and shapes, by tasting, smelling, hearing, and seeing. It comes to know what suits the nature of its body.[87] This is the stage of habit formation, which man shares with the animals. The third degree of the soul is the stage of art (*ars*). The activity of the soul is directed to understanding the natural world and the ways in which its materials are used by man to serve his needs. Augustine shows evidences for it such as many arts of craftsmen, the building of cities, the inventions of so many signs in letters, words, gesture, and paintings, languages, the great number of books and similar documents for preserving memory, and music. However, he argues that "this heritage, common to all rational souls, is shared in by the learned and the unlearned, by the good and the wicked."[88] The fourth degree of the soul is the stage of moral goodness (*virtus*).[89] From this grade the soul commences to direct its attention toward itself by striving to gain its rightful mastery over own body and material world.[90] It leads to purifying itself from the dominance of false values and develops a more humane outlook. The fifth degree of the soul is tranquility (*tranquillitas*). The soul is freed from all disease and cleansed of all its stains, and then finally it possesses itself in all joy and is not disturbed at all for any reason of its own.[91] This is the stage of self-purification; "It advances toward God that is, to the contemplation of Truth itself, that Truth, the highest and most hidden reward for all the labor it has exerted."[92] The six degree of the soul is advance (*ingressio*). This activity is "the soul's highest vision."[93] The seventh degree of the soul is contemplation (*contemplatio*). This is not only the last step but also "a dwelling place" to which the

---

87. *quant.* 33.71.
88. *quant.* 33.72.
89. *quant.* 33.73.
90. *quant.* 33.74.
91. *quant.* 33.74. cf. Michael S. Northcott, "Being Silent: Time in the Spirit," in *the Blackwell Companion to Christian Ethics*, ed. Stanley Hauerwas and Samuel Wells (Oxford: Balckwell Publishing Ltd, 2004), 414.
92. *quant.* 33.74.
93. *quant.* 33.75.

previous steps have brought us.[94] In this step, soul perceives it supreme good and rejoices in the knowledge of it by distinguishing vanity and truth. Even though all visible things seem to be marvelous, they are nothing in comparison with the unseen realities. In obedience to the divine law corporeal nature undergoes so many changes and vicissitudes. "In the contemplation of truth, no matter from what side we study it, so great is the joy, so great the purity, the sincerity, and the certainty of faith that one at length comes to think that the previous knowledge he thought he is really nothing. Then death, which was an object of fear and an obstacle to the soul's fullest union with the full truth, death, namely, the sheer flight and escape from this body, is now yearned for as the greatest boon."[95] In Augustinian contemplation, it is also necessary to recognize his contemplation is always a gift from above, for humans are unable to come to such an understanding without divine aid.[96] These seven steps can be named also in this way: "of the body; through the body; about the body; toward itself; in itself; toward God; in God."[97] Soul's force and power are great in that nothing is nearer to God among all the things God created than the human soul.[98] According to Augustine, reason insists that a single soul is of far greater value than all material things, if only lovers of the truth will dare to pursue with unfaltering and respectful steps the path the soul points out, a path that is hard because it lies the well-worn road of common experience.[99] God who alone is the maker of soul is alone to be adored and worshiped by soul.[100]

Contemplative Souls at Ostia

According to Augustine, contemplation must rely upon the mediation of the ideas as the intelligible expressions of divine truth in the present life.[101] It is required to distinguish such an imperfect mode of contemplation

---

94. *quant.* 33.76.
95. *quant.* 33.76.
96. *Trin.* 15.10.
97. *quant.* 35.79.
98. *quant.* 34.77.
99. *quant.* 34.77.
100. *quant.* 34.78.
101. *quant.* 27.53

from the pure, unimpeded vision of God reserved for the life to come.[102] At best, the soul can enjoy only a sporadic knowledge of true being. In this regard, Augustine frequently explains the act of contemplation in the dimension of mystical experiences.[103] Given that Augustine regards contemplation as the practice of transcendence for the interior access of the soul to God, his most famous account of contemplation must be situated the vision at Ostia in *Confessions* IX, which is following Augustine's baptism. It shows a vivid and consistent account of Augustine's efforts to engage in the practice of contemplation. The theological purpose of the Ostian narrative is to demonstrate exactly what salvific value can be discovered through contemplation, and how deeply the baptized soul can reach into eternity.[104] Through it, where Platonism succeeds and where it fails are revealed in the dimension of its cognitive value and its salvific inadequacy. According to Augustine, Platonism provides knowledge of God, but not salvation. The mystical experience at Ostia is presented in two initial sections, 23 and 24, followed by a further meditation in section 25 on the significance of the ascension. Here is the text of the first two narrative sections as follows:

> Not long before the day on which she was to leave this life—you knew which day it was to be, O Lord, though we did not—my mother and I were alone, leaning from a window which overlooked the garden in the courtyard of the house where we were staying at Ostia. We were waiting there after our long and tiring journey, away from the crowd, to refresh ourselves before our sea-voyage. I believe that what I am going to tell happened through the secret working of your providence. For we were talking alone together and our conversation was serene and joyful. We had forgotten what we had left behind and were intent on what lay before us (Phil. 3:13). In the presence of Truth, which is yourself, we were wondering what the eternal life of the saints would be like, that life which no eye has seen, no ear has heard, no human heart conceived (1 Cor. 2:9). But we laid the lips of our hearts to the heavenly stream that flows from your fountain, the source of all life which is in you (Ps. 35:10), so that as far as it was in our power to do so we might be sprinkled with its waters and

---

102. N. Joseph Torchia, "Contemplation and Action," 234.

103. *ord.* 2.19.51; *Gn. Litt.* 12.26.53-12.28.56. trans. Edmund Hill in *a Translation for the 21st Century*, vol. 13 (New York: New City Press, 2006). Hereafter I use this translation; *epp.* 92.3, 147.31.

104. Kenney, *The Mysticism of Saint Augustine*, 78.

in some sense reach an understanding of this great mystery. Our conversation led us to the conclusion that no bodily pleasure, however great it might be and whatever earthly light might shed luster upon it, was worthy of comparison, or even of mention, beside the happiness of the life of the saints. As the flame of love burned stronger in us and raised us higher towards the eternal God, our thoughts ranged over the whole compass of material things in their various degrees, up to the heavens themselves, from which the sun and the moon and the stars shine down upon the earth. Higher still we climbed, thinking and speaking all the while in wonder at all that you have made. At length we came to our own souls and passed beyond them to that place of everlasting plenty, where you feed Israel for ever with the food of truth. There life is that Wisdom by which all these things that we know are made, all things that ever have been and all that are yet to be. But that Wisdom is not made: it is as it has always been and as it will be forever—or, rather, I should not say that it has been or will be, for it simply is, because eternity is not in the past or in the future. And while we spoke of the eternal Wisdom, longing for it and straining for it with all the strength of our hearts, for one fleeting instant we reached out and touched it. Then with a sigh, leaving our spiritual harvest bound to it (Rom 8:23), we returned to the sound of our own speech, in which each word has a beginning and an ending—far, far different from your Word, our Lord, who abides in himself for ever, yet never grows old and gives new life to all things.[105]

The text begins with the dramatic announcement of its poignant context.[106] This conversation between Augustine and Monica took place in Ostia just a fortnight before her death. Augustine sketches the garden scene in the hope of Monica's heavenly future. He surmises her future salvation and devises his setting accordingly. They converse about the eternal life of the saints, establishing a dialogue which frames the ascension narrative, one that is superseded only at the apex of contemplation. This narrative is, as Kenny argues, a Christian explanation of contemplation, not a Plotinian one.[107] The vision at Ostia is a Christian experience rather than a philosophical one. In the Ostian narrative, scriptural texts are effective in securing a deeper Christian resonance. Augustine's points are developed both by the force of the passage's explicit autobiographical

---

105. *conf.* 9.10.23,24.
106. Kenney, *The Mysticism of Saint Augustine*, 79.
107. Ibid., 79.

details and by the continued use of imbedded scriptural references, particularly Pauline ones. In the passage, Augustine and Monica's discussion introduced by Philippians 3:13, a resurrection text. This Pauline references serves to secure a specifically Christian outlook on this episode by focusing on its Christ centric character. Not only does it provoke Monica's aspiration for resurrection to Christian reader, it also gives a forceful sanction for Augustine's pilgrimage.[108] In order to gain Christ, he gives up ambition, marriage, and sexuality. Adapting Paul's rejection of legal righteousness to his own ends, Augustine describes himself as seeking God, not through the willed perfection of Platonic philosophy, but through the power of Christ. Furthermore, through discussion by Monica and Augustine the promise of a higher Christian wisdom, superior to that of the pagans, is presented by the use of 1 Corinthians 2:9. Their conversation pertains to eternal life of the saints and attempt to reflect on this eternal life. Spiritual truths are obtainable only to those who possess the Spirit who alone can search for the depths of God. Because the Spirit comes upon them at Ostia, mother and son will know each other's inner thoughts and achieve for a moment the mutual lucidity of the saints. Augustine then demonstrates a formal pattern of ascent: the bodily senses, corporeal objects, the heavens, the mind, and Divine Wisdom.[109] The pilgrim souls begin with the levels of temporal existence. In the last level, the souls return upon completion of the ascent as the stage of internal reflection, dialogue, and reflection upon empirical knowledge. At Ostia the contemplative souls ascend from discursive reasoning directly into eternity and divine wisdom, so that they transcend their own minds and move beyond the temporal self. God rarely grants humans mystical experience, but it is not impossible. As Augustine said that humans touched divine wisdom in some small degree by a moment of total concentration of the heart, contact with divine wisdom is a matter of the moral self. As Augustine mentions from Romans 8 that the contemplative souls sigh and leave behind the first fruit of the Spirit, for him contemplation is inherently eschatological unlike Plotinus.[110] Contemplation is momentary insight and glimpse from a fallen world through an aperture opened by the grace of Christ emergent within the soul. The contemplative soul cannot discover its real self within eternal wisdom, but only be an exercise in

---

108. Ibid., 80.
109. Ibid., 81.
110. Ibid., 82.

hope. Eschatological hope is not realized by the embodied soul, but only be actualized after death. Even though Monica and Augustine achieve in contemplation an initial hold on wisdom, and discover their place of hope, their true place within the divine wisdom, this option cannot be exercised until the soul has followed Christ into both death and resurrection.[111] Augustine then reflects upon the ascension that he and Monica experienced at 25 as follows:

> And so our discussion went on. Suppose, we said, that the tumult of a man's flesh were to cease and all that his thoughts can conceive, of earth, of water, and of air, should no longer speak to him; suppose that the heavens and even his own soul were silent, no longer thinking of itself but passing beyond; suppose that his dreams and the visions of his imagination spoke no more and that every tongue and every sign and all that is transient grew silent—for all these things have the same message to tell, if only we can hear it, and their message is this: We did not make ourselves, but he who abides for ever made us (Ps. 79:3, 5). Suppose, we said, that after giving us this message and bidding us listen to him who made them, they fell silent and he alone should speak to us, not through them but in his own voice, so that we should hear him speaking, not by any tongue of the flesh or by an angel's voice, not in the sound of thunder or in some veiled parable, but in his own voice, the voice of the one whom we love in all these created things; suppose that we heard him himself, with none of these things between ourselves and him, just as in that brief moment my mother and I had reached out in thought and touched the eternal Wisdom which abides over all things; suppose that this state were to continue and all other visions of things inferior were to be removed, so that this single vision entranced and absorbed the one who beheld it and enveloped him in inward joys in such a way that for him life was eternally the same as that instant of understanding for which we had longed so much—would not this be what we are to understand by the words Come and share the joy of your Lord (Matt. 25:21)?1 But when is it to be? Is it to be when we all rise again, but not all of us will undergo the change (1 Cor 15:51)?[112]

According to this section 25, there are two sorts of voices such as that of creatures and that of the creator.[113] The text contrasts mediated

111. Ibid., 82.
112. *conf.* 9.10.25.
113. Kenney, *The Mysticism of Saint Augustine*, 84.

reports about Wisdom, whether through human, angelic, or symbolic form of representation, with direct encounter. In contemplation, the soul closes the gap of its separation from God. The contemplative souls at Ostia seek to discover the authentic voice of a divine being wholly distinct from their souls. The God discerned at Ostia is not just the source of the soul, a power like the One distinct from its products. The soul only hears directly the God for which it yearns momentarily, and only achieves unmediated contact with him for a limited time. The embodied soul, even after baptism and under the direction of divine grace, can only achieve an instance of unmediated association. Contemplation is not an act of salvation, so that it cannot accomplish this in our present life. By drawing upon a Pauline resurrection text, 1 Corinthians 15:51, Augustine demonstrates the limited value of contemplation. This text shows a model of our final state, which is both psychic and corporeal, over against the merely psychic character of the vision at Ostia. Contemplation at Ostia leaves the body behind while Christian resurrection does not. Salvation is once again shown to be distinct from contemplation. Augustine demonstrates the limit of contemplation when he wrote *Confessions*. He recognizes his utter dependence upon God in both metaphysical and moral terms by rejecting the Neoplatonic and Stoic ideals of the autonomous, self-sufficient sage which he embraced in his earliest writings.[114] The aftermath of his personal moral struggles and his subsequent conflicts with Pelagianism, as Torchia argues, led to developing firm in his conviction of our radical contingency and the necessity of grace for our salvation.[115] Since from this later perspective only Christ can enable us to accomplish what we could never achieve on our own in our sinful condition, the soul's contemplative movement to God must be interpreted as the gift of grace.[116]

Unlike the ascent of Book Seven of *Confessions*, the vision at Ostia allows the pilgrim souls to find happiness with God in anticipation of their final state of eternal association with him. However, despite enjoying this vision at Ostia, Monica's soul in need of redemption. In this context, Augustine prays after her death.[117] For Augustine contemplation is transformed into a double-edged recognition of the certain existence

114. Torchia, "Contemplation and Action," 235.

115. *Conf.* 7.21.27, *ep.* 145, Torchia, "Contemplation and Action," 235,

116. *en. Ps.* 41.9. trans. J. E. Tweed in *Nicene and Post-Nicene Fathers*, vol. 8 (New York: Christian Literature Publishing Co., 1888). Hereafter I use this translation. Torchia, "Contemplation and Action," 235.

117. *conf.* 9.13.35.

of transcendent Wisdom together with the soul's tragic loss and fall. Contemplation secures the transcendental hope of the soul at the expense of its equanimity.[118]

Contemplation of Scripture

Augustine's contemplation is contemplation of scripture to be closer to divine wisdom. His exegesis of the scriptural accounts of contemplation is inextricably related to the matter of action. He perceives a real tension between the active and contemplative ways of life. Augustine's exegeses on action and contemplation as ways of life are grounded upon three pairs of contrastive figures: Martha and Mary, Leah and Rachel, and Peter and John.[119] Mary, Rachel, and John who devote to religious contemplation seeks fulfillment in prayer or intellectual endeavors while Martha, Leah, and Peter who emphasize active ministry commit to the performance of charitable works of mercy.[120] The active life symbolized by Martha, Leah, and Peter provides paradigms of temporal existence, while Mary, Rachel, and John point to the peace and stability of eternal life and an unimpeded devotion to God.[121]

By drawing upon Luke 10:38, Augustine describes the matter of action and contemplation in Martha and Mary.[122] When Jesus was invited by a religious woman Martha into her house, she was occupied in the care of serving in contrast to her sister Mary who was sitting at the Lord's Feet, and hearing His Word. Martha was busy and giving out but Mary was still and was being filled. Hence, Martha appealed to the Lord, and complained of her sister, for she did not help her in her labor. But the Lord answered Martha for Mary; and He became her Advocate, who had been appealed to as Judge. Jesus said that Martha occupied about many things, when one thing is necessary. Mary has chosen the better part, which shall not be taken from her. Mary was intent on the sweetness of the Lord's word. Martha was intent, how she might feed the Lord; Mary intent how she might be fed by the Lord. By Martha a feast was being prepared for the Lord, in whose feast Mary was even now delighting herself. As Mary

118. Kenney, *The Mysticism of Saint Augustine*, 86.
119. *Jo. ev. tr.* 124.1-7.
120. Torchia, "Contemplation and Action," 233.
121. Ibid., 233.
122. *s.* 104.1. cf. *s.* 103, 179, 255

then was listening with sweet pleasure to Jesus' most sweet word, and was feeding with the most earnest affection, when the Lord was appealed to by her sister. For by a wondrous sweetness was she held; a sweetness of the mind which is doubtless greater than that of the senses. She was excused, she sat in greater confidence. In this context, Augustine pays attention to how she was excused. According to Augustine, Martha is occupied about many things, when one thing is needful.[123] Mary has chosen the better part. Martha did not choose a bad part, but Mary a better. And how better? Martha is about many things, while Mary about one thing. One is preferred to many. It is because one does not come from many, but many from one:

> The things which were made, are many, He who made them is One. The heaven, the earth, the sea, and all things that in them are, how many are they! Who could enumerate them? Who conceive their vast number? Who made all these? God made them all. Behold, they are very good. Very good are the things He made; how much better is He who made them![124]

What Martha did for Jesus is about mortal flesh. Yet, he is not in it. As Augustine stresses that in the beginning was the Word, and the Word was with God, and the Word was God, he focuses on what Mary was listening to. Jesus did not blame Martha's work, but distinguished between their services. Martha is occupied about many things, but one thing is needful. That is why Mary chose this for herself. The labor of manifoldness passes away and the love of unity abides. Therefore, what she chose shall not be taken from her, but what Martha chose shall be taken away. Hence, Augustine said that Mary is already in port, but Martha is still on the sea.[125] Through these two women, Augustine shows there are two lives; the life present, and the life to come, the life of labor, and the life of quiet, the life of sorrow, and the life of blessedness, the life temporal, and the life eternal.[126] For Augustine Martha's life does not a wicked one. He thinks that both praiseworthy; the one of labor, the other of ease; neither vicious, neither slothful. "In Martha was the image of things present, in

---

123. *s.* 104.3.
124. *s.* 104.3.
125. *s.* 104.3.
126. *s.* 104.4.

Mary of things to come. What Martha was doing, that we are now; what Mary was doing, that we hope for."[127]

In the *Contra Faustum Manicheum* written around 400, Augustine's exegesis on action and contemplation is discussed through Leah and Rachel. According to Augustine, the two wives of Jacob signify the two lives. They were daughters of the remission of sins of Laban.[128] One is loved, the other is borne. But she that is borne is the most and the soonest fruitful, that she may be loved, if not for herself, at least for her children. The toil of the righteous is especially fruitful in those whom they beget for the kingdom of God, by preaching the gospel amid many trials and temptations. Through two lives of Leah and Rachel, Augustine shows paradigms of temporal existence and eternal life as follows:

> Such births result most easily and plentifully from the word of faith, the preaching of Christ crucified, which speaks also of His human nature as far as it can be easily understood, so as not to hurt the weak eyes of Leah. Rachel, again, with clear eye, is beside herself to God (2 Corinthians 5:13), and sees in the beginning the Word of God with God, and wishes to bring forth, but cannot; for who shall declare His generation? So the life devoted to contemplation, in order to see with no feeble mental eye things invisible to flesh, but understood by the things that are made, and to discern the ineffable manifestation of the eternal power and divinity of God, seeks leisure from all occupation, and is therefore barren. In this habit of retirement, where the fire of meditation burns bright, there is a want of sympathy with human weakness, and with the need men have of our help in their calamities. This life also burns with the desire for children (for it wishes to teach what it knows, and not to go with the corruption of envy), and sees its sister-life fully occupied with work and with bringing forth; and it grieves that men run after that virtue which cares for their wants and weaknesses, instead of that which has a divine imperishable lesson to impart. This is what is meant when it is said, "Rachel envied her sister." (Genesis 30:1) Moreover, as the pure intellectual perception of that which is not matter, and so is not the object of the bodily sense, cannot be expressed in words which spring from the flesh, the doctrine of wisdom prefers to get some lodging for divine truth in the mind by whatever material figures and illustrations occur, rather than

127. *s.* 104.4.

128. *c. Faust.* 22.54. trans. Roland Teske, S.J. in *a Translation for the 21st Century*, vol. I/20 (New York: New City Press, 2007). Hereafter I use this translation.

to give up teaching these things; and thus Rachel preferred that her husband should have children by her handmaid, rather than that she should be without any children. Bilhah, the name of her handmaid, is said to mean old; and so, even when we speak of the spiritual and unchangeable nature of God, ideas are suggested relating to the old life of the bodily senses.[129]

Even though all who seek it must be warned that here it will bring no exemption from the "toil of righteousness" which is its condition, Augustine thinks of an attainment of wisdom and understanding in this life. Augustine insists that the same thing happens constantly in the church; "In all their labors they aim chiefly at this, that their chosen way of life may have greater and wider renown, as having supplied the people with such leaders; as Jacob consents to go with Leah, that Rachel may obtain the sweet-smelling and good-looking fruit. Rachel, too, in course of time, by the mercy of God, brings forth a child herself, but not till after some time; for it seldom happens that there is a sound, though only partial, apprehension, without fleshly ideas, of such sacred lessons of wisdom."[130]

In the *In Johannis evangelium tractatus*, Augustine deals with action and contemplation through Peter and John by drawing upon John 21:19-25. He pays attention to why Jesus said to the Apostle Peter, "Follow me," when he manifested himself to the disciples a third time but the Apostle John, "So I will have him to remain till I come. What is it to you?" For Augustine, it is interesting that why Jesus loved John more when Peter loved the Jesus himself more. John adds this fact that Jesus loved him whenever John mentions himself, so that by this sign he might be distinguished from the others.[131] According to Augustine, "the Apostle John was more loved by Christ precisely because he did not take a wife and lived most chastely from the beginning of his childhood."[132] Even though this does not appear in canonical Scriptures, it aids the appropriateness of this opinion that that life has been signified by him where there will be no marriages. According to Augustine, there are two lives as follows:

> one in the time of sojourning abroad, the other in a eternity of dwelling; one in toil, the other in rest; one in the way, the other in one's homeland; one in the effort of action, the other in

129. *c. Faust.* 22.54.
130. *c. Faust.* 22.58.
131. *Jo. ev. tr.* 124.4. trans. Edmund Hill in *a Translation for the 21st Century*, vol. 12 (New York: New City Press, 2009). Hereafter I use this translation.
132. *Jo. ev. tr.* 124.7.

the reward of contemplation; one turns aside from evil and does good, the other has not evil from which it turns aside and has great good which it is to enjoy; one fights with the enemy, the other reigns without the enemy; one is strong in adversity, the other perceives nothing of adversity; one reins in carnal lusts, the other is free for spiritual delights; one is anxious with a care for conquering, the other is secure in the peace of victory; one is given help in temptations, the other rejoices in the Helper himself without any temptation; one comes to the aid of the needy, the other is there where it comes upon no one in need; one forgives another's sins that its own may be forgiven it, the other neither suffers what it may forgive nor does what it may ask to be forgiven it; one is scourged by evils that it may not be exalted in its goods, the other by so great a fullness of grace lacks every evil so that without any temptation to pride it adheres to the highest good; one sees the difference between goods and evils, the other sees things which are only good; therefore, one is good but still wretched, the other is better and happy.[133]

Augustine perceives a real tension between the active and contemplative ways of life.[134] He stresses their relationship and interaction rather than viewing them as mutually exclusive. In this regard, he considers action the necessary means to contemplation, both now and in the life to come. For example, "we find Christ on earth in the poor in our midst (s. 345.4), and likewise, we secure a place in heaven by performing charitable works on their behalf (s. 178.4). Service to those in need, then, is nothing less than a means to the contemplation and love of God. For Augustine, each way of life must be permitted to flourish, but only in such a way that neither encroaches upon the other's good. And while he designates contemplation as the better part (*melior pars*), this does not imply that action is bad, but only that it must give way to something more perfect (s. 103.5)."[135] For Augustine, the first life is signified by the Apostle Peter, that other by John. He regards the Apostle Peter in the effort of action as being still wretched, but the Apostle John in the reward of contemplation as being happy. It is because corruptible body weighs down the soul.[136] In this context, Augustine understands Jesus' questions as follows; "Do you follow me through the imitation of enduring temporal evils, let him wait

133. *Jo. ev. tr.* 124.5.
134. Torchia, "Contemplation and Action," 233.
135. Ibid., 233.
136. *Jo. ev. tr.* 124.2.

till I come to restore everlasting good?"[137] He explains this meaning more clearly follows:

> Let perfected action follow me, shaped by the example of my passion, but let contemplation only begun remain till I come, to be perfected when I come. For the pious plenitude of patience, reaching even to death, follow Christ; however, the plentitude of knowledge remains till Christ comes, then to be made manifest. For indeed here are tolerated the evils of this world in a land of the dying; there will be seen the goods of the Lord in a land of the living. For his words, I will have him to remain till I come, must not be understood in such a way as if he said to remain behind or to continue to remain, but to wait because what is signified by him will be fulfilled, not now, of course, but when Christ comes.[138]

This indicates that true happiness cannot be achieved in this world in contrast with Mencius who claim that one can be perfect by developing virtues bestowed by the Heaven. Such differences derive from the understanding of human nature.

SUMMARY

In this chapter, I highlighted Confucius and Mencius's self-reflection and Augustine's contemplation. In terms of Confucius' self-reflection, it is essential in relation to the process of moral learning. Basically, Confucius thought study is more important than self-reflection. Particularly, when it comes to the essence of self-reflection, it does not indicate abstract and theoretical cogitation. It indicates to keep one's attention engaged with something, often a goal or ideal which one intends to achieve. In contrast to Confucius, however, for Mencius self-reflection has great importance in self-cultivation in connection with human nature in the formation of moral self. It is because one can retake benevolence embedded in his nature through self-reflection. This leads to knowing Heaven. For him, the way to serve Heaven is to preserve one's mental constitution, and nourish one's nature. Mencius focused on the importance of self-reflection in order to find virtues originally in our mind such as benevolence, righteousness, ritual propriety, and wisdom. Theses virtues are not infused

---

137. *Jo. ev. tr.* 124.5.
138. *Jo. ev. tr.* 124.5.

from outside and universal to all people. In this context, Mencius thought there are no differences between sages and people in finding such virtues in mind. Likewise, for him the man of virtue is not a unique being but the one who preserves such virtues in his heart. Like Confucius, of course, Mencius emphasizes the importance of habitual self-reflection because it enhances man of virtue's faith on the Way. In the course, suffering is an essential course for the man of virtue in that it makes one's character patient and improves his ability. Unlike Mencius, Augustine thought contemplation in the perspective of purifying our mind. He regards contemplation of God as the supreme good. In other words, contemplation is not an advanced form of prayer. Contemplation of eternal things is connected with wisdom as knowledge of God, not knowledge of temporal matter. Given that his understanding of contemplation drives from his depiction of human nature as a substantial unity of soul and body, contemplation is a binding of the mind to God. Above all, his contemplation is based on his experience at Ostia. Considering that soul can enjoy only a sporadic knowledge of true being, Augustine explained the act of contemplation in connection with mystical experiences. Contemplation is momentary insight and glimpse from a fallen world through an aperture opened by the grace of Christ emergent within the soul. The contemplative soul cannot discover its real self within eternal wisdom, but only be an exercise in hope. Furthermore, his contemplation is contemplation of scripture to be closer to divine wisdom.

4

Li (禮) and Sacrament

INTRODUCTION

IN THIS CHAPTER I will arrange the comparative exegesis of Confucius and Mencius' ritual propriety (*li* 禮) and Augustine's sacraments as ways for the formation of moral self according to internal, communitarian, and transcendental dimensions including Augustine's sacraments and Confucian ritualistic ceremonies. For them, music plays an important role in the formation of moral self in relation to ritual propriety and sacrament. In this chapter, I first outline Confucius' account of ritual propriety. This deals with why he highlights ritual propriety in relation to establishing harmonious government and how speech, action, and the mean are interconnected with it. And then I begin to show Mencius' account of ritual propriety. This includes how his ritual propriety is inextricably related to benevolence and righteousness and why his ritual propriety is not antiutilitarianism by explaining his understanding of shame, government officer, and funeral. Lastly, I examine Augustine's account of the formation of moral self through the sacraments including baptism and marriage in ordering the mind toward the love of God rather than self since such sacraments are representative rituals in his thought.

CONFUCIUS' RITUAL PROPRIETY

Returning to Ritual Propriety

When the Duke Ling of Wei asked Confucius about tactics, Confucius replied "I acquired some knowledge of the business of sacrificial vessels, but I have never studied military matters" and then he took his departure the next day.[1] This indicates his main academic interest was not military matters (軍) but ritual propriety. Why did he seek to study ritual rather than tactics? In terms of relation between ritual propriety and study, he states that "the virtue of man, extensively studying all literatures, and keeping himself under the restraint of the requirement of ritual propriety, may thus likewise not overstep what is right."[2] For Confucius, moral learning ought to be kept pace with ritual propriety in order to follow the Way. For instance, when he was asked about a boy from Que village who was employed by Confucius to carry the messages between him and his visitors, Confucius stated that "he is the sort of person who wants to get results quickly" since according to his observation "he sits in an adult's place and I see that he walks together with his elders."[3] He argued that a person without ritual propriety may be not the one who is seeking to make progress in learning. Thus, he stresses to practice ritual propriety in accordance with one's role. When Confucius was inquired about government, he replied that "there is government, when the prince is prince, and the minister is minister; when the father is father, and the son is son."[4]

Beyond this relation between moral learning and ritual propriety, he explains why ritual propriety is pivotal in the matter of how to morally behave;

> Respectfulness, without the rules of ritual propriety, becomes laborious bustle; carefulness, without the rules of ritual propriety, becomes timidity; boldness, without the rules of ritual propriety, becomes insubordination; straightforwardness, without the rules of ritual propriety, becomes rudeness. When the man of virtue deals sincerely with their kinsfolk, then the people are stimulated towards benevolence. When old friends are not neglected, then the people will not behave irresponsibly.[5]

---

1. *Analects*, 15.1. Translation adapted from Dawson. 衛靈公問陳於孔子。孔子對曰：「俎豆之事，則嘗聞之矣；軍旅之事，未之學也。」明日遂行。

2. *Analects*, 6.27. Translation adapted from Legge. 子曰：「君子博學於文，約之以禮，亦可以弗畔矣夫！」

3. *Analects*, 14.44. 闕黨童子將命。或問之曰：「益者與？」子曰：「吾見其居於位也，見其與先生並行也。非求益者也，欲速成者也。」

4. *Analects*, 12.11. As translated in Legge. 齊景公問政於孔子。孔子對曰：「君君，臣臣，父父，子子。」

5. *Analects*, 8.2. Translation adapted from Legge. 子曰：「恭而無禮則勞，慎而無禮則葸，勇而無禮則亂，直而無禮則絞。君子篤於親，則民興於仁；故舊不遺，則民不偷。」

The reason why he emphasizes studying ritual propriety along with music is that it is prerequisite to be a government officer:

> Those who first approached me were rustics as far as ritual propriety and music were concerned, and those who approached me afterwards were the man of virtue as far as rites and music were concerned. If I put them to use, I follow those who first approached me.[6]

It is because ritual propriety can make harmony (和) possible in government with the rules of propriety as Master You said as follows:

> In the practice of the rites harmony is regarded as the most valuable thing, and in the ways of the ancient kings this is regarded as the most beautiful thing. It is adopted in all matters, both small and great. But sometimes it does not work. If you behave harmoniously because you understand harmony, but do not regulate your conduct with ritual, surely that cannot be made to work.[7]

Fundamentally, ritual propriety is inextricably linked to the man of virtue, given that for Confucius the man of virtue is suitable to a government official. About the question of the man of virtue raised by Sima Niu, Confucius replied the man of virtue is neither worried nor afraid since when he looks within he is not diseased.[8] The man of virtue, as Zixia argues, does not need to worry even about not having brothers since "if the man of virtue is reverent and avoids error, if he is courteous in his dealings with others and observes the obligations of ritual, then all within the Four Seas are his brothers," given that death and life are predestined, and riches and honors depend on Heaven.[9] As a result, the man of virtue can have a dignified ease without pride, avoiding inconstant in his virtue that causes disgrace.[10] Therefore, Confucius himself exerted all possible effort

---

6. *Analects*, 11.1. Translation adapted from Dawson. 子曰：「先進於禮樂，野人也；後進於禮樂，君子也。如用之，則吾從先進。」

7. *Analects*, 1.12. 有子曰：「禮之用，和為貴。先王之道斯為美，小大由之。有所不行，知和而和，不以禮節之，亦不可行也。」

8. *Analects*, 12.4. 司馬牛問君子。子曰：「君子不憂不懼。」曰：「不憂不懼，斯謂之君子已乎？」子曰：「內省不疚，夫何憂何懼？」

9. *Analects*, 12.5. Translation adapted from Dawson. 司馬牛憂曰：「人皆有兄弟，我獨亡。」子夏曰：「商聞之矣：死生有命，富貴在天。君子敬而無失，與人恭而有禮。四海之內，皆兄弟也。君子何患乎無兄弟也？」

10. *Analects*, 13.26. 子曰：「君子泰而不驕，小人驕而不泰。」; *Analects*, 13.22. 子曰：「南人有言曰：『人而無恆，不可以作巫醫。』善夫！」「不恆

to practice ritual propriety in his life as he states that "Abroad, to serve the high ministers and nobles; at home, to serve one's father and elder brothers; in all duties to the dead, not to dare not to exert one's self; and not to be overcome of wine—which one of these things do I attain to?"[11]

Understanding Confucian thought entails, as Hagen argues, understanding a Confucian concept cluster, which includes a number of terms that are notoriously difficult to translate. Among these terms, *li* is one of the challenging concepts. *li* can be translated as ritual (Waley), ritual propriety (Behuniak), and rite (Slingerland, Lau) according to contexts. Regarding these various translations, one may raise a question about whether there is single word in any of the European languages that covers the same range.[12] Even though there is no single word for *li*, for Confucius there should exist the unchangeable essence of *li*. What is this? Confucius defined ritual propriety in relation to benevolence (仁) as follows:

> Yan Hui asked about benevolence. The Master said: "To subdue oneself and return to ritual is to practice benevolence. If someone subdued himself and returned to ritual for a single day, then all under Heaven would ascribe benevolence to him. For the practice of benevolence does surely proceed from the man himself, or does it proceed from others?" Yan Hui said: "I beg to ask for the details of this." The Master laid: "Do not look at what is contrary to ritual propriety, do not listen to what is contrary to ritual propriety, do not speak what is contrary to ritual propriety, and make no movement which is contrary to ritual propriety." Yan Hui said: "Although I am not clever, I beg to put this advice into practice."[13]

According to Confucius, returning to ritual propriety is to practice benevolence. In the dimension of subduing one's self, more specifically, he shows how to return to ritual propriety. It is not supernatural. Returning to ritual propriety is not to look at what is contrary to ritual propriety, not to listen to what is contrary to ritual propriety, not to speak what

---

其德, 或承之羞。」子曰：「不占而已矣。」

11. *Analects*, 9.16. As translated in Legge. 子曰：「出則事公卿，入則事父兄，喪事不敢不勉，不為酒困，何有於我哉？」

12. Kurtis Hagen, "The Propriety of Confucius: A sense-of-Ritual," *Asian Philosophy* 20 (March 2010), 4.

13. *Analects*, 12.1. Translation adapted from Dawson. 顏淵問仁。子曰：「克己復禮為仁。一日克己復禮，天下歸仁焉。為仁由己，而由人乎哉？」顏淵曰：「請問其目。」子曰：「非禮勿視，非禮勿聽，非禮勿言，非禮勿動。」顏淵曰：「回雖不敏，請事斯語矣。」

is contrary to ritual propriety, and not to make no movement which is contrary to ritual propriety. It is about human behavior. This indicates that the matter of practicing humaneness depends on the will of man. Hence, he offers "courtesy, tolerance, good faith, diligence, and kindness" as five things in the form of ritual propriety for achieving humaneness since these can be conducted by human will.[14]

Speech, Naming, and Mean

In contrast to Augustine who dealt with action in relation to contemplation, Confucius stresses that the man of virtue ought to practice consistency of speech and action in accordance with ritual propriety:

> The man of virtue in everything considers righteousness to be essential. He performs it according to the rules of propriety. He brings it forth in humility. He completes it with sincerity. This is indeed the man of virtue.[15]

It is because "the man of virtue is modest in his speech, but exceeds in his actions."[16] As a result, the man of virtue, as Zi Xia describes, undergoes three changes; "Looked at from a distance, he appears stern; when approached, he is mild; when he is heard to speak, his language is firm and decided."[17] He hated glib-tongued people without action unlike the man of virtue:

> Zi Lu got Zi Gao appointed governor of Fei. The Master said, "You are injuring a man's son." Zi Lu said, "There are common

---

14. *Analects*, 17.6. Translation adapted from Dawson. "Zizhang asked Confucius about humaneness. Confucius said: One who can bring about the practice of five things everywhere under Heaven has achieved humaneness. When he begged to ask about them, he said: Courtesy, tolerance, good faith, diligence, and kindness. If one is courteous, one is not treated with rudeness; if one is tolerant, one wins over the multitude; if one is of good faith, others give one responsibility; if one is diligent, one obtains results; and if one is kind, one is competent to command others." 子張問仁於孔子。孔子曰：「能行五者於天下，為仁矣。」請問之。曰：「恭、寬、信、敏、惠。恭則不侮，寬則得眾，信則人任焉，敏則有功，惠則足以使人。」

15. *Analects*, 15.18. Translation adapted from Legge. 子曰：「君子義以為質，禮以行之，孫以出之，信以成之。君子哉！」

16. *Analects*, 14.27. Translation adapted from Legge. 子曰：「君子恥其言而過其行。」

17. *Analects*, 19.9. As translated from Legge. 子夏曰：「君子有三變：望之儼然，即之也溫，聽其言也厲。」

people and officers; there are the altars of the spirits of the land and grain. Why must one read books before he can be considered to have learned?" The Master said, "It is on this account that I hate your glib-tongued people."[18]

Hence, Confucius notes that "the virtuous will be sure to speak correctly, but those whose speech is good may not always be virtuous. Men of principle are sure to be bold, but those who are bold may not always be men of principle."[19] Rather, Confucius regarded the one who is hesitant in his speech as the humane person since he already penetrated how difficult narrowing the gap between speech and action is in spite of human will.[20] According to him, "The firm, the enduring, the simple, and the modest (訥) are close to humaneness."[21] In this context, he emphasized that those who are sincere and truthful in speech can put in practice as follows:

> Zi Zhang asked how a man should conduct himself, so as to be everywhere appreciated. The Master said, "Let his words be sincere and truthful and his actions honorable and careful—such conduct may be practiced among the rude tribes of the South or the North. If his words be not sincere and truthful, and his actions not honorable and careful, will he, with such conduct, be appreciated, even in his neighborhood? When he is standing, let him see those two things, as it were, fronting him. When he is in a carriage, let him see them attached to the yoke. Then may he subsequently carry them into practice." Zi Zhang wrote these counsels on the end of his sash.[22]

If so, what does being hesitant in speech mean? For Confucius, it is linked to the matter of moderation; "Since I cannot get men pursuing the due medium, to whom I might communicate my instructions, I must find the ardent and the cautiously-decided. The ardent will advance and lay hold of truth; the cautiously-decided will keep themselves from what is

---

18. *Analects*, 11.25. As translated from Legge. 子路使子羔為費宰。子曰：「賊夫人之子。」子路曰：「有民人焉，有社稷焉。何必讀書，然後為學？」子曰：「是故惡夫佞者。」

19. *Analects*, 14.4. As translated from Legge. 子曰：「有德者，必有言。有言者，不必有德。仁者，必有勇。勇者，不必有仁。」

20. *Analects*, 12.3. 司馬牛問仁。子曰：「仁者其言也訒。」曰：「其言也訒，斯謂之仁已乎？」子曰：「為之難，言之得無訒乎？」

21. *Analects*, 13.27. As translated in Dawson. 子曰：「剛毅、木訥，近仁。」

22. *Analects*, 15.6. As translated from Legge. 子張問行。子曰：「言忠信，行篤敬，雖蠻貊之邦行矣；言不忠信，行不篤敬，雖州里行乎哉？立，則見其參於前也；在輿，則見其倚於衡也。夫然後行。」子張書諸紳。

wrong."[23] Hence, he states that "when respect is shown according to what is proper, one keeps far from shame and disgrace."[24] For example, he notes that "when good government prevails in a state, language may be lofty and bold, and actions the same. When bad government prevails, the actions may be lofty and bold, but the language may be with some reserve."[25]

In speech, more specifically, Confucius made an emphasis on rectifying names as a specific method for rightly realizing ritual propriety in managing government as follows:

> Zi Lu said, "The ruler of Wei has been waiting for you, in order with you to administer the government. What will you consider the first thing to be done?" The Master replied, "What is necessary is to rectify names." "So! indeed!" said Zi Lu. "You are wide of the mark! Why must there be such rectification?" The Master said, "How uncultivated you are, You! The man of virtue, in regard to what he does not know, shows a cautious reserve. If names be not correct, language is not in accordance with the truth of things. If language be not in accordance with the truth of things, affairs cannot be carried on to success. When affairs cannot be carried on to success, ritual and music will not flourish. When ritual and music do not flourish, punishments will not be properly awarded. When punishments are not properly awarded, the people do not know how to move hand or foot. Therefore, the man of virtue considers it necessary that the names he uses may be spoken appropriately, and also that what he speaks may be carried out appropriately. What the man of virtue requires is just that in his words there may be nothing incorrect."[26]

Confucius illustrates how harmful incorrect names are to people. It is because inappropriate names give rise to producing language apart from the truth of thing results in failure of affairs which might prevent accurately conducting ritual and music. The decline of ritual and music may lead to a situation that punishments are not properly awarded. As a

---

23. *Analects*, 13.21. As translated in Legge. 子曰：「不得中行而與之，必也狂狷乎！狂者進取，狷者有所不為也。」

24. *Analects*, 1.13. 有子曰：恭近於禮，遠恥辱也

25. *Analects*, 14.3. 子曰：「邦有道，危言危行；邦無道，危行言孫。」

26. *Analects*, 13.3. Translation adapted from Legge. 子路曰：「衛君待子而為政，子將奚先？」子曰：「必也正名乎！」子路曰：「有是哉，子之迂也！奚其正？」子曰：「野哉由也！君子於其所不知，蓋闕如也。名不正，則言不順；言不順，則事不成；事不成，則禮樂不興；禮樂不興，則刑罰不中；刑罰不中，則民無所措手足。故君子名之必可言也，言之必可行也。君子於其言，無所苟而已矣。」

result, the people nervously do not know how to behave. Rectifying names is not just an erroneous belief in word-magic or a pedantic elaboration of his concern with teaching tradition.[27] It is essential for executing ritual propriety. It leads to the harmony and beauty of social forms in that ritual propriety is public, shared, transparent.[28] Like Xunzi, in particular, it is noticeable for Confucius to state the necessity of punishments in relation to ritual propriety. This statement seems to be against his idea of governing people by virtue and ritual rather than laws and punishments:

> If the people be led by laws, and uniformity sought to be given them by punishments, they will try to avoid the punishment, but have no sense of shame. If they be led by virtue, and uniformity sought to be given them by the rules of propriety, they will have the sense of shame, and moreover will become good.[29]

However, this contradiction is about the matter of order. In other words, Confucius must have preferred virtue and ritual in administer people like Mencius, but he did not ignore the value of punishments.

Along with the matter of speech and action, Confucius extensively discusses ritual propriety in relation to the Mean (中庸). As he states that "Supreme indeed is the Mean as virtue, but for a long time it has been rare among the people,"[30] he lamented absence of the Mean in his time. Considering Cheng's question about the value of ornamental accomplishments in ritual, there seemed to be some scholars against Confucian's idea of ritual propriety as follows:

> Ji Zi Cheng said, "In the man of virtue it is only the substantial qualities which are wanted; why should we seek for ornamental accomplishments?" Zi Gong said, "Alas! Your words, sir, show you to be the man of virtue, but four horses cannot overtake the tongue. Ornament is as substance; substance is as ornament. The hide of a tiger or a leopard stripped of its hair, is like the hide of a dog or a goat stripped of its hair."[31]

27. Fingarette, *Confucius*, 15

28. Ibid., 16.

29. *Analects*, 2.3. As translated in Legge. 子曰：「道之以政，齊之以刑，民免而無恥；道之以德，齊之以禮，有恥且格。」

30. *Analects*, 6.29. As translated in Dawson. 子曰：「中庸之為德也，其至矣乎！民鮮久矣。」

31. *Analects*, 12.8. As translated in Legge. 棘子成曰：「君子質而已矣，何以文為？」子貢曰：「惜乎！夫子之說，君子也。駟不及舌。文猶質也，質猶文也。虎豹之鞟，猶犬羊之鞟。」

The matter of absence of the mean is about ritual propriety and the man of virtue. About the critique of ritual propriety, Zi Gong argues ornament and substance are equally important in the dimension of the Mean. In this context, Confucius stated that "Where the solid qualities are in excess of accomplishments, we have rusticity; where the accomplishments are in excess of the solid qualities, we have the manners of a clerk. When the accomplishments and solid qualities are equally blended, we then have the man of virtue."[32] For all that, Confucius did not praise too much ornament beyond substance as he insisted that "to go beyond is as wrong as to fall short."[33] Rather, about the essence of ritual propriety in the dimension of festive ceremonies he stated that "it is better to be frugal than lavish."[34] Like Mencius Confucius is not anti-asceticism.

MENCIUS' RITUAL PROPRIETY

Essence of Ritual Propriety: Benevolence and Righteousness

Mencius hugely emphasizes the roles of ritual propriety (*li* 禮) in the formation of moral self. Virtually, *li* can be translated into ceremony, ritual, rites, propriety, rules of propriety, good custom, ritual propriety, decorum, and good form, given that its concept is linked to others.[35] For Mencius, ritual propriety is more valuable than eating and sex. When he was asked about embarrassing question on ritual propriety by Wu Lu, he simply replied if, by twisting your elder brother's arm, and snatching from him what he is eating, you can get food for yourself, while, if you do not do so, you will not get anything to eat, will you so twist his arm? If by getting over your neighbor's wall, and dragging away his virgin daughter, you can get a wife, while if you do not do so, you will not be able to get a wife, will you so drag her away?[36] As etymologically *li* symbolizes a religious sacrifice, Mencius states that even an ugly man would be fit to

---

32. *Analects*, 6.18. As translated in Legge. 子曰：「質勝文則野，文勝質則史。文質彬彬，然後君子。」

33. *Analects*, 11.16. As translated in Legge. 子貢問：「師與商也孰賢？」子曰：「師也過，商也不及。」曰：「然則師愈與？」子曰：「過猶不及。」

34. *Analects*, 3.4. As translated in Dawson. 林放問禮之本。子曰：「大哉問！禮，與其奢也，寧儉；喪，與其易也，寧戚。」

35. Tu, *Humanity and Self-Cultivation*, 21.

36. *Mencius*, 6B1. 紾兄之臂而奪之食，則得食；不紾，則不得食，則將紾之乎？踰東家牆而摟其處子，則得妻；不摟，則不得妻，則將摟之乎？

offer sacrifices to God if he cleanses himself.[37] For him, cleaning himself does not just indicate bathing but self-cultivation. Explaining that the actions of the sages have been different, he demonstrates that some have kept remote from court, and some have drawn near to it. For example, it is possible for Yi Yin to seek an introduction to Tang by the Way of Yao and Shun, not his knowledge of cookery. Mencius stresses that the purpose of those different courses is to keep their persons ethically pure.[38] For Mencius, furthermore, along with moral learning ritual propriety is a matter of ups and downs in a nation. According to him, it is not the exterior and interior walls being incomplete, and the supply of weapons offensive and defensive not being large, which constitutes the calamity of a kingdom. It is not the cultivable area not being extended, and stores and wealth not being accumulated, which occasions the ruin of a State. He states that "when superiors do not observe ritual propriety, and inferiors do not learn, then seditious people spring up, and that State will perish in no time."[39] It is because government officers serve their prince without righteousness and do not follow the Ways of the ancient kings when ritual propriety is not properly conducted.

In particular, Mencius shows the essence of ritual propriety in relation to benevolence and righteousness. Contrary to Confucius, Mencius frequently mentions benevolence and righteousness at the same time. When Mencius went to see king Hui of Liang, the king presumed that Mencius has some way of profiting his kingdom. Unlike his expectation, Mencius clearly states that his topics for counseling with him are only benevolence and righteousness since the king's interest for profit makes superiors and inferiors try to snatch this profit the one from the other and the kingdom will be endangered. Mencius warns that those above and below will not be satisfied without snatching all if righteousness is put last, and profit is put first. He underlines there never has been a benevolent and righteous man who neglected his parents and made his sovereign an after consideration.[40]

---

37. *Mencius*, 4B25. 雖有惡人，齊戒沐浴，則可以祀上帝。

38. *Mencius*, 5A7. 聖人之行不同也，或遠或近，或去或不去，歸潔其身而已矣。吾聞其以堯舜之道要湯，未聞以割烹也。

39. *Mencius*, 4A1. Translation adapted from Legge. 上無禮，下無學，賊民興，喪無日矣。

40. *Mencius*, 1A1. 未有仁而遺其親者也，未有義而後其君者也。

Anti-Utilitarianism: Shame, Government Officer, and Funeral

For Mencius, ritual propriety is based on benevolence and righteousness. This indicates that ritual propriety is not utilitarian as follows:

> Mencius said, "Yao and Shun were what they were by nature; Tang and Wu were so by returning to natural virtue. When all the movements, in the countenance and every turn of the body, are exactly what is proper, that shows the extreme degree of the complete virtue. Weeping for the dead should be from real sorrow, and not because of the living. Following the path of virtue and not violating ritual propriety are not for taking up an office. When one invariably keeps one's word it is not to establish the rectitude of one's actions. The man of virtue performs the norm and awaits his Destiny."[41]

This passage shows three essential points on his ritual propriety: shame, government officer, and funeral. Firstly, it is noteworthy that Mencius states the man of virtue carries out ritual propriety according to his nature. For Mencius, simply aiming at what is right is the way of the man of virtue who does not think beforehand of his words that they may be sincere, nor of his actions that they may be resolute.[42] He argues that is a distinctive difference between men and animals. Unlike animals, humans have the sense of shame. The sense of shame plays an important role in ritual propriety. Mencius insists that "a man must not be without shame, for the shame of being without shame is shameless indeed."[43] The sense of shame is to a man of great importance in that those who form contrivances and versatile schemes distinguished for their artfulness, do not allow their sense of shame to come into action.[44] Mencius thinks that those who do violence to themselves and throw themselves away are shameless. It is because to disown ritual propriety in one's conversation is to violate one's self. Given that benevolence is the tranquil habitation of man, and righteousness is his straight path, rejecting to dwell in

---

41. *Mencius*, 7B33. Translation adapted from Legge. 孟子曰：「堯舜，性者也；湯武，反之也。動容周旋中禮者，盛德之至也；哭死而哀，非為生者也；經德不回，非以干祿也；言語必信，非以正行也。君子行法，以俟命而已矣。」

42. *Mencius*, 4B11. 孟子曰：「大人者，言不必信，行不必果，惟義所在。」

43. *Mencius*, 7A6. As translated in Lau. 孟子曰：「人不可以無恥。無恥之恥，無恥矣。」

44. *Mencius*, 7A7. 恥之於人大矣。為機變之巧者，無所用恥焉。

benevolence or pursue the path of righteousness is to throw one's self away.[45] He offers Shun as an example of practicing benevolence and righteousness. According to Mencius, Shun, who clearly understood the multitude of things and closely observed the relations of humanity, does not exploit benevolence and righteousness as a means. He merely walked along the path of benevolence and righteousness.[46] In this context, Shun could be regarded as the great man. Mencius defines the great man according to ritual propriety. For him, the great man is the one who lives in benevolence as the spacious dwelling, stand in ritual propriety as the correct seat, and goes along righteousness as the great path. When the great man achieves his ambition, he shares these with the people; when he fails to do so he practices the Way alone. He cannot be led into excesses when wealthy and honored or deflected from his purpose when poor and obscure, nor can he be made to bow before superior force.[47]

Secondly, it is noticeable that Mencius deals with the matter of how to obtain a government position in connection with ritual propriety as he states that "following the path of virtue and not violating ritual propriety are not for taking up an office." He acknowledges how important taking office is for the man of virtue in that the loss of his place to an officer is like the loss of his State to a prince. For example, when Confucius was not in the service of a lord for a period of three months, he looked anxious and unhappy. According to the *Book of Rituals*, it is because the scholar unemployed for three months cannot supply the grain and animals for performing sacrifice. Hence, in ancient times when a man was not in the service of a lord for a period of three months he was offered condolences. Why the man of virtue ought to take office according to ritual propriety in spite of its urgent matter? Mencius uses the metaphor of marriage to explain it. According to him, every parent wishes to find a wife and a husband one day when their children are born. If the young people, without waiting for the orders of their parents, and the arrangements of the go-betweens, shall bore holes to steal a sight of each other, or get over the

---

45. *Mencius*, 4A10. 自暴者，不可與有言也；自棄者，不可與有為也。言非禮義，謂之自暴也；吾身不能居仁由義，謂之自棄也。仁，人之安宅也；義，人之正路也。

46. *Mencius*, 4B19. 孟子曰：「人之所以異於禽於獸者幾希，庶民去之，君子存之。舜明於庶物，察於人倫，由仁義行，非行仁義也。」

47. *Mencius*, 3B2. 居天下之廣居，立天下之正位，行天下之大道。得志與民由之，不得志獨行其道。富貴不能淫，貧賤不能移，威武不能屈。此之謂大丈夫。

wall to be with each other, then their parents and all other people will despise them. In ancient times, likewise, the man of virtue was indeed eager to take office, but he disliked seeking it by dishonorable means against ritual propriety, for to seek office by an improper way is no different from the man and women who bore holes in the wall.[48] Even Mencius demonstrates that the man of virtue ought to be responded to a summons by a prince when he takes proper ritual propriety:

> When a prince wishes to see a man of talents and virtue, and does not take the proper course to get his wish, it is as if he wished him to enter his palace, and shut the door against him. Righteousness is the road and the ritual propriety is the door. Only the man of virtue follows this road and goes in and out through this door.[49]

With regard to taking up an office, Mencius also advises that individuals should not change their places to speak with one another, nor may they pass from their ranks to bow to one another in the court according to ritual propriety.[50] This indicates the man of virtue should live everywhere according to ritual propriety.

Thirdly, it is significant that Mencius mentions the matter of funeral in the dimension of ritual propriety. Through the *Book of Mencius*, the matter is frequently dealt with. Why did he focus on funeral in relation with the formation of moral self? In order to understand it, it is necessary to comprehend who were his counterparts such as Yang Zhu and Mo Di. Mencius states as follows:

> Once more, sage sovereigns cease to arise, and feudal lords give the reins to their lusts. Unemployed scholars indulge in unreasonable discussions. The words of Yang Zhu and Mo Di fill the Empire. The teachings current in the Empire are those of the school of Yang or of the school of Mo. Yang's principle is each one for himself, which does not acknowledge the claims of the sovereign. Mo's principle is to love all without discrimination,

---

48. *Mencius*, 3B3. As translated in Legge. 孟子曰：「丈夫生而願為之有室，女子生而願為之有家。父母之心，人皆有之。不待父母之命、媒妁之言，鑽穴隙相窺，踰牆相從，則父母國人皆賤之。古之人未嘗不欲仕也，又惡不由其道。不由其道而往者，與鑽穴隙之類也。」

49. *Mencius*, 5B7. As translated in Legge. 欲見賢人而不以其道，猶欲其入而閉之門也。夫義，路也；禮，門也。惟君子能由是路，出入是門也。

50. *Mencius*, 4B27. 禮，朝廷不歷位而相與言，不踰階而相揖也。我欲行禮，子敖以我為簡，不亦異乎？

which amounts to a denial of one's father. To ignore one's father on the one hand, and one's prince on the other, is to be no different from the beast ... If the principles of Yang and Mo be not stopped, and the principles of Confucius not set forth, then those perverse heresies will delude the people, and stop up the path of benevolence and righteousness. When benevolence and righteousness are stopped up, beasts will be led on to devour men, and men will devour one another. I am alarmed by these things, and address myself to the defense of the doctrines of the former sages, and to oppose Yang and Mo. I drive away their licentious expressions, so that such perverse speakers may not be able to show themselves. Their delusions spring up in men's minds, and do injury to their practice of affairs. Shown in their practice of affairs, they are pernicious to their government. When sages shall rise up again, they will not change my words.[51]

According to Mencius, political disorders in the Empire result from the principles of Yang Zhu and Mo Di, for their teachings ignore loyalty to one's king and filial piety to one's father contrary to the Way of sage kings. Mencius warns affairs and politics are interfered when their delusions spring up in men's minds. It is because holding to one point is the injury it does to the way of right principle by taking up one point and disregarding a hundred others.[52] Hence, he is convinced that "those who are fleeing from the errors of Mo naturally turn to Yang, and those who are fleeing from the errors of Yang naturally turn to Confucianism."[53] In this context, the purpose of his moral education is to defend the doctrines of the former sages such as Yu, Zhou Gong, and Confucius and rectify men's hearts by driving away Yang and Mo's licentious expressions. Mencius states:

> In former times, Yu repressed the vast waters of the inundation, and the country was reduced to order. Zhou Gong's achievements extended even to the barbarous tribes of the east and north, and he drove away all ferocious animals, and the people enjoyed repose. Confucius completed the *Spring and Autumn*

---

51. *Mencius*, 3B9. As translated in Legge. 聖王不作，諸侯放恣，處士橫議，楊朱、墨翟之言盈天下。天下之言，不歸楊，則歸墨。楊氏為我，是無君也；墨氏兼愛，是無父也。無父無君，是禽獸也。... 楊墨之道不息，孔子之道不著，是邪說誣民，充塞仁義也。仁義充塞，則率獸食人，人將相食。吾為此懼，閑先聖之道，距楊墨，放淫辭，邪說者不得作。作於其心，害於其事；作於其事，害於其政。聖人復起，不易吾言矣。

52. *Mencius*, 7A26. 為其賊道也，舉一而廢百也。

53. *Mencius*, 7B26. 逃墨必歸於楊，逃楊必歸於儒。

Annals, and rebellious ministers and villainous sons were struck with terror ... These father-deniers and king-deniers would have been smitten by Zhou Gong. I also wish to rectify men's hearts, and to put an end to those perverse doctrines, to oppose their one-sided actions and banish away their licentious expressions—and thus to carry on the work of the three sages. Do I do so because I am fond of disputing? I am compelled to do it. Whoever can, with words, combat Yang and Mo is a true disciple of the sages.[54]

As Mencius claims that the true disciple of the sages is the one who is verbally able to combat Yang and Mo, he himself heartily takes part in refuting them. Particularly, this is shown in a debate between Mencius and the Mohist Yi Zhi on funeral.[55] According to Yi Zhi, follow the way of frugality in funerals, for frugal funerals could change the customs of the

---

54. *Mencius*, 3B9. As translated in Legge. 「昔者禹抑洪水而天下平，周公兼夷狄驅猛獸而百姓寧，孔子成《春秋》而亂臣賊子懼。... 無父無君，是周公所膺也。我亦欲正人心，息邪說，距詖行，放淫辭，以承三聖者；豈好辯哉？予不得已也。能言距楊墨者，聖人之徒也。」

55. Behuniak thinks that it is wrong to read Mencius as expounding a fixed human nature which is essentially good. He denies the essentialist reading of the goodness of human nature in the Mencius and argues for a more dynamic possibility of the development of the seeds or sprouts, which he reads not as human nature but as "dispositions." This means that human beings cannot be said to possess an antecedent, predetermined, and natural end. More important to Mencius and the Confucians in general are the sensibilities that develop within the ideal family setting into which each and every human being is born. Given that for Mencius *shan* (善) as good is fundamentally relational, it is noticeable that Behuniak discusses the problem of the extension of family feeling (*xin* 心). The development of moral character involves "drawing out" or "extending" (*da* 達) the feelings that attend the spontaneous revulsion toward that which one cannot bear. In the Mencian framework, the "extension" of feeling is an integral expression of the growth of one's disposition (*xing* 性); "Feeling is the root of all human virtue for Mencius, and it is the engine that advances the human way. Human virtue emerges as the fruit of concrete, felt experiences. It does not emerge from anything outside of such experience." Mencius appeals to the sages as models (*fa* 法) of moral cultivation based on the filial piety they exhibit in their persons. According to Behuniak, Shun is offered as an exemplar of "family affection" (親). In terms of sages as exemplars of conduct, there seems to be no difference between Mencius and Mozi. However, for Mozi, the morality (*yi* 義) of sages is ultimately the expression of a standard (*fa* 法) far removed from the sages' own concrete circumstances, while for Mencius human virtue comes from particular humans. In spite of the importance of family affection, Mencius does not identify it as a sprout and it is more likely that family affection is the "soil" from which the "four sprouts" emerge. James Behuniak, *Mencius on Becoming Human* (Albany: State University of New York Press, 2005), 4, 23, 55, 69, 70.

kingdom. However, Mencius points out the limit of frugality in funerals in connection with filial piety.[56] In the most ancient times, according to him, there were some who did not bury their parents. When their parents died, they took them up and threw them into some water-channel. Afterwards, when passing by them, they saw foxes and wild-cats devouring them, and flies and gnats biting at them. The perspiration started out upon their foreheads, and they looked away, unable to bear the sight. Mencius shows it was not on account of other people that this perspiration flowed, for it was an outward expression of their innermost heart. Hence, they instantly went home, and came back with baskets and spades and covered the bodies. Through this story, Mencius demonstrates the filial sons and virtuous men ought to act in accordance with ritual propriety if it was truly right for them to bury the remains of their parents. In this context, Mencius buried his mother with a good coffin unlike the Mohists, for he thought the man of virtue would not skimp on expenditure where his parents are concerned.[57] According to him, contrary to high antiquity where there was no rule for the size of either the inner or the outer coffin, in middle antiquity the inner coffin was made seven inches thick, and the outer one the same. This was done by all, from the sovereign to the common people, and not simply for the beauty of the appearance, but because they thus satisfied the filial piety of their hearts. It is because there is no satisfaction to the natural feelings of a man, in preventing the earth from getting near to the bodies of his dead. Mencius warns that men cannot have the feeling of pleasure if prevented by statutory regulations from making their coffins as the Mohists suggests. Fundamentally, Mencius' emphasis on funerals is based on his understanding of filial piety in connection with ritual propriety as Zeng defines it. Mencius states:

> When parents are alive, they should be served according to ritual propriety; when they are dead, they should be buried according to ritual propriety; and they should be sacrificed to according to ritual propriety—this may be called filial piety.[58]

56. *Mencius*, 3A5. 蓋上世嘗有不葬其親者。其親死，則舉而委之於壑。他日過之，狐狸食之，蠅蚋姑嘬之。其顙有泚，睨而不視。夫泚也，非為人泚，中心達於面目。蓋歸反虆梩而掩之。掩之誠是也，則孝子仁人之掩其親，亦必有道矣。

57. *Mencius*, 2B7. 曰：「古者棺椁無度，中古棺七寸，椁稱之。自天子達於庶人。非直為觀美也，然後盡於人心。不得，不可以為悅；無財，不可以為悅。得之為有財，古之人皆用之，吾何為獨不然？且比化者，無使土親膚，於人心獨無恔乎？吾聞之君子：不以天下儉其親。」

58. *Mencius*, 3A2. Translation adapted from Legge. 曾子曰：『生事之以禮；死

Hence, he claims that "the nourishment of parents when living is not sufficient to be accounted the great thing. It is only in the performing their obsequies when dead that we have what can be considered the great thing."[59] For him, in discharging the funeral duties to parents, men indeed feel constrained to do their utmost.[60] Furthermore, as Mencius makes an emphasis on sacrifice after burying according to ritual propriety, he presents to hold three years as the mourning period, mourning dress made of rough hemp with a hem, the eating of nothing but rice gruel, for these were observed in the Three Dynasties by men of all conditions alike from the sovereign to the mass of the people.[61] Compared to the Mohists, the funeral procession guided by Mencius seems to be ineffective. Nevertheless, why did Mencius stress funeral according to ritual propriety? When the duke Ding of Teng died, the prince tried to do the three years' morning. In contrary to his desire, all his officers opposed to his plan. Regarding this concern, Mencius advised to him as follows:

> In this matter the solution cannot be sought elsewhere. Confucius said, "When a prince dies, his successor entrusts the administration to the prime minister. He sips the congee. His face is of a deep black. He approaches the place of mourning, and weeps. Of all the officers and inferior ministers there is not one who will presume not to join in the lamentation, he setting them this example. What the superior loves, his inferiors will be found to love exceedingly. The relation between superiors and inferiors is like that between the wind and grass. The grass must bend when the wind blows upon it." The business depends on the will of the prince.[62]

Mencius urges the prince to do three years mourning with a firm will. It is because conducting funeral according to ritual propriety as moral education could lead to political authority just as highly respected old men such as Bo Yi and Tai Gong decided to follow king Wen as soon

---

葬之以禮，祭之以禮，可謂孝矣。』

59. *Mencius*, 4B13. As translated in Legge. 孟子曰：「養生者不足以當大事，惟送死可以當大事。」

60. *Mencius*, 3A2. 親喪固所自盡也

61. *Mencius*, 3A2. 三年之喪，齊疏之服，飦粥之食，自天子達於庶人，三代共之。

62. *Mencius*, 3A2. As translated in Legge. 孟子曰：「然。不可以他求者也。孔子曰：『君薨，聽於冢宰，歠粥，面深墨。即位而哭，百官有司，莫敢不哀，先之也。』上有好者，下必有甚焉者矣。『君子之德，風也；小人之德，草也。草尚之風必偃。』是在世子。」

as they heard of the rise of him, for they heard that he knows well how to nourish the old with sincerity.[63] His people, as Mencius presents, will follow what the sovereign loves just as the grass must bend when the wind blows upon it. This indicates that filial piety could be the source of political authority. According to Mencius, those who wish to win the confidence of their sovereign ought to make their parents pleased. How can they make their parents pleased? Mencius highlights the value of "sincerity" (誠) in serving parents just as he stresses honoring and respecting in treating a scholar since to feed a scholar and not love him is to treat him as a pig and to love him and not respect him is to keep him as a domestic animal.[64] Given that there has never been a man possessed of complete sincerity who did not move others, sincerity is the pivotal attitude in filial piety. Contrary to the Mohists, Mencius insists customs in the kingdom can be changed by sincere funeral procession rather than frugal one. For Mencius, thinking of how to be sincere is the way of man. In this context, he regards sincerity as the way of Heaven in that understanding what is good is a way to the attainment of sincerity in one's self.[65] Therefore, Mencius asks the prince to do three years mourning with a firm will in the dimension of sincerity, for the good is practicing filial piety which is the source of political authority. From the perspective of Mencius, this shows the absence of the true good in Mohism. In the debate between Mencius and Yi Zhi, a Mohist on funeral, this issue can be deeply expounded through the matter of graded love as follows:

> Yi Zhi said "The Confucians praised the ancient rulers for acting as if they were watching over an infant. What does this expression mean? To me it sounds that we are to love all without difference of degree; but the manifestation of love must begin with our parents."... Mencius said "Does Yi Zhi truly believe that a man's affection for the child of his brother is merely like his affection for the infant of a neighbor? What is to be approved in that expression is simply this: that if an infant crawling about is likely to fall into a well, it is no crime in the infant. Moreover, Heaven gives birth to creatures in such a way that they have one root, and Yi Zhi makes them to have two roots. This is the cause of his error."[66]

63. *Mencius*, 4A13. 吾聞西伯善養老者。
64. *Mencius*, 7A37. 食而弗愛，豕交之也；愛而不敬，獸畜之也。恭敬者，幣之未將者也。
65. *Mencius*, 4A12. 誠身有道：不明乎善，不誠其身矣。是故誠者，天之道也；思誠者，人之道也。
66. *Mencius*, 3A5. As translated in Legge. 夷子曰：「儒者之道，古之人『若保

Notwithstanding his emphasis on frugal funeral, as Mencius points out, Yi Zhi ironically gave his parents lavish burials. With regard to Mencius' critique, Yi Zhi defends by combining his Mohist commitment to universal love with this Mencian idea of benevolence as an apology for his own act of filial piety. Regarding to this argument, Mencius points out that Yi Zhi misunderstood the parable of the "child in peril" as a case of natural compassion shown to any child. Mencius argues under more normal or less urgent circumstances one would not love all children equally. One naturally loves a nephew more than a neighbor's child. According to Mencius, we learn to love the neighbor's child as an extension of the love we feel for our nephew. In this context, Mencius stresses "one root" of Heaven which is naturally graded in his moral universe. This indicates that Heaven produced the natural distinctions of superior and inferior.[67] It is not some homogeneous substance found in all things as Taoist and Buddhist would have it.[68] Mencius makes an emphasis on the order of love in connection with living creatures, people, and parents:

> In regard to living creatures, the man of virtue loves them but show no benevolence towards them. In regard to people generally, he shows benevolence towards them but not affectionate. He is affectionate to his parents, but is merely benevolent towards the people. He is benevolent towards the people but is merely love living creatures.[69]

For example, the benevolence of Yao and Shun did not extend to love everything. Instead, they earnestly devoted themselves to what was important and good and wise men.[70] In other words, even such sages did not conduct love without discrimination. In Mencius' ritual propriety, three years' mourning is regarded as one of important priorities. Hence, he demonstrates for a man to observe meticulously three years mourning, while failing to observe three years' mourning, or for him to ask whether he is guilty of breaking the food with his teeth while bolting

---

赤子』，此言何謂也？之則以為愛無差等，施由親始。」... 孟子曰：「夫夷子，信以為人之親其兄之子為若親其鄰之赤子乎？彼有取爾也。赤子匍匐將入井，非赤子之罪也。且天之生物也，使之一本，而夷子二本故也。」

67. Whalen Lai, "In defence of graded love three parables from Mencius," *Asian Philosophy* 1 (Spring 1991), 57.

68. Ibid., 57.

69. *Mencius*, 7A45. Translation adapted from Lau and Legge. 孟子曰：「君子之於物也，愛之而弗仁；於民也，仁之而弗親。親親而仁民，仁民而愛物。」

70. *Mencius*, 7A46. 堯舜之仁不遍愛人，急親賢也。

down his food and drink is for him to show an ignorance of priorities.[71] For Mencius, three years' mourning is ritual propriety.

AUGUSTINE'S SACRAMENT

Confucius and Mencius stress human efforts such as ritual propriety in order to cultivate moral self. By comparison Augustine did not insist that personal effort alone can take care of soul in attaining happiness. For Augustine there is a complex relationship between the formation of moral self and the grace of God in which ritual as well as the interior life, and contemplation, play significant roles. In the following exposition, I will unfold the relevant passages of Augustine on the role ritual of moral formation in order to highlight the contrast with the emphasis on ritual propriety in Confucius and Mencius as well as music. The key question I intend to address is where and how grace enters into his account. It is also an interesting question to ask if there is any equivalent to the role of grace in Confucius and Mencius or if their accounts solely reliant on outward mimesis having an interior effort in forming the moral self toward the Way. Though partaking in the sacraments, we are ordered to God rather than to self.[72] As Augustine states that "there can be no religious society, whether the religion be true or false, without some sacrament or visible symbol to serve as a bond of union,"[73] he initially has a very broad understanding of sacrament. But especially through his debate with the Manichees, the Donatists, and Pelagians his sacrament shows its clarity. In this section, Augustine's baptism and marriage as sacraments and music are intensively expounded in relation to formation of moral self.

Baptism: Forgiveness of Sins and Starting Point of Salvation

Many research of Augustine concentrates on the inward drama of conversion in *Confessions*, but Augustine himself saw the event of baptism as having equal or in all likelihood greater importance in comparison with the moment of conversion. Augustine was not baptized until age thirty-three. In *Confessions*, he describes the dramatic journey of his

71. *Mencius*, 7A46. Translation adapted from Lau. 不能三年之喪，而緦小功之察；放飯流歠，而問無齒決，是之謂不知務。

72. Herdt, *Putting on Virtue*, 67.

73. *c. Faust.* 19.11.

conversion. He had been made catechumen in his child, and would have undergone the traditional rite of entry. Augustine states:

> While still a boy I had been told of the eternal life promised to us by Our Lord, who humbled himself and came down amongst us proud sinners. As a catechumen, I was blessed regularly from birth with the sign of the Cross and was seasoned with God's salt, for, O Lord, my mother placed great hope in you.[74]

However, Augustine delayed his baptism as his ill was quickly recovered as follows:

> Once as a child I was taken suddenly ill with a disorder of the stomach and was on the point of death. You, my God, were my guardian even then, and you saw the fervor and strength of my faith as I appealed to the piety of my own mother and to the mother of us all, your Church, to give me the baptism of Christ your Son, who is my God and my Master. My earthly mother was deeply anxious, because in the pure faith of her heart, she was in greater labor to ensure my eternal salvation than she had been at my birth. Had I not quickly recovered, she would have hastened to see that I was admitted to the sacraments of salvation and washed clean by acknowledging you, Lord Jesus, for the pardon of my sins. So my washing in the waters of baptism was postponed.[75]

As a catechumen, Augustine would have been considered a Christian and a member of the church even though he was not baptized yet. While in Carthage in his late teens, Augustine left the Catholic Church and joined the Manichees. When he arrived in Milan in 384 as a Manichee and city orator, he began to attend the sermons of Ambrose, the Christian bishop of Milan. Augustine was deeply impressed not only by his rhetoric but especially by his philosophical and exegetical sophistication. Soon after, he gave up the Manichees and began to consider himself Christian catechumen as follows:

> Next I tried my utmost to find some certain proof which would convict the Manichees of falsehood. If I had been able to conceive of a spiritual substance, all their inventions would at once have been disproved and rejected from my mind. But this I could not do. However, the more I thought about the material

---

74. *conf.* 1.11.17.
75. *conf.* 1.11.17.

> world and the whole of nature, as far as we can be aware of it through our bodily senses, and the more I took stock of the various theories, the more I began to think that the opinions of the majority of the philosophers were most likely to be true. So, treating everything as a matter of doubt, as the Academics are generally supposed to do, and hovering between one doctrine and another, I made up my mind at least to leave the Manichees, for while I was in this state of indecision I did not think it right to remain in the sect now that I found the theories of some of the philosophers preferable. Nevertheless I utterly refused to entrust the healing of the maladies of my soul to these philosophers, because they ignored the saving name of Christ. I therefore decided to remain a catechumen in the Catholic Church, which was what my parents wanted, at least until I could clearly see a light to guide my steps.[76]

However, even after listening to Ambrose's sermon, he postponed receiving baptism again. Augustine still pursued the advance of his career. Only after his dramatic conversion experience in the garden in the summer of 386 he wrote to Ambrose with acknowledging his past errors and formally put in his name for baptism as follows:

> When the autumn vacation was over, I notified the people of Milan that they must find another vendor of words for their students, because I had chosen to be your servant and also because the difficulty I had in breathing and the pain in my lungs made me unfit for the duties of a professor. I wrote to your bishop, the saintly Ambrose, to tell him of my past errors and the purpose I now had in mind. I asked him to advise me which books of Scripture it would be best for me to study, so that I might be better prepared and more fitted to receive so great a grace. He told me to read the prophet Isaiah, presumably because the Gospel and the calling of the gentiles are foretold more clearly in that book than in any other. But I did not understand the first chapters and, on the assumption that the rest of the book would be equally difficult, I laid it aside to be taken up again later, when I should be more used to the style in which God's word is spoken.[77]

Eventually, at the Easter vigil, 24-25 April 387, Augustine was baptized. "While the term baptism can refer specifically to the rite of

---

76. *conf.* 5.14.25.
77. *conf.* 9.5.13.

immersion, patristic authors often used it to refer to the whole complex of initiation rites that took place at the Easter vigil, including what we now call confirmation."[78] He was joined by his son, Adeodatus, and his friend Alypius. In the *Confessions*, he discusses nothing of the ceremonial, emphasizing instead the inner intensity of the experience. Augustine states:

> We were baptized, and all anxiety over the past melted away from us. The days were all too short, for I was lost in wonder and joy, meditating upon your far-reaching providence for the salvation of the human race. The tears flowed from me when I heard your hymns and canticles, for the sweet singing of your Church moved me deeply. The music surged in my ears, truth seeped into my heart, and my feelings of devotion overflowed, so that the tears streamed down. But they were tears of gladness.[79]

Why was Augustine happy by baptism? It is because for Augustine baptism is the way in which God's grace acts on us to forgive and wash away of all previous our sins, and the beginning of membership in the church, the body of Christ here on Earth, oriented toward its heavenly head, that is, Christ. For Augustine baptism as a sacrament is the starting point of forgiving sins while for Confucius and Mencius ritual propriety make it possible to return to benevolence and righteousness. For Augustine, Christ is the one who opens up the way to our heavenly country by forgiving our sins. Augustine states:

> when we are on the way, and that not a way that lies through space, but through a change of affections, and one which the guilt of our past sins like a hedge of thorns barred against us, what could He, who was willing to lay Himself down as the way by which we should return, do that would be still gracious and more merciful, except to forgive us all our sins, and by being crucified for us to remove the stern decrees that barred the door against our return?[80]

Without this cleansing bath, humans are still trapped in sin, and will receive no real benefit from any of the spiritual exercises. Augustine writes on the forgiveness of sins by baptism as follows:

---

78. William Harmless, "Baptism," in *Augustine through the Ages: An Encyclopedia*, ed. Allan D. Fitzgerald (Cambridge: Wm. B. Eerdmans Publishing Company, 1999), 84.

79. *conf.* 9.6.14.

80. *disc. Chr.* 1.17.16.

If this were not to be had in the Church, there would be no hope. If the forgiveness of sins were not to be had in the Church, there would be no hope of a future life and eternal liberation. We thank God, who gave his Church such a gift. Here you are; you are going to come to the holy font, you will be washed in saving baptism, you will be renewed in *the bath of rebirth* (Ti 3:5), you will be without any sin at all as you come up from that bath. All the things that were plaguing you in the past will there be blotted out. Your sins will be like the Egyptians, hard on the heels of the Israelites; pursuing them, but only as far as the Red Sea. What does it mean, as far as the Red Sea? As far as the font, consecrated by the cross and blood of Christ . . . That's why baptism is signed with the sign of Christ.[81]

Augustine frequently draws on the image of the exodus to explain baptism. Just as the Israelites had passed through the Red Sea while the pursuing Egyptians were drowned, the candidates would pass through the Red Sea of baptism, a sea reddened and consecrated by the blood of Christ, while their sins would be left to drown in the waters of the font.[82] For Augustine baptism that provides the only hope of human salvation is efficacious ritual of purification committed to the reality of the Catholic Church's social role as divinely ordained custodian of grace on Earth.[83] However, Augustine does not regard baptism as the completion on the way of salvation. He is against those who overemphasize the effects of baptism:

> For they fail to observe that men severally become sons of God when they begin to live in newness of spirit, and to be renewed as to the inner man after the image of Him that created them. For it is not from the moment of a man's baptism that all his old infirmity is destroyed, but renovation begins with the remission of all his sins, and so far as he who is now wise is spiritually wise.[84]

Baptism gives us new start on the way of salvation and the full renewal of the image of God within our minds is only completed in the afterlife. This indicates that we need to struggle for the rest of our lives with the will to evil which remains in us after baptism.[85] The road to

---

81. *s.* 213.9.

82. Harmless, "Baptism," 88.

83. Stalnaker, *Overcoming Our Evil*, 210.

84. *pecc. mer.* 2.7.9. trans. Roland J. Teske, S.J. in *a Translation for the 21st Century*, vol. I/23 (New York: New City Press, 1997). Hereafter I use this translation.

85. G. R. Evans, *Augustine on Evil* (Cambridge: Cambridge University Press,

perfection so long that Augustine questions whether anyone comes to the end of it in this life.

Fundamentally, Augustine developed theology of baptism in his debate with the Donatists. When Augustine returned to Africa in 388, church was divided. The Donatist Church, born of the disputes which followed the Diocletianic persecution about the validity of sacraments conducted by those alleged to have been guilty of the sin of *traditio*, but with a lineage extending back to the days of St Cyprian and reflecting only too well the stormy African temperament, had, in three-quarters of a century, grown and expanded until it more than equaled the Catholic as the church of Africa.[86] According to Bonner, whereas the Catholics were indissolubly related in the eyes of the African peasant with the Roman state, the pagan oppressor, the Donatists were the sons of the martyrs, members of a church which had never compromised with the godless tyrant but had retained that spirit of defiance, implicit in the fulminations of Tertullian and expressed in the life and death of the great Cyprian, the hero of all Africans, to whom Catholic and Donatist alike looked as the doctor of the African Church.[87] The Donatists maintain two positions that they had inherited from Cyprian.[88] First, there is no salvation outside the Church, for if one is to have God as Father, one must first have the Church as Mother. Second, baptism given by heretics can have no validity, since heretics who cannot possess the Holy Spirit cannot give what they do not have. The Donatists claimed that Catholics had descended from those who had betrayed the church during the persecution of Diocletian and were therefore not just sinners, but traitors, the "church of Judas." Therefore, Donatists routinely rebaptized converts from the Catholic camp.

Against such views Augustine developed three key positions in his treatise *On Baptism against Donatists*.[89] Firstly, he demonstrated that the purity of the minister was irrelevant, that it was the purity and power of Christ that made baptism effective. Much of Augustine's teachings on the sacraments were in response to the Donatists' misleading views on the theology of the sacraments. The Donatists had taught that the validity and

---

1982), 162.

86. Gerald Bonner, *St Augustine of Hippo: Life and Controversies* (Norwich: Canterbury Press, 2002), 237.

87. Bonner, *St Augustine of Hippo*, 238.

88. Harmless, "Baptism," 88.

89. Ibid., 89.

the proper operation of the sacraments depended on the state of the minister of the sacraments whom they regarded as the giver, if not the subject of the sacraments. They also believed that the origin (*origo*), root (*radix*) and head (*caput*) of the baptized person is none other than the human minister by whom he is baptized. Such a doctrinally incorrect position on the sacraments not only undermined the credibility and the authority of Christ as the sole giver and subject of baptism, but was also largely seen as the root cause of rebaptism blasphemy which was a characteristic error of the Donatists in African Christianity.[90] Augustine wrote:

> Nor is the water "profane and adulterous" over which the name of God is invoked, even though it be invoked by profane and adulterous persons; because neither the creature itself of water, nor the name invoked, is adulterous. But the baptism of Christ, consecrated by the words of the gospel, is necessarily holy, however polluted and unclean its ministers may be; because its inherent sanctity cannot be polluted, and the divine excellence abides in its sacrament, whether to the salvation of those who use it aright, or to the destruction of those who use it wrong. Would you indeed maintain that, while the light of the sun or of a candle, diffused through unclean places, contracts no foulness in itself therefrom, yet the baptism of Christ can be defiled by the sins of any man, whatsoever he may be? For if we turn our thoughts to the visible materials themselves, which are to us the medium of the sacraments, everyone must know that they admit of corruption. But if we think on that which they convey to us, who can fail to see that it is incorruptible, however much the men through whose ministry it is conveyed are either being rewarded or punished for the character of their lives?[91]

Augustine's view of the sacraments is based upon the conception of Christ, the high priest without sin, who is the sole giver of sacramental grace because to Him alone belongs the power of conferring it, but who administers it by human agents. What these administer is the baptism of Christ, whose sanctity cannot be corrupted by unworthy ministers, any more than the light of the sun is corrupted by shining through a sewer. Like water passing through a stone irrigation channel, the power of

---

90. Victor N. Mbanisi, "Baptism and the Ideal of Unity and Universality of the Church in St. Augustine's Ecclesiology: An Exposition of His Theology of Baptism in Light of Donatist Controversy" (Ph.D. diss., Fordham University, 2000), 140-41.

91. *bapt.* 3.10.15. trans. J. R. King in *Nicene and Post-Nicene Fathers*, vol. 4 (New York: Christian Literature Publishing Co., 1887). Hereafter I use this translation.

Christ passes through a sinful minister unpolluted and bears fruit in the recipient. A little consideration will demonstrate this, since we are well aware that the materials with which the sacraments are administered-water, wine, bread, and the like-are corruptible, but the grace which they convey is not corruptible. So it is with human ministers; good or bad, their character does not affect the validity of the sacrament.[92] In the *In Johannis evangelium tractatus*, Augustine expounds this matter by draws upon John 1:33 as follows:

> Still living in the darkness of this life, we are walking by the lamp of faith; let us too hold on to the lamp which John was, let us use it also to put Christ's enemies to confusion; or rather, let him confound his enemies himself with his own lamp. Let us also ask the question which the Lord put to the Jew, let us ask it and say, John's baptism, where is it from? From heaven or from men? What are they going to say? If they say, "From men." Even their own people will stone them; while if they say, "From heaven," we will say to them, *Why then did you not believe him?* Perhaps they say, "We do believe him." "Then how can you say that you are the ones who baptize, and John says, *This is the one who baptizes?*" "But," they say, "the ministers of such a great judge, the ministers through whom baptism is given, should be just." I too say (and we all say) that the ministers of such a great judge should be just. Let the ministers be just if they are willing; but if they are not willing to be just-those who occupy the chair of Moses-my master, about whom his Spirit said, This is the one who baptizes, has assured me. How has he assured me? The scribes and Pharisees, he said, occupy the chair of Moses; do what they say, but do not do what they do; for they say and do not do (Mt 23:2-3). If the minister is just, I regard him as I regard Paul, as I regard Peter; with them do I count ministers who are just because ministers who are really just do not seek their own glory; they are, after all, ministers; they do not want to be taken for judges; they shudder at the thought of hope being placed in themselves. So I reckon the just minister as one with Paul. After all, what does Paul say? I planted, Apollos wanted; but God caused the growth. Neither the one who plants not the one who waters is anything, but God is the one who causes the growth. (1 Cor 3:6-7) Yes, a proud minister is to be aligned with Zabulus, but Christ's gift is not contaminated; what flows through the minister remains pure, the liquid that passes through him reaches fertile soil. Think of the proud minister as made of stone, because he cannot produce

---

92. Bonner, *St Augustine of Hippo*, 292.

fruit when watered; and the water passes along a stone channel, the water passes along to the little garden beds. It produces no fruit in the stone channel, but nonetheless it makes the gardens very fruitful indeed. The spiritual power of the sacrament, you see, is like light; and it is received pure by those to be enlightened, and if it passes through tainted beings, it is not defiled. Certainly let the ministers be just and not seek their own glory but the glory of the one whose ministers they are. Let them not say, "It is my baptism," because it is not theirs. Let them pay attention to John himself. John was full of the Holy Spirit, and he had a baptism from heaven, not from men. But up to when did he have it? He said himself, Prepare a way for the Lord. But, when he was made known, the Lord himself became the way; there was no longer any need for the baptism of John which prepared a way for the Lord.[93]

Augustine demonstrates that the sacrament of holy baptism is of God and not of men. He relativized the importance and the status of the minister of baptism (just as Optatus did) by likening him to an instrument rather than the causal agent or the source of grace and the origin of baptism itself. He reminded the Donatists that baptism, which is an exclusive property of Christ, is neither characteristically ascribed to any human agent nor is it an attribute of any minister. In other words, it is never called the baptism of Caecilianus, or of Donatus, or of Petilianus, or even of himself, Augustine, but essentially the baptism of Christ.[94]

Secondly, Augustine claimed that baptism marked one as belonging to the flock of Christ in an indelible way, what he called the "dominicus character." The analogy he often appealed to was a military one. Roman soldiers received brand, known as a *stigma*, on the back of the right hand. Just as soldiers who deserted were not re-tattooed, so those who received baptism outside the church were not to be rebaptized. Augustine states:

> Further, if any one fails to understand how it can be that we assert that the sacrament is not rightly conferred among the Donatists, while we confess that it exists among them, let him observe that we also deny that it exists rightly among them, just as they deny that it exists rightly among those who quit their communion. Let him also consider the analogy of the military mark, which, though it can both be retained, as by deserters,

---

93. *Jo. ev. tr.* 5.15.

94. Mbanisi, "Baptism and the Ideal of Unity and Universality of the Church in St. Augustine's Ecclesiology," 142.

and, also be received by those who are not in the army, yet ought not to be either received or retained outside its ranks; and, at the same time, it is not changed or renewed when a man is enlisted or brought back to his service. However, we must distinguish between the case of those who unwittingly join the ranks of these heretics, under the impression that they are entering the true Church of Christ, and those who know that there is no other Catholic Church save that which, according to the promise, is spread abroad throughout the whole world, and extends even to the utmost limits of the earth.[95]

Augustine was careful not to adopt and appropriate the Donatists' popular slogan or practice of referring to baptism frequently as the "baptism of heretics" or the "Catholic baptism." He repeatedly identified baptism specifically as the baptism of Christ. That is, for him, there is nothing like the baptism of heretics in the strict sense. It is basically the baptism of Christ administered by the heretics. Therefore, Augustine admitted that Donatists possessed valid baptism, that they bore the brand-mark of Christ; but since they had broken from the unity of the church, they were in effect deserters from the militia of Christ.[96]

Therefore Cyprian writes to Jubaianus as follows, "concerning the baptism of heretics, who, being placed without, and set down out of the Church," seem to him to "claim to themselves a matter over which they have neither right nor power. Which we," he says, "cannot account valid or lawful, since it is clear that among them it is unlawful." Neither, indeed, do we deny that a man who is baptized among heretics, or in any schism outside the Church, derives no profit from it so far as he is partner in the perverseness of the heretics and schismatics; nor do we hold that those who baptize, although they confer the real true sacrament of baptism, are yet acting rightly, in gathering adherents outside the Church, and entertaining opinions contrary to the Church. But it is one thing to be without a sacrament, another thing to be in possession of it wrongly, and to usurp it unlawfully. Therefore they do not cease to be sacraments of Christ and the Church, merely because they are unlawfully used, not only by heretics, but by all kinds of wicked and impious persons. These, indeed, ought to be corrected and punished, but the sacraments should be acknowledged and revered.[97]

95. *bapt.* 1.4.5.
96. Harmless, "Baptism," 89.
97. *bapt.* 3.10.13.

Augustine further argued that there are not two baptisms. For him, the just and the unjust have not two different baptisms but only one baptism, and he believed that both heretics and schismatics, as well as Donatists and Catholics, all equally and commonly possessed and administered the one baptism of Christ. He maintained that baptism, strictly speaking, is not putting on the Donatist or the Catholic Church, but it is putting on Christ. Augustine did not regard a baptized person as having been converted unto the minister that baptized him, "but unto the living God"; nor did he the recipient of baptism believe in the minister; "but in the Father, the Son, and the Holy Ghost," Augustine insisted. The baptism of Christ according to Augustine does not make one a heretic or a schismatic, it is rather, the wicked perfidy of separation from the unity of the Church that does that.[98] The Donatist attempt to defend rebaptism by the example of Apostle Paul at Ephesus, who caused certain men who had been baptized with the baptism of John to be baptized with the baptism of Christ, is wholly misleading, since that Apostle did not reiterate the baptism of John but gave the baptism of Christ to those who lacked it. The schismatic and the heretic are in a quite different situation. The baptism they receive is the baptism of Christ, and it is not the Christian sacraments which they receive which make them heretical but their wicked separation. For this reason, Augustine does not command the Donatists to cease to give the sacraments, but to cease to give them in separation; nor does he forbid their lay people to cease to receive, but to cease to receive in separation; nor does he forbid their lay people to cease to receive, but to cease to receive in separation. Indeed, he lays it down as a principle that, in a case of extreme necessity, a Catholic catechumen who cannot find a Catholic priest may receive baptism from a Donatist, so long as he guards in his heart the Catholic peace. If he should then die, the Catholic Church will reckon him among her members; and if he should survive and return to a Catholic congregation, his action will not merely be condemned but will be applauded.[99]

Thirdly, Augustine distinguished between the validity of baptism and its fruitfulness. By this distinction Augustine would claim that the Donatists were validly baptized, but they would not enjoy the fruits of baptism—forgiveness of sins, eternal life—unless they ended their schism and rejoined the church as follows:

98. Mbanisi, "Baptism and the Ideal of Unity and Universality of the Church in St. Augustine's Ecclesiology," 143.

99. Bonner, *St Augustine of Hippo*, 293.

"Can the power of baptism," says Cyprian, "be greater or better than confession? Than martyrdom? That a man should confess Christ before men, and be baptized in his own blood? And yet," he goes on to say, "neither does this baptism profit the heretic, even though for confessing Christ he be put to death outside the Church." This is most true; for, by being put to death outside the Church, he is proved not to have had charity, of which the apostle says, "Though I give my body to be burned, and have not charity, it profits me nothing." (1 Co 13:3) But if martyrdom is of no avail for this reason, because it has not charity, neither does it profit those who, as Paul says, and Cyprian further sets forth, are living within the Church without charity in envy and malice; and yet they can both receive and transmit true baptism. "Salvation," he says, "is not without the Church." Who says that it is? And therefore, whatever men have that belongs to the Church, it profits them nothing towards salvation outside the Church. But it is one thing not to have, another to have so as to be of no use. He who has not must be baptized that he may have; but he who has to no avail must be corrected, that what he has may profit him. Nor is the water in the baptism of heretics "adulterous," because neither is the creature itself which God made evil, nor is fault to be found with the words of the gospel in the mouths of any who are astray; but the fault is theirs in whom there is an adulterous spirit, even though it may receive the adornment of the sacrament from a lawful spouse. Baptism therefore can "be common to us, and the heretics," just as the gospel can be common to us, whatever difference there may be between our faith and their error—whether they think otherwise than the truth about the Father, or the Son, or the Holy Spirit; or, being cut away from unity, do not gather with Christ, but scatter abroad, (Mt 12:30)—seeing that the sacrament of baptism can be common to us, if we are the wheat of the Lord, with the covetous within the Church, and with robbers, and drunkards, and other pestilent persons of the same sort, of whom it is said, "They shall not inherit the kingdom of God,"(1 Co 6:10) and yet the vices by which they are separated from the kingdom of God are not shared by us.[100]

Because his theology represented a break from the traditional theology of North Africa, Augustine found it important to explain why Cyprian and other venerable figures had denied that heretics or schismatics could validly baptize.

100. *bapt.* 4.17.25.

Along with debate with Donatists, it is necessary to take a look at controversy with the Pelagians in the dimension of caring for infant's soul. This indicates that Augustine paid attend to infants as well as adults while Confucius and Mencius offer moral education for adults. A pivotal aspect of Augustine's debate with the Pelagians was the interpretation of infant baptism. In 411, he faced a tribunal headed by Aurelius, Augustine's friend and episcopal colleague in Carthage when Caelestius, one of Pelagius disciples, applied to be ordained for the church of Carthage. At this tribunal Paulinus, a deacon from Milan and Ambrose's biographer, accused Caelestius of unorthodox stances: that the sin of Adam injured no one but himself and that newborn infants are in that state which Adam was in before the fall. While Caelestius was willing to grant the legitimacy of infant baptism, he was unwilling to accept that the transmission of original sin was part of Christian teaching.[101] Augustine wrote:

> And I suspect that there are still some here, especially in Carthage, but they now whisper in hiding, fearing the most well-founded faith of the Church. For in the church of the same city one of them by the name of Caelestius had already deviously begun to seek the honor of the priesthood, but he was brought by the solid faith and freedom of the brothers straight to an episcopal court on account of these discourses opposed to the grace of Christ. He was, however, forced to confess that infants must be baptized because they too need redemption. Although at the time he refused to say there anything more explicit about original sin, he did, nonetheless, do considerable harm to his position by the mention of redemption.[102]

In *On the Merits and Remission of Sins and on the Baptism of Infants* and *On the Grace of Christ and Original Sin,* Augustine argues that Jesus and the apostles handed down the church's practice of infant baptism in the aspect of the remission of sin.[103] If infants were baptized, then they were baptized for the remission of some sin:

> Catholic Church . . . truly baptizes infants for the remission of sins—not, indeed, sins which they have committed by imitation owing to the example of the first sinner, but sins which

---

101. Harmless, "Baptism," 89.
102. *ep.* 157.22.
103. *pecc. mer.* 1.26.39.

they have contracted by their very birth, owing to the corruption of their origin.[104]

Early in the debate Augustine suggested that unbaptized infants were not saved, though he conceded that they would suffer only "the mildest condemnation of all":

> Accordingly, one can correctly say that little ones who leave the body without baptism will be under the mildest condemnation of all. But one who preaches that they will not be under any condemnation misleads others very much and is himself very mistaken. For the apostle says, *Judgment starts from one sin and leads to condemnation* (Rom 5:16) and a little later, *The sin of one led to the condemnation of all human beings* (Rom 5:18).[105]

What deeply offended him in Pelagian claims about infant sinlessness was that such claims implicitly denied that Jesus had saved infants, for if they were truly sinless, then there would be nothing for him to save them from.[106] Augustine states:

> Those who say that infancy has nothing in it for Jesus to save, are denying that Christ is Jesus for all believing infants. Those, I repeat, who say that infancy has nothing in it for Jesus to save, are saying nothing else than that for believing infants, infants that is who have been baptized in Christ, Christ the Lord is not Jesus. After all, what is Jesus? Jesus means Savior. Jesus is the Savior. Those whom he doesn't save, having nothing to save in them, well for them he isn't Jesus. Well now, if you can tolerate the idea that Christ is not Jesus for some persons who have been baptized, then I'm not sure your faith can be recognized as according with the sound rule. Yes, they're infants, but they are his members. They're infants, but they receive his sacraments. They are infants, but they share in his table, in order to have life in themselves.[107]

With regard to the Pelagians' argument that infant baptism is unnecessary and meaningless, Augustine stresses that Christ must have died for infants as "the Savior"; "After all, *Christ died for sinners* (Rom 5:6). But, if they are not held by any bond of sinfulness stemming from

---

104. *gr. et pecc. or.* 2.17. trans. Roland J. Teske, S.J. in *a Translation for the 21st Century*, vol. I/23 (New York: New City Press, 1997). Hereafter I use this translation.
105. *pecc. mer.* 1.16.21.
106. Harmless, "Baptism," 90.
107. *s.* 174.7.

their origin, how did Christ, who died for the sinners, die for these infants who obviously have done nothing sinful in their own lives?"[108] In fact, he took the anxiety of mothers who brought their children for baptism and the crying of the infants themselves as signs of the inner yearning for the liberation that only Christ could bring. By their baptism, infants came to enjoy the "benefits of the Mediator": they were delivered from evil from evil, reconciled with God, enlightened by the Spirit, and incorporated into the body of Christ, the church.[109]

Marriage: Procreation, Fidelity, and Sacramental Bond

Augustine's thought on marriage developed throughout his lifetime. His thought on marriage developed as the result of dealing with these different situations and controversies. Augustine reflected upon marriage soon after his conversion to Christianity. He then modified and expanded his thought on this topic largely in response to challenges to marriage proposed by different heretical groups. Early in his life as a Christian, Augustine addressed the Manichean view of marriage. Shortly after the year 400, Augustine addressed the errors of Jovinianism. Finally, at the end of his life Augustine entered theological battles with the Pelagians. In each of these controversies and throughout his life as a Christian Augustine upheld the goodness of marriage.[110]

He addressed the topic of Christian marriage in several of his works from his early writings. In the *Soliloquia* written between his conversion in 386 and his baptism in 387, for example, he writes that "I have decided that there is nothing I should avoid so much as much as marriage. I know nothing which brings the manly mind down from the heights more than a woman's caresses and that joining of bodies without which one cannot have a wife."[111] Such as perspective still dominates the *Confessions*, where

---

108. *pecc. mer.* 1.18.23.

109. *pecc. mer.* 1.26.39.

110. Perry J. Cahall, "Saint Augustine and the Communion of Persons: The Relationship of the Bishop of Hippo's Theology of Marriage to His Theology of the Trinity" (Ph.D. diss., Saint Louis University, 2001), 1-2; John Witte, *From Sacrament to Contract: Marriage, Religion, and Law in the Western Tradition* (Louisville: Westminster John Knox Press, 1997), 65.

111. *sol.* 1.10.17. trans. Kim Paffenroth (New York: New City Press, 2000). Hereafter I use this translation.

Augustine describes marriage primarily as a safe harbor from the shipwrecks caused by youthful sexual desire:

> Was there no one to lull my distress, to turn the fleeting beauty of these new-found attractions to good purpose and set up a goal for their charms, so that the high tide of my youth might have rolled in upon the shore of marriage? The surge might have been calmed and contented by the procreation of children, which is the purpose of marriage, as your law prescribes, O Lord. By this means you form the offspring of our fallen nature, and with a gentle hand you prune back the thorns that have no place in your paradise.[112]

Between his baptism (387) and his ordination to the priesthood (391) Augustine wrote *De Genesi contra Manichaeos* around 388-389 in order to refute the Manichean interpretation of the book of Genesis. The Manichees taught a dualistic cosmology in which the forces of light and darkness (good and evil, God and matter) were opposed to each other. Under the Manichean scheme marriage and sexuality were evil because procreation led to the imprisonment of spiritual souls of light in material bodies. Augustine was a follower of Manichaeism from around 373-383/84 and was intent upon refuting the errors which had once seduced him. In particular, Augustine was concerned to uphold the goodness of God's creation. This over-arching purpose must be kept in mind when one reads what Augustine writes in this work and other anti-Manichean works regarding marriage, because Augustine goes to great lengths to show that as a part of God's creation marriage is good:[113]

> This good, in fact, is threefold: fidelity, offspring, sacrament. What fidelity means is that neither partner should sleep with another person outside the marriage bod; offspring means that children should be welcomed with love, brought up with kindness, given a religious education; sacrament means that the union should not be broken up, and that if either for embellishing the fertility of nature, or putting straight the crookedness of lust.[114]

Against the Manichees and their rejection of sexual intercourse and procreation as inherently evil, Augustine defended the goodness of the

---

112. *conf.* 2.2.3.
113. Cahall, "Saint Augustine and the Communion of Persons," 57.
114. *Gn. Litt.* 9.7.12.

married state and the fact that marriage was instituted by God at the beginning of creation by citing the sayings of Jesus (Matt. 19:3-9) and the letters of Paul (1 Cor. 7; Eph. 5).[115]

By devoting three different treatises specifically to the topic of marriage such as *De bono coniugali* (401), *De adulter inis coniugiis* (419/420), and *De nuptiis et concupiscentia* (419/420) a new phase in Augustine's reflections on marriage began. In his *Retractationes*, Augustine states that he wrote *De bono coniugali* in response to the controversy surrounding the monk Jovinian:

> The heresy of Jovinian, by equating the merit of consecrated virgins and conjugal continence, was so influential in the city of Rome that even some nuns, about whose incontinence there had been no suspicion heretofore, were precipitated into marriage, it was said, especially by the following argument: he kept urging them saying: "Are you, then, better than Sarah, better than Susanna or Anna?" and by mentioning other women, highly praised according to the testimony of Holy Scripture, to whom they could not think themselves superior or even equal. In this way, too, he shattered the holy celibacy of holy men by reminding them of and comparing them with fathers and husbands.[116]

In *De bono coniugali* and *De sancta virginitate*, Augustine began to engage a new opponent, the monk Jovinian who had been condemned in the early 390s at Rome and Milan for teaching that Christian marriage and celibacy were equally pleasing to God. Augustine not only responded by arguing that celibacy is superior to marriage but also tried to show the genuine goodness of the marital relationship since some of Jovinian's previous opponents such as Jerome had radically devalued marriage in their defense of celibacy. In other words, against Jerome and against those heretics such as the Manichees, who regarded sex and marriage as something evil, Augustine clearly delineates a variety of "goods" in Christian marriage. In *De bono coniugali* Augustine articulated the idea of the three goods of marriage that was to become classic in Catholic moral theology: offspring (*proles*), mutual fidelity (*fides*), and the sacramental bond (*sacramentum*). According to Augustine, the primary and original good of marriage is the procreation of children. Although at the time of writing

---

115. David G. Hunter, "Marriage," in *Augustine through the Ages: An Encyclopedia*, ed. Allan D. Fitzgerald (Cambridge: Wm. B. Eerdmans Publishing Company, 1999), 535.

116. *retr.* 2.22.49. trans. Boniface Ramsey in *a Translation for the 21st Century*, vol. I/2 (New York: New City Press, 2010). Hereafter I use this translation.

De bono coniugali Augustine had not yet made up his mind on the question of how the human race might have reproduced at the very beginning of creation, he was convinced that "in that condition of being born and dying with which we are acquainted, and in which we were created, the union of man and woman is something of value."[117] Augustine shows that why God created human beings as men and women as follows:

> Every human being is part of the human race, and human nature is a social entity, and has naturally the great benefit and power of friendship. For this reason God wished to produce all persons out of one, so that they would be held together in their social relationships not only by similarity of race, but also by the bond of kinship. The first natural bond of human society, therefore, is that of husband and wife. God did not create them as separate individuals and bring them together as persons of a different race, but he created one from the other, making the side, from which the woman was taken and formed, a sign of the strength of their union. For those who walk together, and look ahead together to where they are walking, do so at each other's side. The result is the bonding of society in its children, and this is the one honorable fruit, not of the union of husband and wife, but of their sexual conjunction. For even without that kind of intimacy, there could have been between the two sexes a certain relationship of friendship and kinship where one is in charge and the other compliant.[118]

Marriage is the "first natural bond of human society," and the producing of children is "the first social union of the human race."[119] Precisely because human nature is social, Augustine argues, God arranged for human beings to be connected to one another not only as members of the same species, but also by the bonds of physical kinship. Augustine acknowledges there could have been between the two sexes a certain relationship of friendship and kinship without sexual conjunction, but he explains that marriage leads to "the bonding of society in its children, and this is the one honorable fruit, not of the union of husband and wife, but of their sexual conjunction." Augustine states:

---

117. *b. conjug.* 3.3. trans. Ray Kearney in *a Translation for the 21st Century*, vol. I/9 (New York: New City Press, 1999). Hereafter I use this translation.

118. *b. conjug.* 1.1.

119. *b. conjug.* 6.6.

marriages also have the benefit that sensual or youthful incontinence, even though it is wrong, is redirected to the honorable purpose of having children, and so out of the evil of lust sexual union in marriage achieves something good. Furthermore, parental feeling brings about a moderation in sensual desire, since it is held back and in a certain way burns more modestly. For a certain seriousness attaches to the ardor of the pleasure, when in the act whereby man and woman come together with each other, they have the thought of being father and mother.[120]

Marriage is a way for the formation of moral self in that becoming parents might make them virtuous. For Augustine, sexual intercourse is allowed in the condition of marriage. It is because sexual union is for the health of the race just as what food is for the health of a person.[121] Augustine states:

> Neither is devoid of pleasure for the senses, and when this is regulated and put to its natural use under the restraint of moderation there cannot be passion. On the other hand, what forbidden food is in relation to sustaining life, fornication and adultery are in relation to seeking to have offspring; and what forbidden food is in the case of gluttony, unlawful intercourse is in the case of passion without desire for offspring; and what excessive appetite for lawful food is for some people, the intercourse that is excusable is for married persons.[122]

Hence, Augustine claims that it is better to die without children than to look for descendants by an illicit union just as it is better to die of hunger than to eat food that has been sacrificed to idols.[123] In other words, Augustine does not allow having children through concubinage. He images that one takes a concubine for a certain period and seeks only to have children from that relationship but the one do not want to marry her. He explains this situation as follows:

> In the same way, if anyone unfairly and wrongly usurped some land so as to give generously to charity with its produce, that would not justify the theft; and if another selfish and greedy person occupies land as a family estate or by legitimate acquisition, this is no reason to blame the legal regulation that makes him

120. *b. conjug.* 3.3.
121. *b. conjug.* 16. 18.
122. *b. conjug.* 16. 18.
123. *b. conjug.* 16. 18.

the legitimate owner. Similarly, the illegitimacy of a tyrannical government will not become praiseworthy, because a tyrant treats the subject people with regal gentleness, nor the institution of royalty become detestable, because a king rages with tyrannical cruelty. Choosing to use unjust power justly is one thing; using just power unjustly is another.[124]

Accordingly, Augustine claims that if temporary concubines have intercourse for the sake of having children, they do not thereby make their concubinage right while married women who are lascivious with their husbands do not make the institution of marriage responsible for their guilt.[125] Nevertheless, according to Augustine, children of concubinage can be honorable and saved if they do not follow the vices of their parents and give God due worship: "Whatever person it comes from, the human seed is created by God, and while it will go badly for anyone who uses it badly, it will never itself be bad. Even so, just as the good children of adulterers do not justify the adulteries, so too the bad children of married persons are not the fault of marriage."[126] In this context, Augustine defends the fathers of the Old Testament. Augustine states:

> There is no comparison at all between the fathers of New Testament times who took nourishment because it was their duty, even though they ate it with natural physical enjoyment, and the pleasure of those who ate the food from sacrifices (1 Cor 8:7), or those who over-indulged even in food that was not forbidden. So too the fathers of the Old Testament had intercourse because it was their duty, and their natural enjoyment of it was never let go to the point of becoming irrational or sinful passion, and there is no comparison between this and the depravity of adultery or married persons' excesses. Children have had to be provided for our mother Jerusalem, now spiritually and at that time physically, but always from the same source, love.[127]

Augustine stresses that the fathers of the Old Testament had intercourse for "their duty." Just as those who already longs to die and be with Christ, no longer takes nourishment because of a desire to go on living here but out of duty to remain in the body because of the needs of others, for holy men the lawful act of intercourse in marriage was an

124. *b. conjug.* 14.16.
125. *b. conjug.* 14.16.
126. *b. conjug.* 16.18.
127. *b. conjug.* 16.18.

act of duty, not sensuality.[128] Augustine regards the marriages of the holy fathers as life of celibacy. It is not that Augustine does not find marriages comparable to their marriages for the same gift to mortal human nature is present in all of them equally; but he does not find persons making use of marriage whom Augustine would compare to the persons of those times who made use of marriage in a very different way. Augustine shows Abraham as a specific example for it:

> For this reason we have to go further, and ask what celibate persons might be comparable to those married persons. The alternative is to think that Abraham could not refrain from marriage for the sake of the kingdom of heaven, although for the sake of the kingdom of heaven he could resolutely sacrifice his only guarantee of descendants, which is the reason why marriage is held dear.[129]

The particular significance of the sacrament in marriage varies according to its location in salvation history. For example, in the Old Testament divorce and polygamy were allowed; in the New Testament and subsequent Christian history, strict monogamy is the rule. Holy fathers possessed their own unique kind of sacramentality even though marriages were neither monogamous nor indissoluble in the Old Testament. Augustine wrote:

> Therefore, just as the sacrament of polygamous marriages of that age was a symbol of the plurality of people who would be subject to God in all nations of the earth, so too the sacrament of monogamous marriage of our time is a symbol that in the future we shall all be united and subject to God in the one heavenly city.[130]

For Augustine, hence, the indissolubility of marriage is fundamental to its sacramentality in the Christian era.[131]

In addition to procreation, for Augustine the good of marriage is the mutual fidelity of spouses. Fidelity is the commitment to engage in sexual relations only with one's spouse to avoid adultery. But fidelity also involves the mutual responsibility of married persons to engage in sex with each other by relieving the pressure of sexual desire in order to help

---

128. *b. conjug.* 15.
129. *b. conjug.* 20.24.
130. *b. conjug.* 18.21.
131. Hunter, "Marriage," 536.

the other to refrain from adultery. Augustine shows marriage as a remedy for sensuality for those who are lack in self-control as follows:

> In the same way there are men who are so lacking in self-control that they do not spare their wives even when they are pregnant. Whatever married people do between themselves that is impure or shameful or sordid, therefore, is a sin of the persons, not the fault of marriage. When the performance of the marriage duty is insisted on unreasonably, so that they have intercourse even when it is not for the purpose of having children, the apostle allows this as something that can be excused, though it is not something he lays down as a command. So, even if a perverted morality motivates them to have intercourse like that, marriage still saves them from adultery or fornication. It is not that conduct of that kind is accepted because of marriage, but it is forgiven because of marriage. Married people, therefore, not only owe each other fidelity in relation to sexual union for the sake of having children, which in this mortal state is the human race's first social union, but also in a certain way they owe each other a mutual service to relieve each other's weakness, and thereby avoid illicit unions. As a result even if one of them favors permanent abstinence, this is not possible unless the other agrees to it. It is for this reason that *the wife does not have authority over her own body, but the husband does; and likewise the husband does not have authority over his own body, but the wife does* (1 Cor 7:4), so that they will not refuse each other what the husband looks for from the marriage or the wife looks for from the husband, even when it is not for the sake of having children but because of weakness and lack of self-control. In this way, with Satan tempting them, they will not lapse into depraved conduct deserving of damnation because of the lack of restraint of one or other or both of them. Marital intercourse for the sake of procreating is not sinful. When it is for the purpose of satisfying sensuality, but still with one's spouse, because there is marital fidelity it is a venial sin. Adultery or fornication, however, is a mortal sin.[132]

Augustine argues that it is no sin to have sex with one's partner for this reason, even apart from the intention to procreate. The married person who seeks sexual relations out of excessive desire ("the concupiscence of the flesh") commits a sin that is forgivable, but adultery is

---

132. *b. conjug.* 6.6.

a sin.[133] Augustine describes fidelity as "a mutual service to relieve each other's weakness, and thereby avoid illicit unions." Why does he focus on the weakness of will? It derived from his experience. Before conversion into Christianity, Augustine was not interested in fulfilling the duties of maintaining a well-ordered marriage and raising a family. At this time, he was "a prisoner of habit" due to "suffering cruel torments through trying to satisfy a lust that could never be sated."[134] He was bound down by this

---

133. *b. conjug.* 10.11.

134. *conf.* 6.12.22. In contrast to Augustine, Aristotle stresses the importance of habit in acquiring virtue (*EN* 1098b28). For Aristotle the relation between happiness and virtues is quite ambiguous to be regarded as "means-end relationship," but for Augustine their relationship is much clear. From his earliest writings he appeals to the distinction between means and ends. Created things are to be used (*uti*); only God can be enjoyed (*frui*); "if we wish to return to our Father's home, this world must be used, not enjoyed, that so the invisible things of God may be clearly seen, being understood by the things that are made,—that is, that by means of what is material and temporary we may lay hold upon that which is spiritual and eternal" (*doc. Chr.* 1.4.). In *Resurrection and Moral Order*, Oliver O'Donovan raises the question about whether virtue ethics can provide soteriological answer as follows; "An ethic of character, therefore, raises the soteriological question in relation to morality; that is why the Catholic tradition of moral theology has been right to retain it. However, it does not answer that question sufficiently; that is why the Protestant tradition has been right to suspect its possible pretention. We shall not learn how to save our souls by talking about the formation of virtuous characters" (O'Donovan, *Resurrection and Moral Order*, 224). In *Augustine and the Limits of Virtue* Wetzel overlooks, as O'Donovan points out, the doctrine of grace in the explanation of virtue (Wetzel, *Augustine and the Limits of Virtue*, 164). Instead, he argues the divided will in terms of habit in the *Confessions*. Wetzel explains habit as the temporally extended residue of previous states of will, formed by past visions of the good that are no longer viable to reason, but that have left competing desires in the memory. Temporal extension of will is the key concept here. Temporal extension makes it impossible for agents to remake their own wills *ex nihilo*—and also explains why both Pelagian and modern concepts of the will as sheer volition go wrong when they abstract the will from time and memory. However, for Augustine virtues as the gift of God "enable us to work at attaining salvation" (Kent, 'Augustine's ethics', 212). For Augustine salvation is the purpose of life while virtues are a mean to attain it. Augustine insists that no one can have true virtue without true piety such as true worship of the true God rather than habit and learning Aristotle suggested (*civ. Dei.* 5.19, 19.4). "It is for this reason that the virtues which it seems to itself to possess, and by which it restrains the body and the vices that it may obtain and keep what it desires, are rather vices than virtues so long as there is no reference to God in the matter" (*civ. Dei.* 19.25.). Habituation simply anchors them more deeply in pride and self-love. He regards habit as the enemy of virtue. For Augustine character depends on the will by which one might break the bonds of habit and turn away from one's own past, so the importance of conversion, the "turning around" that marks the decisive moment in a Christian's life. God is external good so that through human efforts virtue cannot be achieved (*civ. Dei.* 19.4.).

disease of the flesh and was afraid to be freed from it.[135] In book VIII of the *Confessions*, Augustine shows the conflict of two wills at the scene of his conversion in relation to sexual desire:

> I longed to do the same, but I was held fast, not in fetters clamped upon me by another, but by my own will, which had the strength of iron chains. The enemy held my will in his power and from it he had made a chain and shackled me. For my will was perverse and lust had grown from it, and when I gave in to lust habit was born, and when I did not resist the habit it became a necessity. These were the links which together formed what I have called my chain, and it held me fast in the duress of servitude. But the new will which had come to life in me and made me wish to serve you freely and enjoy you, my God, who are our only certain joy, was not yet strong enough to overcome the old, hardened as it was by the passage of time. So these two wills within me, one old, one new, one the servant of the flesh, the other of the spirit, were in conflict and between them they tore my soul apart.[136]

Even though the new will that would worship and enjoy God emerges in his mind, it struggles to overcome the old will as the legacy of habit for sexual desire. The force of habit leads to devastating the new will.[137] Augustine demonstrates the grace of God, through Jesus Christ our Lord can cure it.[138] In other words, sexual desire is an inevitable matter for those who are lack in self-control. In this context, he shows that the pressure of sexual desire can be relieved in the condition of marriage.

The third good of marriage that Augustine shows is what he calls its *sacramentum*, that is, its significance as a sacred symbol or sign. Augustine defines marriage as an outward and visible sign of an inward and invisible grace. Augustine is among the very first to articulate the notion of the sacramentality of Christian marriage, which to him means its character as a union that is both monogamous and indissoluble until the death of one of the spouses. In *De nuptiis et concupiscentia*, Augustine demonstrates the indissolubility of marriage through the sacramentality of Christian marriage as follows:

---

135. *conf.* 6.12.21.
136. *conf.* 8.5.10.
137. *conf.* 8.5.12.
138. *conf.* 8.5.12.

> It is certainly not fecundity only, the fruit of which consists of offspring, nor chastity only, whose bond is fidelity, but also a certain sacramental bond in marriage which is recommended to believers in wedlock. Accordingly it is enjoined by the apostle: Husbands, love your wives, even as Christ also loved the Church. Of this bond the substance undoubtedly is this, that the man and the woman who are joined together in matrimony should remain inseparable as long as they live; and that it should be unlawful for one consort to be parted from the other, except for the cause of fornication. For this is preserved in the case of Christ and the Church; so that, as a living one with a living one, there is no divorce, no separation forever. And so complete is the observance of this bond in the city of our God, in His holy mountain—that is to say, in the Church of Christ—by all married believers, who are undoubtedly members of Christ, that, although women marry, and men take wives, for the purpose of procreating children, it is never permitted one to put away even an unfruitful wife for the sake of having another to bear children.[139]

For Augustine, marriage is "a certain sacramental bond," so that divorce is not allowed. Just as Christ loved the Church, the man and the woman who are joined together in matrimony should remain inseparable as long as they live:

> We can say now that in that condition of being born and dying with which we are acquainted, and in which we were created, the union of man and woman is something of value. The divine Scripture is so much in favor of this union that it is not lawful for a woman put aside by her husband to marry another as long as the husband lives, nor for a man put aside by his wife to take another, unless the woman who has separated from him has died. As even in the Gospel the Lord confirmed that marriage is something of value, not only because he forbade divorce except for the reason of adultery, but also because he attended a wedding as a guest, so with good reason one asks in what lies its value.[140]

This indicates that divorce or separation is not acceptable when a wife cannot procreate children. For Augustine, the good of marriage is:

---

139. *nupt. et conc.* 1.11. trans. Roland J. Teske, S.J. in *a Translation for the 21th Century*, vol. I/24 (New York: New City Press, 1998). Hereafter I use this translation.

140. *b. conjug.* 3.3.

not only because of the procreation of children, but also because of the natural sociability that exists between the different sexes. Otherwise in the elderly it would no longer be called marriage, especially if they had lost their children or had not had any. As it is, however, in a good marriage, even with older people, although the passion of youth between man and woman has waned, the relationship of love between husband and wife continues strong, and the better persons they are, the earlier they begin by mutual consent to abstain from carnal union. So what happens is not that later on, by necessity, they are not able to do what they would like to do, but that beforehand, to their credit, they choose not to do what they are able to do. If, therefore, they are faithful to the duty of honor and respect of one sex for the other, even though their bodies are feeble and deathlike, the chastity of minds properly joined in marriage is so much more honorable for being more genuine, so much more secure for being more fully accepted.[141]

Furthermore, Augustine deals with divorce in relation to apostasy since both of them are linked to the matter of sacrament; "In like manner the soul of an apostate, which renounces as it were its marriage union with Christ, does not, even though it has cast its faith away, lose the sacrament of its faith, which it received in the laver of regeneration. It would undoubtedly be given back to him if he were to return, although he lost it on his departure from Christ. He retains, however, the sacrament after his apostasy, to the aggravation of his punishment, not for meriting the reward."[142] Likewise, Augustine claims that divorce is guilty of adultery on the basis of the law of the gospel. He makes an emphasis on enduring as the rights of marriage between those who have contracted them as long as they both live. To be sure, "if the husband die, with whom a true marriage was made, a true marriage is now possible by a connection which would before have been adultery. Thus between the conjugal pair, as long as they live, the nuptial bond has a permanent obligation, and can be cancelled neither by separation nor by union with another. But this permanence avails, in such cases, only for injury from the sin, not for a bond of the covenant."[143] Augustine shows the marriage of Joseph and Mary who are parents of Christ as the perfect good of the nuptial institution. It is because there was, offspring, faithfulness, and the bond

---

141. *b. conjug.* 3.3.
142. *nupt. et conc.* 1.11.
143. *nupt. et conc.* 1.11.

in that as offspring the Lord Jesus Himself; the fidelity, in that there was no adultery; the bond, because there was no divorce:

> Only there was no nuptial cohabitation; because He who was to be without sin, and was sent not in sinful flesh, but in the likeness of sinful flesh (Rom 8:3) could not possibly have been made in sinful flesh itself without that shameful lust of the flesh which comes from sin, and without which He willed to be born, in order that He might teach us, that everyone who is born of sexual intercourse is in fact sinful flesh, since that alone which was not born of such intercourse was not sinful flesh.[144]

How did Joseph become the father of Christ? Augustine demonstrates that it derives from true wedlock between Mary and Joseph as follows:

> But God forbid that the nuptial bond should be regarded as broken between those who have by mutual consent agreed to observe a perpetual abstinence from the use of carnal concupiscence. Nay, it will be only a firmer one, whereby they have exchanged pledges together, which will have to be kept by a special endearment and concord—not by the voluptuous links of bodies, but by the voluntary affections of souls. For it was not deceitfully that the angel said to Joseph: Fear not to take unto you Mary your wife. (Mt 1:20) She is called his wife because of her first troth of betrothal, although he had had no carnal knowledge of her, nor was destined to have. The designation of wife was neither destroyed nor made untrue, where there never had been, nor was meant to be, any carnal connection. That virgin wife was rather a holier and more wonderful joy to her husband because of her very pregnancy without man, with disparity as to the child that was born, without disparity in the faith they cherished. And because of this conjugal fidelity they are both deservedly called parents (Lk 2:41) of Christ (not only she as His mother, but he as His father, as being her husband), both having been such in mind and purpose, though not in the flesh.[145]

Joseph had no carnal connection with Mary, so it was not necessary to marry her. Nevertheless, he did not withdraw. For Joseph the virgin wife was a holier and more wonderful joy because of her very pregnancy without man. Augustine states:

---

144. *nupt. et conc.* 1.13.
145. *nupt. et conc.* 1.13.

since she bore Him without his engendering, they could not surely have both been His parents, of that form of a servant, if they had not been conjugally united, though without carnal connection. Accordingly the genealogical series (although both parents of Christ are mentioned together in the succession) had to be extended, as it is in fact, down rather to Joseph's name, that no wrong might be done, in the case of this marriage, to the male, and indeed the stronger sex, while at the same time there was nothing detrimental to truth, since Joseph, no less than Mary, was of the seed of David, of whom it was foretold that Christ should come.[146]

Thus, they are both deservedly called parents of Christ owing to the conjugal fidelity.

In his later two books *De adulterinis conjugiis*, Augustine intensively defends indissolubility of marriage on the basis of the Scripture. There Augustine focuses on the biblical grounding of the prohibition of divorce and remarriage. It is because it was written in the course of responding to questions proposed by Pollentius who read Augustine's two books, *The Lord's Sermon on the Mount*, and was troubled by his strict interpretation of Jesus' teaching on divorce in Matthew 5:31-32 and Matthew 19:9. Book one is concerned primarily with the interpretation of 1 Corinthians 7:10-18 and Matthew 19:9. Reading Paul in the light of Matthew, Pollentius claims that a distinction should be made between divorce that takes place because of unchastity and divorce that occurs on other grounds. In both cases, Pollentius argued, divorce is allowed. When adultery has occurred, Pollentius suggested, remarriage is allowed as well, because of Matthew's exception. Paul's prohibition of remarriage, he argued, applies only in cases where spouses separated for reasons other than adultery.[147] With regard to Pollentius' views, Augustine strongly rejects. He argues that Matthew 19:9 implies that the only legitimate reason for the separation of spouses is adultery. Augustine notes that neither the gospel nor Paul admits any other grounds for divorce; unilateral separation, even for the sake of pursuing a life of continence, is to be rejected. And in cases of divorce because of adultery, Augustine maintains, the marriage remains intact, and remarriage is forbidden. He states:

---

146. *nupt. et conc.* 1.12.

147. *adul. conjug.* 1.1. trans. Ray Kearney in *a Translation for the 21st Century*, vol. I/9 (New York: New City Press, 1999). Hereafter I use this translation.

> Since, therefore, we say that even the woman who divorces a husband who commits adultery is not allowed to remarry, whereas you say it is allowed, but not advisable, without argument we both say that the one who divorces a husband who commits adultery ought not remarry. What is at issue is that we say that, when both the partners are Christians, a woman is not allowed to remarry if she leaves a husband who commits adultery, but if the husband does not commit adultery she is not allowed to leave him at all, whereas you say that if a woman leaves a husband who is not guilty of adultery, it is not right for her to remarry because of a commandment, but if she leaves a husband who is guilty of adultery, it is not advisable for her to remarry because of the scandal. You say, therefore, that, if she intends to remain unmarried, a woman is allowed to leave her husband, whether or not he commits adultery.[148]

In response to Pollentius' objection that in Matthew 19:9 Jesus makes a clear exception for divorce in the case of adultery, Augustine suggests that this exception means that remarriage after a spouse has been divorced because of adultery is less culpable than remarriage in other cases; nonetheless, remarriage is prohibited in all cases:

> Who are we to say that one person who marries again after divorcing his wife commits adultery, but someone else who does this does not commit adultery, when the gospel says that everyone who does it commits adultery? Hence, if anyone, that is everyone, who does this—divorces his wife and marries someone else—commits adultery, then without doubt this includes the two, both the one who divorces his wife when it is not for adultery and the one who does so on account of adultery. This is what *Whoever divorces* means; this is what *Everyone who divorces* means.[149]

Augustine appeals to the fact that the gospels of Mark (10:11-12) and Luke (16:18) contain the prohibition of divorce in an unqualified form and, therefore, the qualified prohibition of Matthew 19:9 must be read in the light of these other gospels.[150] How did Augustine deal with the matter of adultery? He shows the ground of forgiving the sin of adultery in Christ. For Augustine, it is not difficult for a husband or wife to forgive the other partner who committed adultery because if there is faith. Through

---

148. *adul. conjug.* 1.6.6.
149. *adul. conjug.* 1.10.
150. *adul. conjug.* 1.11.12.

baptism and penance, they were cleansed and healed. These crimes were not washed away by any sacrifices in the Old Testament where it was absolutely forbidden to take a wife contaminated by another man. Yet, these ones were washed away by the blood of the New Testament. Regarding this views, Augustine shows David and Jesus as examples:

> although David unhesitatingly accepted back the daughter of Saul, whose own father had taken her from him and given her to another man, he did this as a sign of what was to come in the New Testament. Now, however, Christ has said to the woman who committed adultery, *Neither do I condemn you; go now and sin no more* (Jn 8:11). After that, is there anyone who does not understand that a husband should forgive what the Lord, the Lord of both of them, has forgiven, and a woman one believes has repented and had her crime wiped away by the divine mercy should no longer be called an adulteress?[151]

In terms of divorce with a non-Christian spouse, Augustine interprets the text of 1 Corinthians 7:12-16 in the perspective of the indissolubility of marriage. In the text, Paul demonstrates that Christians are not bound to remain in marriages with non-Christians, if the non-Christian spouse wishes to separate. In this case, Augustine acknowledges, the apostle has made an allowance for separation between a Christian and a non-Christian when the faith of the Christian is endangered. However, He stresses that a lawful (*licere*) separation may not always be "beneficial" (*expedire*).[152] Augustine wrote:

> It is permitted [to divorce an unbelieving spouse], but it is not good to do, because people might take offense at the breakup of marriages and abhor the very doctrine of salvation that forbids the things that are not permitted. They would then continue on in the same state of unbelief, worse than before and destined to perish. For this reason the apostle intervenes with the advice forbidding us to do what is permitted though not good. While the Lord does not forbid the faithful, men and women, to leave husbands or wives who are not believers, at the same time he does not command them to do so. If he did command it, the apostle's advice not to act in that way would be out of place.

---

151. *adul. conjug.* 1.6.5.
152. *adul. conjug.* 1.14.15.

The Lord's faithful slave would never forbid doing what the Lord commands us to do.[153]

When the non-Christian partner presents no obstacle to the Christian's faith, charity dictates that the spouses should remain together, so that the non-Christian partner might be converted.

In book two of *De adulterinis conjugiis*, Augustine disputes Pollentius' claim on spiritual death by adultery as follows:

> You say this because you think those words of the same apostle, *A woman is bound to her husband, as long as he lives; but if her husband dies, she becomes free, and she may marry as she chooses* (1 Cor 7:39), should be taken to mean that a husband or wife who has committed adultery should be regarded as having died, and therefore after adultery the other partner, husband or wife, is allowed to marry again, in the same way as after the partner's death.[154]

According to Augustine, Pollentius presents that the death to which Paul refers is the spiritual death caused by adultery. In this way Pollentius had taken Paul to agree with Matthew 19:9, the passage in which Jesus allowed an exception to the rule against divorce and remarriage in cases where one spouse was guilty of adultery. Augustine rejects Pollentius' interpretation, arguing that even when a spouse has been legitimately divorced because of adultery, the "bond of marriage" lasts until the death of one of the spouses. For example, if a wife divorces an adulterer, she too may not enter a union with anyone else; for she is bound as long as her husband is alive, and only if he dies is she freed from the law of her husband and so able to be with another man without being an adulteress.[155] Like the sacrament of baptism, which remains valid even after serious sin and excommunication, Augustine argues, the bond of marriage remains intact even when a divorce has occurred because of adultery:

> When someone guilty of some crime is excommunicated, the sacrament of rebirth remains present in that person, and that person does not lose that sacrament even if he or she is never reconciled with God. In the same way, when a wife is divorced for committing adultery, the bond of the marriage union remains in her, and she does not lose that bond even if she is

---

153. *adul. conjug.* 1.18.
154. *adul. conjug.* 2.2.2.
155. *adul. conjug.* 2.5.4.

never reconciled with her husband. She will lose it, however, if her husband dies. The person who suffers the penalty of excommunication, on the other hand, will never lose the sacrament of rebirth, even if he or she is never reconciled, because God never dies.[156]

In this context, just as Christ forgives the sin of adultery, Augustine urges Christians to forgive the adulterous spouse. Augustine criticizes false advice that simply divorce those adulteresses and marry someone else who can comfort you while the first spouse is still alive. He thinks that the purpose of such arguments is not "out of respect for God, but for the freedom to marry again":

> Finally, I ask you whether, either by the old law of God or by Roman law, a Christian husband is allowed to take the life of an adulteress? If it is allowed, then it is better for him to refrain from both actions, namely, the punishment that is lawful because the woman has sinned, and the marriage that is unlawful because she is still living. If he insists on choosing one or the other, it is more acceptable for him to do what is lawful for him to do, have the adulteress punished, than to do what is not lawful, commit adultery while she is still living.[157]

However, everyone cannot forgive the other partner who commits adultery. In this case, Augustine advises that it is better for those who are afraid to take back partners who committed adultery to stay celibate rather than remarry.[158] It is because this is not broken, even when the wife is separated after being divorced by an innocent husband. Augustine states:

> For, whether he is an adulterer or chaste, *a woman is bound to her husband, as long as he lives* (1 Cor 7:29), and she commits adultery if she marries anyone else; and the man, since he is tied to his wife as long as she lives, whether she is an adulteress or chaste, commits adultery if he marries another woman.[159]

According to Augustine, it is broken only by the death of the husband, not when he commits adultery but when he leaves the body. Hence, he advises that if a woman leaves a husband who commits adultery, and she does not choose to be reunited with him, she must remain unmarried;

---

156. adul. conjug. 2.5.4.
157. adul. conjug. 2.15.
158. adul. conjug. 2.13.13.
159. adul. conjug. 2.13.13.

and if a man divorces a wife who commits adultery, and he does not choose to take her back, even after she has repented, then he must stay celibate. Augustine warns that if they do not this out of desire to choose the greater good, then certainly they must do it to avoid deadly evil:

> So then, even after divorcing a wife who is an adulteress, with any other woman he is an adulterer, since not just this particular one or that particular one, but *everyone who divorces his wife and marries someone else commits adultery* (Lk 16:18). Consequently if there is little desire for the life of the saints free from the bond of marriage, let there be dread of the punishment of adulterers, and if celibacy is not chosen out of love, at least let the desires of the flesh be curbed by fear. If the effort is made because there is fear, because the effort is made there will also be love. We must not trust in our own strength, but must combine effort with prayer, so that the one who deters us from evil will fill us with goodness.[160]

Augustine advises that celibacy must not be conducted by our won strength but by prayer. Augustine presents celibacy is possible with God's help; "If the burden is Christ's, it will be light; and it will be Christ's, if there is faith, as this procures from the one who commands it the accomplishment of what he commands."[161] Augustine's sacramental aspect of marriage is clearly different from that of Confucius and Mencius.

SUMMARY

In this chapter, I showed huge differences between classical Confucians and Augustine in *li* (禮) and sacrament in the formation of moral self. Confucius highlighted ritual propriety because it makes harmony (和) possible in government. Hence, he urged to return to ritual propriety. According to Confucius, returning to ritual propriety is to practice benevolence by subduing one's self. It is not supernatural. Returning to ritual propriety is not to look at what is contrary to ritual propriety, not to listen to what is contrary to ritual propriety, not to speak what is contrary to ritual propriety, and not to make any movement which is contrary to ritual propriety. It is about personal effort. In particular, Confucius stresses that the man of virtue ought to practice consistency

---

160. *adul. conjug.* 2.13.13.
161. *adul. conjug.* 2.19.20.

of speech and action in accordance with ritual propriety. Interestingly, he stressed to rectify names as a specific method for rightly realizing ritual propriety in managing government in the discussion of speech. In addition, Confucius extensively discussed ritual propriety in relation to the Mean (中庸). Like Confucius, Mencius also highlighted the role of ritual propriety in relation to benevolence and righteousness. This indicates that ritual propriety is not utilitarian. Mencius states that the man of virtue carries out ritual propriety according to his nature which is the sense of shame unlike animals. In obtaining a government position, he emphasized to follow ritual propriety even though for the man of virtue taking an office is deeply important. He thought that funeral ought not to be dealt with utilitarian aspect but ritual propriety. In contrast to Confucius and Mencius who emphasized human efforts to conduct ritual propriety, Augustine offered how grace enters to the formation of moral self through sacraments such as baptism and marriage in the course of ordering mind to God rather than self. Augustine thinks that personal effort is not sole means for caring of moral self. Contrary to Confucius and Mencius, Augustine makes a room for grace through sacraments in the formation of moral self. Augustine's view of the sacraments is based upon the conception of Christ, the high priest without sin, who is the sole giver of sacramental grace. However, it is necessary to observe that Augustine did not regard baptism as the completion on the way of salvation. He is against those who overemphasize the effects of baptism. Baptism gives us new start on the way of salvation and the full renewal of the image of God within our minds is only completed in the afterlife. In terms of marriage, he developed his idea on it in controversies with different heretical groups such as Manicheans, Jovinians, and Pelagians. According to him, advantages of marriage are procreation of children, mutual fidelity of spouses, and sacramentality of Christian marriage which means its character as a union that is both monogamous and indissoluble until the death of one of the spouses and in the situation of spouse's adultery. If it is not acceptable, celibate is only available instead of remarriage. This indicates that for Augustine family is not utilitarian like Mencius. Confucius and Mencius focus on filial piety, so that funeral is hugely emphasized. However, for Augustine family is a place where the virtue of forgiveness takes place on the basis of sacramental bond beyond the functions of procreation of children and funeral.

5
Yue (樂) and Music

INTRODUCTION

IN THIS CHAPTER, I first examine Confucius' account of music (*yue* 樂). This covers the role of music in the formation of moral self in relation to harmony in the course of achieving happiness. I then survey Mencius' account of music. This deals with how music is connected with virtues and filial piety in communitarian dimension. In the last section, I discuss Augustine's music. This presents two aspects of music, music as a liberal discipline, and immutable truth of music.

CONFUCIUS' MUSIC

Sacrificial Music

The role of music in Confucian moral and political teachings has often been overlooked in contemporary studies. However, music was, as Cook argues, of paramount interest to the early Confucians for a number of reasons and was framed particularly in the era of the Eastern Zhou (東周) and Warring States (戰國).[1] In this period a breakdown of the feudal structure upon which society had formerly laid its foundations led to the importance of music in order to promote the appropriate balance between the desire to recover the old ways ruler ship lost from China's

---

1. Cook, "Unity and Diversity in the Musical Thought of Warring States China," iv; Jia Chen, "How Can One be Perfected by Music?: Contemporary Educational Significance of Chinese Pre-Qin Confucian Thought on Yue Jiao (Music Education)," (Ph.D. diss., University of Illinois, 2012), 38.

past, and the need to institute new forms of governance to respond to the changing nature of society and the times.[2] Music offerings were played as a part of state sacrificial ceremonies for ensuring the continued good will of the ancestral spirits. It drives from the fact that ancient Chinese societies were based on ceremonies in contrast with the Western societies based on laws.[3] Musical instruments such as bronze bell-sets were thought to have the power to communicate directly with such spirits with their harmonious sounds. The order inherent within the structure of music itself reflected the structure of the cosmos as a whole with its twelve-month cycles and alternating five phases. By helping to establish the ritual calendar in such a way that ensured sacrificial music would be performed in the proper keys and modes for the different times of the year, the music masters assisted their rulers in tapping and harnessing the very strength of Heaven and Earth.[4] This made music possible to become a pivotal part of the hierarchical system of ritual control that pervaded all aspects of ruling-class life. Music also became an important part of state educational institutions, through which were imparted to the young members of the ruling class a strong sense of noble virtues and social functions.[5] From the standpoint of the performer, music was for some the perfect metaphor for the process of self-cultivation and the maturation of the completely virtuous individual. In terms of public performance and the listening audience, recognition of the overwhelming influential power of music led the nobility into using music as a toll by which to instill the masses with a sense of social harmony, to both allay their tendencies toward unrest and direct them as a unitary body toward desired ends. Music masters thus ranked high in the hierarchy of officialdom, and they tended to serve in an important advisory capacity to their rulers.[6]

Harmony

Throughout the *Analects*, Confucius continuously attempts to clarify how one can achieve happiness (樂) in life as follows:

> 2. Cook, "Unity and Diversity in the Musical Thought of Warring States China," vi.
> 3. Yue Ji, 'Confucius on Music Education,' *Nebula* 5, no. 1-2 (2008), 128.
> 4. Cook, "Unity and Diversity in the Musical Thought of Warring States China," v.
> 5. Mary T. Guerrant, "Three Aspects of Music in Ancient China and Greece," *College Music Symposium* 20, no. 2 (1980), 91.
> 6. Cook, "Unity and Diversity in the Musical Thought of Warring States China," iv.

> There are three kinds of happiness which are beneficial and three kinds of pleasure which are harmful. It is beneficial to find happiness in the proper arrangement of ritual and music, to find happiness in talking about the good points of other men, to find happiness in having a large number of friends who are men of quality. It is harmful to take pleasure in the delights of showing off, to take pleasure in a self-indulgent life-style, and to take pleasure in the delights of feasting.[7]

Interestingly, among methods for finding happiness, he first offers the importance of properly arranging ritual propriety and music (樂) prior to taking about the good points of other men and having a large number of excellent friends.[8] In ancient Chinese, the word for happiness and music are written with the same character. However, Confucius did not stress music just for taking pleasure. Why did Confucius focus on music? Confucius taught the Six Arts, which include rites, music, archery, chariot-driving, literature, and mathematics to his students. For him, music is a core subject for moral education among Six Arts.[9] Confucius crystallized inherited traditional teaching of Six arts, particularly the education of music from the three previous dynasties such as Zia, Shang, and Zhou.[10] The most significant saying of Confucius on moral education through music might be:

> Confucius said that self-cultivation begins with studying the *Book of Poetry*, is established by ritual, and is perfected by music.[11]

Given that the finish of something is usually linked to greater importance than other parts, it is noteworthy that Confucius regards music as the finishing strokes in the process of self-cultivation.[12] Music has its own important position in relation to studying the *Book of Poetry* and ritual propriety in Confucius' formation of moral self. This indicates that

---

7. *Analects*, 16.5. As translated in Legge. 孔子曰：「益者三樂，損者三樂。樂節禮樂，樂道人之善，樂多賢友，益矣。樂驕樂，樂佚遊，樂宴樂，損矣。」

8. Erica Brindley, "Music, Cosmos, and the Development of Psychology in Early China," *T'oung Pao* 92, no. 1 (2006), 2.

9. Leonard Tan, "Towards an Ancient Chinese-Inspired Theory of Music Education," *Music Education Research* (2015), 3.

10. Youwei Xu, "Confucius: An Educationalist of Aesthetics in Ancient China," *Journal of Popular Culture* 27, no. 2 (1993), 125.

11. *Analects*, 8.8. Translation adapted from Legge. 子曰：「興於詩，立於禮。成於樂。」

12. Yue, "Confucius on Music Education," 128.

even poetry is inseparable with music since in Confucius' time the lyrics were the *Odes*, one of the basic texts for Confucius' moral education, so singing poetry was a method for his disciples to live in righteousness and to achieve a balanced emotion.[13] For Confucius, music is not a mere pleasant pastime for joyful comfort and amusement, but "stands for a supreme spiritual force for the cultivation of one's moral character" as the purest sound of the heart.[14] According to the *Book of Rituals*, it is in the play of music that the harmony of sky and earth is obtained while rituals represent the order of sky and earth by distinguishing the categories of various beings and arranging them in a proper hierarchy. Due to the importance of music, Confucius himself used to devote to arrange songs; "I returned from Wei to Lu, and then the music was reformed, and the pieces in the Royal songs and praise songs all found their proper places."[15] In other words, just as for him ritual does not only indicate gems and silk, music must be beyond bells and drums.[16] Like other methods of his self-cultivation, music is also focused on how to live in harmony as follows:

> The Master instructing the Grand music master of Lu said, "How to play music may be known. At the commencement of the piece, all the parts should sound together. As it proceeds, they should be in harmony while severally distinct and flowing without break, and thus on to the conclusion."[17]

This indicates that the nature of music is to take part in playing harmoniously together. Given that the role of the highly original composer creates not only new works within old forms, but also creates new forms, in the post-Romantic West the musical-moral analogy is the matter of the fullest realization of that individuality due to the emphasis on the individual as of ultimate value and on free will as the engine of individual self-expression. However, Confucius thought that the individual can have truly human significance only by living communal relationship in a context of mutually shared and valued forms that are authentically

---

13. Yeo, *Musing with Confucius and Paul*, 225.

14. Wenye Jiang, Review of *A Discourse on Confucius's Music*, by Huaiyu Wang, *Dao* 9 (2010), 115.

15. *Analects*, 9.15. As translated in Legge. 子曰：「吾自衛反魯，然後樂正，雅頌各得其所。」

16. *Analects*, 17.11. As translated in Legge. 子曰：「禮云禮云，玉帛云乎哉？樂云樂云，鐘鼓云乎哉？」

17. *Analects*, 3.23. As translated in Legge. 子語魯大師樂。曰：「樂其可知也：始作，翕如也；從之，純如也，皦如也，繹如也，以成。」

embodied in the performance and participated in by the appreciative audience.[18] What make it possible? According to Confucius, it depends on whether someone has the virtues proper to benevolence (仁); "If someone is not benevolent in spite of being a man, ritual propriety and music are meaningless."[19] This indicates that benevolence is the source of ritual and music. The ultimate goal of Confucian education is to learn to be a person of benevolence. In traditional Chinese society its most important aim was to focus how to behave in such a way as to become a person of benevolence. For Confucius music is a tool in the formation of moral self since it was used to help in the teaching of the ritual propriety that develops human relationships and raises society's moral standard, which were regarded as the essence of a peaceful society.[20]

What kinds of music did Confucius recommend for self-cultivation? Regarding this question, he explained it in relation to governing a state, but its explanation can be applied for self-cultivation, given that both concepts are inextricably related in his theory. He urged to adopt the music of the *shao* and *wu* in the dimension of how the government of a country should be administered as follows:

> Yan Hui asked about governing a state. The Master said: "Introduce the seasons of Xia, ride the state carriage of Yin wear the ceremonial cap of Zhou. For music adopt the *shao* and *wu*. Get rid of the songs of Zheng," and banish clever talkers. The songs of Zheng are licentious and clever talkers are a menace.[21]

For Confucius the quality of music is a major concern since it is an essential element in the formation of moral self. Given that Confucius assesses the songs of Zheng are licentious and clever talkers are a menace, the music of the *shao* and *wu* should be different from such songs. In what aspects did Confucius appreciate the music of the *shao* and *wu*? Confucius thinks the important elements of music are beauty (美) and goodness (善). With these criteria, he judges both songs; "The Master

---

18. Herbert Fingarette, "The Music of Humanity in the Conversations of Confucius," *Journal of Chinese Philosophy* 10, no. 4 (1983), 346.

19. *Analects*, 3.3. As translated in Dawson. 子曰：「人而不仁，如禮何？人而不仁，如樂何？」

20. Marina Wong, "A comparison between the Philosophies of Confucius and Plato as Applied to Music Education," *The Journal of Aesthetic Education* 32, no. 3 (1998), 111.

21. *Analects*, 15.11. As translated in Dawson. 顏淵問為邦。子曰：「行夏之時，乘殷之輅，服周之冕，樂則韶舞。放鄭聲，遠佞人。鄭聲淫，佞人殆。」

said of the *Shao* that it was perfectly beautiful and also perfectly good. He said of the *Wu* that it was perfectly beautiful but not perfectly good."[22] To put it another way, according to him, the *Shao* is equipped with beauty and goodness, but the *Wu* has only the element of beauty. For Confucius the music of *Shao* is superior to that of the *Wu*. It derives from their moral contents.[23] The music of *Shao* was composed to praise the Emperor Shun who ascended the throne in peaceful succession to the Emperor Yao, whereas the music of *Wu* was composed to praise the Emperor Wu who attained the throne through armed conquest. Even though the music of *Shao* and the music of *Wu* were both good, Confucius thought that music could be assessed according to the moral representation of its content. For Confucius the piece of music representing peace is regarded as morally good since its morally good ideas can reach the general public, elevate people's moral standard, and eventually bring peace and order to a country while the piece of music representing war is considered to be morally bad since its evil ideas will influence people's minds and confuse their value judgments, and eventually it will lower the moral standard. Confucius preferred music that is morally good and representative of peace since music greatly influences on a person's mind.[24] For him, the music of *Shao* was perfect since the piece of music is good in terms of form as well as content. Confucius thinks the music of *Shao* as the best he had ever heard, and he states that "the music of Shao was so perfect that he could not even tell the taste of meat in three months' time after hearing it."[25]

MENCIUS' MUSIC

Filial Piety

Contrary to Confucius, Mencius rarely mentions on music in the *Book of Mencius*, but it still plays an important part in the formation of moral self. Mencius shows a vision of ebullient happiness resulting from the

---

22. *Analects*, 3.25. As translated in Legge. 子謂韶，「盡美矣，又盡善也。」謂武，「盡美矣，未盡善也」。

23. Wong, "A comparison between the Philosophies of Confucius and Plato as Applied to Music Education," 111.

24. Ibid., 111.

25. *Analects*, 7.14. Translation adapted from Dawson. 子在齊聞韶，三月不知肉味。曰：「不圖為樂之至於斯也！」

balanced practice of the great virtues such as benevolence, righteousness, and wisdom in relation to music as follows:

> The content of benevolence is the serving of one's parents. The content of righteousness is obedience to one's elder brothers. The content of wisdom is to understand those two things, and not departing from them. The content of ritual propriety is the ordering and adorning those two things. The content of music is the happiness that comes of delighting in them. When happiness arises how can one stop it? And when one cannot stop it, then one unconsciously begins to dance with one's feet and wave one's arms.[26]

For Mencius, the nature of music is happiness in that the sense of happiness catalyzes the growth of the virtues, and leads to ecstatic experiences such as dance by delighting the contents of benevolence and righteousness. Given that such virtues are inextricably related to filial piety in the context of family life, the essence of music should be understood in a communitarian way.

Happier Together

In his cultivation of self through music, the happiness does not just abide in family life. Beyond family, the influence of music precisely targets the national life. In other words, music has intense political tendency.[27] For example, when Mencius discusses on music with king Hui of Liang, he expects that the kingdom of Qi would be near to a state of good government because of the king's great fondness for music. Mencius takes no account of what the king loves popular music rather than the music of the ancient sovereigns, for there are no differences between them in effecting the function of music.[28] Mencius believes that music with noble ideology can educate people. For Mencius, the purpose of music is to form a harmonious society and government.

---

26. *Mencius*, 4A27. Translation adapted from Legge. 孟子曰：「仁之實，事親是也；義之實，從兄是也。智之實，知斯二者弗去是也；禮之實，節文斯二者是也；樂之實，樂斯二者，樂則生矣；生則惡可已也，惡可已，則不知足之蹈之、手之舞之。」

27. Junbo Shi, "A Comparison between the Music Concepts of Confucius and Mencius," *Journal of Guan Zi* 4 (2010), 59.

28. *Mencius*, 1B1.

This indicates post-Confucius thinkers such as Mencius and Xunzi share Confucian ideas in spite of their differences of human nature and musical pedagogy.[29] According to Xunzi, music is inextricably linked to the truth. Xunzi defines music as happiness. The man of virtue takes it in attaining the Way, but the small man takes it in attaining the object of his desires. Those who takes the Way to regulate their desires can be happy.[30] Xunzi states that "music has the power to make good the hearts of the people, to influence men deeply, and to reform their manners and customs with facility," so "the former kings guided the people with ritual and music, and the people became harmonious and congenial."[31] Music as "the height of ordering people" makes the people turn toward what is correct.[32] Balanced, peaceful, solemn and majestic music make people harmonious and being uniformly ordered, by which state can be protected.[33] Xunzi conceives music as a corrective measure for chaos.[34]

Mencius highlights how to enjoy music in the perspective of community. Regarding this question, the king states that enjoyment in the company of many is more pleasant rather than enjoyment by himself and enjoyment in the company of a few. For Mencius, this has significant political implication. He explained to the king that why people differently react to the king's fondness for music? When the king enjoys the music by himself alone, the people complains that why does the king's fondness for music bring us to such straits that fathers and sons do not see each other, and brothers, wives and children are parted and scattered? According to him, it is because the king failed to share your happiness with the people. In contrast, if the people enjoy hearing the noise of his bells and drums, and the notes of his fifes and pipes, it is because the king shared his happiness with the people.[35] For Mencius, the way to be a true king is to share his happiness with the people. In other words, music is the expression of the common happiness in social harmony among various relations.

---

29. Xiaojun Tian, "The Musical Pedagogy of Mencius and Xunzi," *Journal of Guizhou University for Ethnic for Ethnic Minorities* 1 (2008), 39.

30. *Xunzi*, 20.6. trans. Eric L. Hutton (Princeton: Princeton University Press, 2014), 221. Hereafter I use Hutton's translation.

31. *Xunzi*, 20.5., 220.

32. *Xunzi*, 20.6., 221.

33. *Xunzi*, 20.5., 219.

34. Scott Cook, "Xun Zi on Ritual and Music," *Monumenta Serica* 45 (1997), 25.

35. *Mencius*, 1B1. As translated in Legge. 與民同樂也。今王與百姓同樂，則王矣。

AUGUSTINE'S MUSIC

Two Aspects of Music

For Augustine the final end is enjoyment of God. Virtue is not an end in itself but a means. In the process of being virtuous there are two kinds of activity on the part of the senses which prevent enjoyment of God: concupiscence of the flesh and eyes.[36] Concupiscence of the flesh is called "pleasure-seeking" which lure us to indulge in the pleasures of all the senses, and brings disaster on its slaves who flee far from God. Concupiscence of the eyes is called "curiosity" which is "subject to a certain propensity to use the sense of the body, not for self-indulgence of a physical kind, but for the satisfaction of its own inquisitiveness."[37] In the Scriptures it is called "gratification of the eye" since sight is the principal sense by which knowledge is acquired.[38] Pleasure through concupiscence of the flesh pursues the beautiful, the melodious, the fragrant, the tasty and the silky, whereas curiosity seeks the opposite to all these, not because it wants to undergo discomfort but from lust to experience and find out.[39] For example, no one obtain sensual pleasure in viewing a mangled corpse, but people congregate in order to experience ashen-faced horror if there is one lying anywhere.

> At the same time they are frightened that it may give them nightmares! Anyone would think they had been forced to look at the thing while awake, or had been persuaded to do so by some rumor of its beauty. The same holds for the other senses, but it would be tedious to pursue the point through them all.[40]

Due to this unhealthy curiosity that freaks and prodigies are put on show in the theatre, likewise, men are led to examine the secrets of nature, which are not relevant to our lives, although such knowledge is of no value to them and they wish to gain it merely for the sake of knowing. It is curiosity, too, which causes men to turn to sorcery in the effort to obtain knowledge for the same perverted purpose. And it even invades our religion, for we put God to the test when we demand signs and wonders from him, not in the hope of salvation, but simply for the love of the

---

36. *conf.* 10.35.54.
37. *conf.* 10.35.54.
38. *conf.* 10.35.54.
39. *conf.* 10.35.55.
40. *conf.* 10.35.55.

experience.[41] Hence, Augustine thinks concupiscence of the eyes is more seductive than concupiscence of the flesh.

When it comes to music, concupiscence of the flesh is more related to it. According to Augustine, concupiscence of the flesh can be activated by sense of touch, taste, sight, smell, and hearing. Augustine shows his experiences of these temptations in *Confessions*. In terms of sense of touch, As God commanded him to abstain from fornication, Augustine took even before he was ordained as a dispenser of sacrament owing to God's grace. However, in his memory sexual images survived because they were imprinted there by "former habit" (*consuetudo*). While he was awake they suggested themselves feebly enough, but in dreams with power to arouse him not only to pleasurable sensations but even to consent, to something closely akin to the act they represent. So strongly does the illusory image in his mind affect his body that these unreal figments influence him in sleep in a way that the reality could never do while he was awake.[42] Augustine also deals with temptation of taste. He was taught to take food at mealtimes as medicine, but when he passed from uncomfortable need to tranquil satisfaction, the snare of concupiscence lies waiting for me in the very passage from one to the other. Augustine said that "for this transition itself was pleasurable and there is no other means of satisfying hunger except the one which we are obliged to take. And although the purpose of eating and drinking is to preserve health, in its train there follows an ominous kind of enjoyment, which often tries to outstrip it, so that it is really for the sake of pleasure that I do what I claim to do and mean to do for the sake of my health."[43] Furthermore, he did not know how much food is required to maintain health. By using this uncertainty, his unhappy soul cheered up and marshalled excuses in its own defense, glad to take advantage of the ambiguity about what temperate preservation of health requires, and cloaked its self-indulgence under the pretense that health is being prudently provided for.[44] In addition, Augustine shows how influential the temptation of sight is. According to him, men make innumerable things by every kind of art and the skill of their hands such as clothes, shoes, pottery, and other useful objects, besides pictures and various works which are the fruit of their imagination. He points out

---

41. *conf.* 10.35.56.
42. *conf.* 10.30.41. Wetzel, *Augustine and the Limits of Virtue*, 128, 135.
43. *conf.* 10.31.44.
44. *conf.* 10.31.44.

that "they make them on a far more lavish scale than is required to satisfy their own modest needs or to express their devotion, and all these things are additional temptations to the eye, made by men who love the worldly things they make themselves but forget their own Maker and destroy what he made in them."[45] Above all, Augustine deals with matter raised by the temptation of hearing in the music of hymns as follows:

> I used to be much more fascinated by the pleasures of sound than the pleasures of smell. I was enthralled by them, but you broke my bonds and set me free. I admit that I still find some enjoyment in the music of hymns, which are alive with your praises, when I hear them sung by well-trained, melodious voices. But I do not enjoy it so much that I cannot tear myself away. I can leave it when I wish. But if I am not to turn a deaf ear to music, which is the setting for the words which give it life, I must allow it a position of some honor in my heart, and I find it difficult to assign it to its proper place. For sometimes I feel that I treat it with more honor than it deserves. I realize that when they are sung these sacred words stir my mind to greater religious fervor and kindle in me a more ardent flame of piety than they would if they were not sung; and I also know that there are particular modes in song and in the voice, corresponding to my various emotions and able to stimulate them because of some mysterious relationship between the two. But I ought not to allow my mind to be paralyzed by the gratification of my senses, which often leads it astray. For the senses are not content to take second place. Simply because I allow them their due, as adjuncts to reason, they attempt to take precedence and forge ahead of it, with the result that I sometimes sin in this way but am not aware of it until later.[46]

Augustine points out the matter raised by the pleasures of sound. He used to be fascinated by the music of hymns of well-trained voices rather than sacred word itself. As a result, it was hard for him to put it in proper place by treating it with more honor than it deserves. He knew that he ought not to allow his mind to be paralyzed by the gratification of my senses. As he was deceived by sensuous gratification, he committed a sin inadvertently, and only realized it later. In order to avoid this trap from over-anxiety he made the mistake of being too strict on music. When this happens, he wished to exclude all the melody of those lovely

45. *conf.* 10.34.53.
46. *conf.* 10.33.49.

chants to which the Psalms of David are habitually sung from my ears, and from the ears of the Church as well. For Augustine, it seemed safer to follow Athanasius' advice, which is to "recite the psalms with such slight modulation of the voice that they seemed to be speaking rather than chanting."[47] On the other hand, Augustine acknowledges the value of music in ordering our self to God; "But when I remember the tears that I shed on hearing the songs of the Church in the early days, soon after I had recovered my faith, and when I realize that nowadays it is not the singing that moves me but the meaning of the words when they are sung in a clear voice to the most appropriate tune, I again acknowledge the great value of this practice."[48]

Music as a Liberal Discipline

Music is an important part of Christian moral formation in being ordered to God rather than to self.[49] When compared to the extensive literature on works such as *Confessions, De civitate Dei, De Trinitate,* or his commentary on the *book of Genesis*, Augustine's *De musica* has been largely ignored in recent times. However, this work was storehouse of vocabulary, conceptualization, topics of discussion or subject matter, as well as a basis for the discussion of music itself. During the medieval period, manuscripts of *De musica* were the major sources of moral learning.[50] Why did music play an important role in moral learning in the medieval period? This can be explained through the role of music as liberal discipline in *De Ordine*, which was written as a catechumen awaiting baptism at Cassiciacum near Milan in 386-87. This treatise deals with the problem of order first at a metaphysical level, examining divine providence, good, and evil, then moves to a full-blown theory of an order of study in the liberal arts, whereby one can proceed from corporeal to incorporeal things. The classic dilemma—can God be both good and

---

47. *conf.* 10.33.50.

48. *conf.* 10.33.50.

49. Carol Harrison, "Getting Carried Away: Why did Augustine Sing?," *Augustinian Studies* 46, no. 1 (2015), 3; Jeremy Begbie, *Theology, Music, and Time* (Cambridge: Cambridge University Press, 2000); Jeremy Begbie, *Music, Modernity, and God essays in Listening* (Oxford: Oxford University Press, 2013).

50. Nacy Van Deusen, "De Musica," in *Augustine through the Ages: An Encyclopedia*, ed. Allan D. Fitzgerald (Cambridge: Wm. B. Eerdmans Publishing Company, 1999), 576.

omnipotent in the face of evil—is quickly dismissed, and the inability of the human mind to grasp the overall divine order is urged instead. The ability to perceive the divine order is achieved through that spiritual and intellectual discipline which leads to knowledge of self and of the spiritual world. Only by withdrawing form knowledge of material things can the true beauty of the universe be understood. Augustine thinks the liberal arts directly contribute to the quality of the Christian quest for love and knowledge of God, which is the pivotal core of happy life. For Augustine, the liberal arts lead the mind to God. Augustine states:

> the truly learned are those who, not allowing all the different realities to distract them, attempt their unification into a simple, true, and certain whole. Having done so, they can soar on to divine realities not rashly and by faith alone, but contemplating, understanding, and retaining them.[51]

He planned to write individual treaties on grammar, dialectic, rhetoric, music, geometry, arithmetic, and astronomy, but he completed only two, on grammar and music. This is the first attestation of the systematization of knowledge at two levels that will later be called the trivium and the quadrivium. The first level consists of grammar, dialectic, and rhetoric. On the first are grammar, the study of language in a very full sense, including literature and even history as part of the study of letters[52]; dialectic, the "discipline of disciplines," which covers reason itself, including how to think, teach, and learn; and because people generally follow their feelings and habits rather than truth, rhetoric is added, to charm the crowd and move them to action for their own good.[53] The second level consists of music, geometry, astronomy, and arithmetic. This is the task of contemplation of eternal truth by way of recognition of truth to the experience of happiness. This second step is made possible by the mathematical disciplines that lead the person from sensible, material things to intelligible numbers. Music is the study of rhythm in language and sound, and numeric proportion as the mathematical discipline. Augustine wrote:

> reason understand that number, both in rhythm and modulation, was supreme and all-encompassing. It scrutinized number, therefore, most minutely. When reason realized that with the

51. *ord.* 2.17.44.
52. *ord.* 2.12.37.
53. *ord.* 2.13.38.

help of number it had organized all the foregoing, it called number divine and almost eternal. And so it grievously tolerated that the splendor and purity of number should be somewhat clouded by the material sound of voices. Now number is a mental construct and, as such, ever present in the mind and understood as immortal. Sound, on the other hand, is temporary and fleeting, but can be memorized.[54]

Geometry is the study of dimensions and thus number and astronomy is the study of distance, dimension, and number in the heavenly realm.[55] These seem to be crowned by mathematics, the study of numbers themselves, which holds the key to the study of metaphysics, which in turn is necessary to successfully investigate basic questions about God and the soul.

Immutable Truth of Music

The representative evidence for Augustine's continued high regard for the liberal disciplines is his *De Musica*.[56] This treatise as an early work began from 387, shortly after Augustine's baptism and shortly before the death of his mother, Monica. In six books, the work represents the only substantial result issuing from an ambitious project conceived of during the period following his return from Casssiciacum. Penetrated with his conviction that the liberal disciplines could provide an excellent ladder for the soul's ascent, as O'Connell demonstrates, he intended to take those liberal disciplines in turn, presenting each of them in such a fashion as to lead the reader's mind upward, through the corporeal to the incorporeal.[57] The purpose of his treaties *De Musica* is to undertake connections of smallest units of sound material within describable, delimited units. In book 1 of *De Musica*, Augustine writes of motion itself, of "rational motions," of complex as well as measured proportional motions, and "intervals of motion, in which two motions, congruent, effected voluptuousness."[58] In books 2-5 Augustine treats of the *copulationes* of

54. *ord.* 2.14.41.

55. *ord.* 2.15.42-43.

56. Robert J. O'Connell, *Art and the Christian Intelligence in St. Augustine* (Oxford: Basil Blackwell, 1978), 63.

57. O'Connell, *Art and the Christian Intelligence in St. Augustine*, 63.

58. *mus.* 1.13.27. trans. Robert Catesby Taliaferro in *the Fathers of the Church*, vol. 4 (Washington: The Catholic university of America Press, 1947). Hereafter I use this

individual sound discretions, as single syllables, into groups, which result in extensions or metric organization—although the writer indicates that both terms, rhythm and meter, raise difficulties of definition. In Book 6 the liberal discipline of music, as Harrison shows, "is effectively transposed into a carefully arranged, systematic theology of God, Creation, the Fall and redemption: God is the eternal, immutable source of music (or rhythm/number); creation is brought into existence from nothing insofar as it possesses music (or rhythm/number); human beings fall insofar as they have become caught up in this music (or rhythm/number) and failed to look beyond it; they are redeemed insofar as they are once again inspired to love and delight in it as God's creation (in other words, to use it rather than enjoy it or take it as an end in itself)."[59] In book 6 Augustine traces out the grades of the various numbers involved in poetic meters. Even the limited focus on meter brings the mind to realize that the universe entire is at every level formed into beauty by the pervasive power of number. He establishes a hierarchy leading from the lowest numbers accessible to sense observation, upward through six higher levels-the familiar septenary scheme remains intact-terminating at the very seat of intelligibility and beauty, the divine.[60] In particular, the doctrine of the fall is discreetly insinuated in Augustine's morality verses. Augustine is bringing his disciple to see that the various operations involved in the investigation of metrics suppose the existence, first, of sounding numbers, numerical proportions embodied in spoken verse; then reacting numbers embodied in the ear's rhythmic reaction to the sounding numbers it hears. Another grade, of advancing numbers, is required to explain the soul's capacity to produce numerically proportioned sounds. Still another grade is needed: the soul must harbor a store of sensible memorial numbers, equipping it to recognize meters it has become familiar with. Finally, but still on the sense-level, a fifth set of judicial numbers must account for the natural, pre-rational judgments of sense whereby sounds are found either pleasant or painful.[61] Augustine sets out to rank these various grades of number hierarchically. The question swiftly arises whether sounding or reacting numbers are superior. Initially, the answer is entertained that the former seem to act toward

---

translation.

59. Harrison, "Getting Carried Away," 15.
60. O'Connell, *Art and the Christian Intelligence in St. Augustine*, 67.
61. Ibid., 72.

production of the latter, and therefore, as causes to effects, must be of a higher order. But this would imply that the body is superior to soul, since the sounding numbers are evidently bodily, whereas the reacting numbers are present in the soul. This power of the body to act upon the soul Augustine concedes to be subject of amazement.[62]

> There is nothing lost in our looking more carefully. For, either we shall find in the human soul superior ones, or, if it should be clear there are none in it higher, we shall confirm these to be the highest in it. For it is one thing not to be, and another not to be capable of being found either by us or any man. But I think when that verse Deus creator omnium we quoted is sung, we hear it through reacting numbers, recognize it through memorial numbers, pronounce it through advancing numbers, are delighted through judicial numbers, and appraise it by still others, and in accordance with these more hidden numbers we bring another judgment on this delight, a kind of judgment on the judicial numbers.[63]

According to Augustine, the mind is raised from the consideration of changeable numbers in inferior things to unchangeable numbers in unchangeable truth itself. The implication is that the sound-embodied numbers, which delight us in measures of verse as they strike our ear, proceed in downward cascade from the eternal numbers, which themselves proceed from God. Augustine states:

> We have only recalled what belongs most to this present discussion, that all this is done by God's Providence He has created and rules all things through, so even the sinful and miserable soul may be moved by numbers and set numbers moving even to the lowest corruption of the flesh. And these numbers can be less and less beautiful, but they can't lack beauty entirely. But God, most good and most just, grudges no beauty whether fashioned by the soul's damnation, retreat, or perseverance. But number also begins from one, and is beautiful in equality and likeness, and bound by order.[64]

This cosmic backdrop for the mind's ascent from lowest to highest numbers and to God, the fount of numerical beauty, is precisely what Augustine had in mind when he conceived of his ambitious project on

---

62. O'Connell, *Art and the Christian Intelligence in St. Augustine*, 73.

63. *mus.* 6.9.23.

64. *mus.* 6.17.56.

the disciplines. The mind must be led through corporeal to incorporeal realities. Augustine wrote:

> But God alone is superior to it, and only body is inferior to it, if you mean the soul whole and entire ... But when the Lord is neglected, intent on its servant with the carnal concupiscence it is seduced by, the soul feels the movements it gives its servant, and is less; yet not so inferior as its servant, even when it is ate the lowest in its own nature.[65]

At the end of Book 6, Augustine suggests that music and the words are not just inseparable but one and the same thing. Augustine thinks that the reason why the immutable rules of music is possible, and the reason why he is able to use classical meter as a way of identifying the immutable truths of music in Books 1–5, is because God is the Creator of that music; He is the eternal, immutable rhythm who is heard in and through the temporal rhythms of music.[66] In other words, the music and the words, the sound and signification of the hymn being sung are inseparable.

SUMMARY

In this chapter, I expounded on Confucius, Mencius and Augustine's music. In terms of Confucius' music, it has an important position in achieving happiness. However, it is not a mere pleasant pastime for joyful comfort and amusement, but represents a supreme spiritual force for the cultivation of one's moral character as the purest sound of the heart. This indicates the transcendental aspect of Confucius' music. Like other methods of his self-cultivation, Confucius' music also focuses on how to live in harmony in communitarian aspect. It is because the nature of music is to take part in playing harmoniously together. Like Confucius, Mencius presented a vision of happiness resulting from the balanced practice of the great virtues such as benevolence, righteousness, wisdom. The content of music is the happiness that comes of delighting in such virtues. Given that such virtues are inextricably related to filial piety in the context of family life, the essence of music should be understood in a communitarian way. Hence, he highlighted how to enjoy music in the perspective of community. Like Confucius and Mencius, for Augustine virtue is not an end in itself but a means to achieve

---

65. *mus.* 6.5.13.
66. Harrison, "Getting Carried Away," 16.

happiness. For Augustine the final purpose of life is the enjoyment of God. He pointed out that the temptation of hearing in the music of hymns prevents the enjoyment of God in the process of ordering our soul to God. On the other hand, in his early work Augustine regarded music as a liberal art that leads the mind to God. It is an important part of Christian moral formation. Music is the study of rhythm in language and sound, and numeric proportion as the mathematical discipline like other liberal arts such as grammar, dialectic, rhetoric, geometry, astronomy, and arithmetic. These seem to be crowned by mathematics, the study of numbers themselves, which holds the key to the study of metaphysics, which in turn is necessary to successfully investigate basic questions about God and the soul. In *De Musica*, Augustine transposed the liberal discipline of music into a carefully arranged, systematic theology of God, Creation, the Fall and redemption: God is the eternal, immutable source of music (or rhythm/number); creation is brought into existence from nothing insofar as it possesses music (or rhythm/number); human beings fall insofar as they have become caught up in this music (or rhythm/number). The music and the words, the sound and signification of the hymn being sung are inseparable.

6

Confucian Augustinianism

IN THIS BOOK MY main aim was to show Confucian Augustinianism as a new theological angle on Confucian-Christian ethics and modern Augustinianism such as Augustinian realism, Augustinian proceduralism, Augustinian civic liberalism, and Radical Orthodoxy by discovering the analogies and differences in Confucius' and Mencius' self-cultivation and Augustine's caring of the soul for cultivating virtue which bridges between Confucians and Augustine. In order to cultivate virtues Confucius and Mencius shows *xue* (學), *si* (思), *li* (禮), and *yue* (樂).[1] These methods offer a framework for comparing with Augustine's moral learning, contemplation, sacrament, and music. As intertextual reasoning, as many scholars such as Gadamer, Clooney, Sugirtharajah, and Yeo argue, points out the limit of neutrality,[2] such a comparison of Confucian and Augustinian accounts of formation in the virtues is not confined in academic discourse to just identifying their similarities and differences conducted by religious scholars in university settings who would seek to find a neutral standpoint. Comparative theology which requires faith is different from comparative religion, but the fields are not entirely separate. The comparative theologian also needs to be an academic scholar in the field of religious study.[3] This research reveals new theological angles on the formation of moral self in the two traditions.

1. *Analects*, 8.8.
2. Gadamer, *Truth and Method*, 387; Clooney, "Comparative Theology," 12; Sugirtharajah, *Asian Biblical Hermeneutics and Postcolonialism*, 3-24; Lee, "Cross-Textual Hermeneutics and Identity in Multi-Scriptural Asia," 200; Yeo, *Musing with Confucius and Paul*, 53.
3. Clooney, "Comparative Theology," 12.

215

This research presents a way to think about what a Confucian Augustinianism might look like, which might in turn inform Christian identities in Asian contexts shaped by Confucianism. Given that some urban Chinese intellectuals are converting to Protestantism, which is deeply formed by the Neoplatonic worldview of Augustine,[4] this intertextual reading of Confucianism and Augustinianism offers theological hermeneutics on the formation of moral self to them.[5] We have observed an antecedent to this book in the dialogues between Confucianism and Christianity initiated by Matteo Ricci, who was influenced by the Aristotelian worldview of Thomas Aquinas. Protestant missionaries to China in the nineteenth and twentieth centuries as non-conformists are thought not to contribute to the East-West cultural exchange in spite of productive results of their charitable works such as hospitals and schools.[6] In this book, we have seen that dialogue between the two traditions which draws on an Augustinian perspective can be fruitful. In conclusion, we find that Confucian Augustinianism can be "a *via media* between the negative anthropology of Augustine and the positive anthropology of China traditional teachings."[7]

This research has used intertextual reasoning between Confucian and Augustinian traditions to crest a conceptual bridge around the acquisition of virtue in moral formation as described variously in the two traditions. For this task, I have sought neither Deontology nor Utilitarianism, neither syncretism nor theological authoritarianism, neither internalism nor transcendentalism, and neither communitarianism nor liberalism.[8] Instead, I have tried to show a middle way between conservative and liberal approaches.[9] If the middle way set forth in this book needs a label to locate it in the context of East Asia, then Confucian Augustinianism would serve well in that the term shows potential for mutual learning in the dimension of constructive theology. Both classical Confucians and Augustine's early works focus on the formation of moral

---

4. Chow, *Theosis, Sino-Christian Theology and the Second Chinese Enlightenment*, 170.

5. Chow, "Calvinist Public Theology in Urban China Today," 158.

6. Loewe, "Imperial China's Reactions to the Catholic Missions," 181.

7. Chow, *Theosis, Sino-Christian Theology and the Second Chinese Enlightenment*, 170.

8. Cf. Bernd Wannenwetsch, *Political Worship* (Oxford: Oxford University Press, 2004), 1.

9. Biggar, *Behaving in Public: How to do Christian Ethics*, xvii.

self in order to acquire virtue which leads to happiness. This comparative work focuses on how to embody the Way of Heaven by cultivating virtue (德) rather than the theology of Heaven (天) or lists of virtues.[10] There are three kinds of Confucian theology according to understanding of Heaven in the Confucian tradition. In the Confucian classics of *Book of Documents*, *Books of Poetry*, and *Analects*, Heaven is regarded as something transcendent of the world, similar to the Christian God. For Neo-Confucians, Heaven is the wonderful life-giving activity transcending the world within the world. For contemporary Confucians such as Xiong Shili, Mou Zongsan, and Tu Weiming Heaven is something "immanently transcendent," the ultimate reality immanent in the world to transcend the world.[11] Contrary to that understanding of Heaven, Confucian Augustinianism focuses on how to live on the basis of cultivating virtues rather than synthesis of the doctrine of God in relation to indigenisation and contextualisation.[12] Confucian Augustinianism is different from the religious-cultural theology of the Korean Methodist Church which was developed through discussions with indigenous traditions such as Shamanism (Yu Dong-Sik), Confucianism (Yun Sung-Bum who suggests that there are some traces of the Trinity in the myth of Dan-gun), and Buddhism (Byun Son-Hwan) in the aftermath of the reawakening of national consciousness after 1960. Confucian Augustinianism shows specific methods for sanctification by linking the self to family, community, nation, and transcendent God.[13] Confucian Augustinianism is different from the belief of many Western missionaries and Chinese Christians. They thought of 'Confucianization' of Christian theology, using the Confucian terminology or framework to articulate Christian theology, as the goal of their theological endeavours, especially before the twentieth century. Given that several frameworks for organising the broad landscape of Chinese and Korean Christian theology in the past has often tended to focus on certain debates and impasses, resulting in the use of labels like 'fundamentalist' or 'patriot,' Confucian Augustinianism provides a new angle of Christian ethics beyond the two poles of religiophilosophical traditions and sociopolitical quests.

---

10. Berthrong, "Chinese (Confucian) Philosophical Theology," 17, 20; Huang, "Confucian Theology: Three Models," 455.

11. Huang, "Confucian Theology," 455.

12. Kim, *Theology in the Public Sphere*, 50.

13. Duara, *The Crisis of Global Modernity*, 2.

This research has revealed a significant and crucial difference. For Confucius and Mencius the public sphere is more critical to identity formation as its end and goal, but Augustine is more drawn to a more inward trajectory in describing the moral formation and the core identity of the Christian. For Augustine the self is the metaphor of the soul in the struggle of both body and soul to construct a view of God in which true happiness exists.[14] For Augustine the formation of moral self is the process of finding truth, God. In moral learning Augustine highlights divine illumination by Christ as the inner Teacher rather than language by external teachers to secure certainty.[15] Our minds have direct access to the eternal truth of reason in that the mind is illuminated with knowledge by the inner Teacher. By the light of Christ or the light of God the mind is able to distinguish the objects of intellectual vision.[16] His moral learning is based on his doctrine of the image of God in that human beings were created to the image of the Trinity in the evidence of memory, understanding, and will.[17] He presents the theological context of memory, understanding, and will as three aspects of the mind in the dimension of the Persons of the Trinity. Like the Persons of the Trinity, which is distinguished as one God, Augustine shows that their relations among memory, understanding, and will are equal to each as a whole and to all as wholes at the same time. For Augustine contemplation of God is to purify the self. As a way of purifying our minds, Augustine makes an emphasis on cultivating pure desires and virtuous habits.[18] For him contemplation of things unseen, as immediate knowledge of a transcendent God discovered within the soul, plays an important role in the formation of moral self. Contemplation of eternal things is connected with wisdom as knowledge of God, not knowledge of temporal matter.[19] Given that his understanding of contemplation drives from his depiction of human nature as a substantial unity of soul and body, contemplation is a binding of the mind to God.[20] For Augustine sacrament is also the

---

14. Cary, *Augustine's Invention of the Inner Self*, 10.
15. *mag.* 11.38.
16. *mag.* 14.45.
17. *Trin.* 10.11.18.
18. *doc. Chr.* 1.10. cf. *Trin.* 1.8.17.
19. *Trin.* 12. 22.
20. *mor.* 1.5.7.

process of ordering the soul to God.²¹ In the process, he shows how grace becomes part of the formation of moral self through sacraments such as baptism and marriage. Augustine's view of the sacraments is based upon the conception of Christ, the high priest without sin, who is the sole giver of sacramental grace. For Augustine baptism is the way in which God's grace acts on us to forgive and wash away all previous sins, and the beginning of membership in the church, the body of Christ here on Earth, oriented toward its heavenly head, that is, Christ. For Augustine, Christ is the one who opens up the way to our heavenly country by forgiving our sins. However, it is necessary to observe that Augustine did not regard baptism as the completion on the way of salvation. He is against those who overemphasize the effects of baptism. Baptism gives us a new start on the way of salvation but the full renewal of the image of God within our minds is only completed in the afterlife. For Augustine the weight of original sin cannot be neglected in the formation of moral self. For Mencius evil is the result of contact between a good human nature and a wicked environment whereas for Xunzi human nature is evil, but both agree in an overall optimism in the human potential in the formation of moral self.²² In Augustine's early work he regards music as a liberal art that leads the mind to God.²³ Music is the study of rhythm in language and sound, and numeric proportion as a mathematical discipline like other liberal arts such as grammar, dialectic, rhetoric, geometry, astronomy, and arithmetic. These seem to be crowned by mathematics, the study of numbers themselves, which holds the key to the study of metaphysics, which in turn is necessary to successfully investigate basic questions about God and the soul.²⁴ In *De Musica*, Augustine transposed the liberal discipline of music into a carefully arranged, systematic theology of God, creation, the fall and redemption. The music and the words, the sound and signification of the hymn being sung are inseparable. This indicates that Confucian Augustinianism is not only a virtue-oriented theology but also a sin-oriented one. In Augustinian realism, Augustine's controversial doctrine of original sin and his dramatic narrative about two cities were reconstructed in the threat of fascism and

---

21. *ord.* 1.9.27.
22. Chow, "The East Asian Rediscovery of Sin," 128.
23. *ord.* 2.17.44.
24. *ord.* 2.14.41.

Marxism.[25] Augustinian realism was closely allied with another kind of realism indebted to Machiavelli and Weber between World War I and the end of the Cold War. In Niebuhr's version of politics, the central fact of human nature this side of the Eschaton is sin, and it is the purpose of government, not to eliminate sin, but to constrain or ameliorate its bad effects. Liberal democracy is the least bad form of government because it recognizes government's limited, sin-constraining role. In defending it, Niebuhr argues it is necessary to have a realistic understanding of human nature and a willingness to use force and the threat of force in the interest of maintaining order and approximating justice. Augustinian realists offer a limited conception of politics as restraining evil, a conception that often travels with a troubling form of moral consequentialism. For Augustinian realists, sentimental attempts to drive a social ethics from the gospel commandment of love are dangerous. However, Confucian Augustinianism highlights the importance of benevolent government by the man of virtue as a way of achieving peace and happiness. In order to raise the man of virtue Confucian Augustinianism offers specific methods such as moral learning, contemplation, sacramental ritual, and music. Confucian Augustinianism seeks economic reform for a just society through political reform by raising the man of virtue. It is different from Augustinian proceduralism which emerges in positive response to the massive influence of John Rawls' theory of "justice as fairness" in 1970s and 1980s.[26] Confucian Augustinianism provides justice in the national dimension whereas Augustinian proceduralism offers a minimalist conception of justice which privatizes important virtues such as friendship and compassion.

For Confucius and Mencius the concept of self is different from Augustine. As Mencius states "the heart of compassion is the germ of benevolence; the heart of shame, of righteousness; the heart of courtesy and modesty, of propriety; the heart of right and wrong, of wisdom."[27] Humans already have potential-self in heart bestowed by Heaven. Such virtues exist in the human heart from the beginning as potential. Hence, Mencius emphasizes self-reflection as a method for forming moral self in order to find virtues originally in the heart. Theses virtues are not infused from outside and universal to all people, so there are no differences

---

25. Gregory, *Politics and the Order of Love*, 10-11.
26. Ibid., 12.
27. *Mencius*, 2A6. As translated in Lau.

between sages and people in finding such virtues in the mind. For him, the way to serve Heaven is to preserve one's mental constitution, and nourish one's nature. The man of virtue is not a unique being but the one who preserves such virtues in his heart. An achieved state of moral excellence is not an individual entity but a tendency.[28] Just as Confucius highlights the importance of practice, Mencius stresses continually learning from sages such as the Way of Yao, Shun, and Confucius in order to overcome sexual desire and poverty which obstruct the goal of becoming the man of virtue.[29] For Confucius and Mencius, the immanence of the Way lies in the human heart, which constitutes the foundation for the human potentiality for transcendence. This capacity for transcendence is what Christianity fails to recognise in the perspective of original sin. In contrast, for Augustine habit cannot make humans perfect. The force of habit bound down by the disease of the flesh devastates the will of overcoming sexual desire.[30] He states that the grace of God, through Jesus Christ our Lord can cure it. Sexual desire is an inevitable matter for those who lack self-control. Hence, he demonstrates that the pressure of sexual desire can be relieved in the condition of marriage. In terms of inward sagehood, it is necessary for Augustine to learn from Confucius and Mencius who present moral pedagogies for "the proper conduct of daily life" as the case for the Confucian Way.[31] Augustine's moral education, as Topping argues, can develop individuals in caring for the soul rather than societies.[32] In Augustine's view, progress is restricted due to the limitation of our knowledge and virtue. In the dimension of an eschatological goal, social progress is primarily in intellectual terms, secondarily in moral terms, and not at all in material terms. Hence, Topping insists, as Wetzel and O'Donovan argue, that Augustine's pedagogy is best understood against the horizon of his evolution on the possibilities of human perfection, and in particular the limits of virtue which "can be encouraged but not guaranteed."[33] Augustine's Christian virtue is far from perfect and his happiness is not complete.[34] Both Confucian Augustinianism

28. *Mencius*, 6B11.

29. *Mencius*, 4A1.

30. *conf.* 8.5.10.

31. Lai, "Chinese Culture and the Development of Chinese Christian Theology," 232; Berthrong, "Chinese (Confucian) Philosophical Theology," 17.

32. Topping, *St. Augustine*, 86

33. Ibid., 90, 94.

34. Herdt, *Putting on Virtue*, 70.

and Augustinian civic liberalism pay attention to rectifying the limit of individualism. Augustinian civic liberalism emerged in 1990 in works by Jean Bethke Elshtain, Timothy P. Jackson, Rowan Williams, and Oliver O'Donovan on the roots of Paul Tillich, Martin Luther King Jr, Paul Ramsey, and Gustavo Gutierrez. Love of God and neighbor play a central role in an Augustinian social vision.[35] Civic liberalism is a virtue-oriented liberalism that aims to avoid individualistic and rationalistic assumptions about human nature as well as romantic or totalitarian conceptions of political community.[36] This relies on a virtue-oriented rather than merely sin-oriented Augustinian politics.[37] Civic liberalism corresponding to liberal perfectionism in contemporary political philosophy allows ideal conceptions of human flourishing into the full light of the public square, conceptions that already shape practical deliberations of public decision-making and normatively evaluate the effects of liberal justice.[38] However, given that Confucian Augustinianism is developed in the context of the rapid growth of East Asian Christians, Confucian Augustinianism realizes Augustine's Christian virtue in the public dimension by introducing methods for Confucian inward sagehood. Confucian Augustinianism leaves ample room for gradual process and transformation for sanctification in order to be renewed in God's image through Confucian self-cultivation and Augustinian caring for soul. Confucian Augustinianism stresses the virtue of humility and sincerity (誠) in the process of cultivating virtues.

I argue that Confucian Augustinianism offers an angle on Christian public engagement in the context of East Asia. Considering the Christian church has a calling to tell the truth about God in the light of Jesus Christ, and about human good and right action in the light of this God, Christians ought to participate in shaping public life by way of prophetic critique.[39] In this context, this intertextual reasoning offers theological implications in public spheres as an important part of "doing" theology in a multi-religious society.[40] Comparing classical Confucians with Augustine enables Chinese public theologians to enlarge their horizons by

---

35. Gregory, *Politics and the Order of Love*, 12.
36. Ibid., 10.
37. Ibid., 14.
38. Ibid., 10.
39. Biggar, *Behaving in Public*, 107.
40. Kim, *Theology in the Public Sphere*, 50.

relating their theology to their own tradition for solving their current socio-political issues as well as religious ones.[41] Confucian Augustinianism as public theology has the aspect of theological contextualisation in the dimension of broader indigenisation.[42] Confucian Augustinianism seeks happiness and virtue through multi-disciplinary engagement and open debate for a fair society. Confucian Augustinianism provides political and public perspectives, but it is different from liberation and political theologies such as Latin American liberation theology (Gustavo Gutiérrez, Leonardo Boff, José Míguez Bonino), Minjung theology (Suh Nam-Dong, Ahn Byeung-Mu), feminist theology (Elisabeth Fiorenza, Rosemary Ruether), black theology (James Cone, Dwight Hopkins, Allan Boesak), Dalit theology (A. P. Nirmal, Nirmal Minz, Sathianathan Clarke), and political theology (Johann Baptist Metz, Jürgen Moltmann). Confucian Augustinianism is not limited in a specific race, ethnicity, gender, and class such as feminist theology, black theology, and Dalit theology. Confucian Augustinianism which is based on virtue ethics as common ground between Confucians and Augustine shows methodologies for engaging in public issues with civil society for its articulation of theology in the public sphere. Particularly, it is different from Latin American liberation theology. Both Confucian Augustinianism and Latin American liberation theology pay attention to the need for a just society for the poor and oppressed. Latin American liberation theology influenced by Marxism has the weak point of lacking spirituality, unlike Confucian Augustinianism. For Latin American liberation theologians, a system is evil or wrong like a Manichean view on the world. Augustine argues marriage was instituted by God at the beginning of creation by citing the sayings of Jesus against the Manichees and their rejection of sexual intercourse and procreation as inherently evil.[43] Every system in Confucian Augustinianism is not evil. In this context, Minjung theology, formed in the context of South Korea and influenced by Latin American liberation theology, faced a lack of support from general church members in spite of its contributions such as justice for minjung, having *han* that indicates the sense of deep despair and reconciliation of two Koreas.[44] Unlike Latin American liberation theology and Minjung theology,

41. Ibid., 50.

42. Wing-hung Lam, "*Patterns of Chinese Theology,*" *Occasional Bulletin of Missionary Research* 4:1 (1980), 20.

43. Hunter, "Marriage," 535.

44. Kim, *Theology in the Public Sphere*, 23.

Confucian Augustinianism offers profound spirituality with the engagement of Augustinian biblical and systematic theology.

Confucian Augustinianism can also help overcome the limit of Augustinian accounts of the self. The Confucian concept of self is deeply situated within the family and society. For Confucius, moral learning is significantly public and political. He stresses the cultivation of virtue as a solution for solving political turmoil in relation to self-cultivation because it leads to benevolent government by fostering the man of virtue.[45] He offers the Zhou dynasty as the ideal model of antiquity for an object of moral learning instead of exploring extraordinary things, feats of strength, disorder, spiritual beings, and death.[46] In relation to ritual propriety, Confucius emphasizes loyalty (忠) and reciprocity (恕) in the *Book of Poetry*.[47] He thought tradition and imitating good teachers are the best methods for the practice of virtue. Given that for Confucius the aim of moral learning is to cultivate moral self, he presents the importance of practicing filial piety (孝) and fraternal submission (弟) as a method of moral learning.[48] Like Confucius, for Mencius becoming the man of virtue is inextricably linked to establishing benevolent government since the purpose of ruler is to protect his people in supporting God.[49] According to Mencius, kings ought to pay attention to the people even in commencing war because Heaven sees and hears through people's eyes and ears.[50] Considering political chaos raised by war in his time, for Mencius human unity created by benevolent government is the most powerful weapon.[51] Mencius regards filial piety as a core of benevolent government, so he enthusiastically insists on reform of economic, social, and educational systems in the perspective of supporting filial piety.[52] In other words, he thought moral learning of filial piety could be possible on the basis of economic and social supports for ordinary people. He stressed the importance of asceticism in moral learning for the superior. His anti-asceticism could be only justified in the relation between a king and the

---

45. *Analects*, 12.10.
46. *Analects*, 7.21.
47. *Analects*, 4.15.
48. *Analects*, 1.2.
49. *Mencius*, 1B3.
50. *Mencius*, 5A5.
51. *Mencius*, 2B1.
52. *Mencius*, 1A7.

people. Ultimately, he stresses a moderate living in dealing only with lifestyle of the king in the evidence of the ancient sovereigns.[53] Given that Protestant individualism emphasising more progressive conception of the role of the individual led to considerable growth of the Protestant churches in Korea since the Second World War by attracting Koreans who were dissatisfied with Confucianism, Confucian Augustinianism can rectify the limit of Protestant individualism based on Augustinian moral education.[54]

Confucius' ritual propriety is also highly public and political. He focuses on how to harmoniously live with others. That is to practice benevolence by subduing one's self.[55] It is about human behavior, not supernatural things. Returning to ritual propriety is not to look at what is contrary to ritual propriety, not to listen to what is contrary to ritual propriety, not to speak what is contrary to ritual propriety, and not to avoid any movement which is contrary to ritual propriety. It is about human behavior. This indicates that the matter of practicing benevolence depends on the will of man.[56] He highlights how the man of virtue maintains consistency of speech and action in accordance with ritual propriety.[57] For Confucius, the man of virtue is modest in his speech, but exceeds in his actions. He regards the one who is hesitant in his speech as the benevolent person since he already understands the problem of narrowing the gap between speech and action. Hence, he emphasizes the Mean (中庸) in ritual propriety.[58] In relation to speech, Confucius made an emphasis on rectifying names as a specific method for rightly realizing ritual propriety in managing government.[59] It is because inappropriate names give rise to producing language apart from the truth of thing results in failure of affairs which might prevent accurately conducting ritual propriety and music. The decline of ritual and music may lead to a situation that punishments are not properly awarded, so that the people do

53. *Mencius*, 1B4.

54. Northcott, "Christianity in Asia," 532; Max Weber, *The Protestant Ethic and the Spirit of Capitalism*, trans. Talcott Parsons (New York: Charles Scribner's Sons, 1958), 47-78; R. H. Tawney, *Religion and the Rise of Capitalism* (Harmondsworth: Penguin Books, 1975), 111.

55. *Analects*, 12.1.

56. *Analects*, 17.6.

57. *Analects*, 15.18.

58. *Analects*, 6.29.

59. *Analects*, 13.3.

not know how to virtuously behave.[60] Mencius also highlights the role of ritual propriety in relation to benevolence and righteousness.[61] This indicates that ritual propriety is not utilitarian.[62] Mencius states the man of virtue carries out ritual propriety according to his nature which includes a sense of shame, unlike animals. In obtaining a government position, he emphasizes the importance of ritual propriety even though for the man of virtue taking an office is highly important. He thought that funerals ought not to be conducted with a utilitarian aspect but ritual propriety.

Like other methods of his self-cultivation, for Confucius and Mencius music shows how to live in harmony and to be happy. For Confucius the nature of music is to take part in playing harmoniously together as a supreme spiritual force for the cultivation of one's moral character.[63] Mencius presented a vision of happiness resulting from the balanced practice of the great virtues such as benevolence, righteousness, wisdom.[64] The content of music is the happiness that comes of delighting in such virtues. Given that such virtues are inextricably related to filial piety in the context of family life, the essence of music should be understood in political dimension.

Compared to Confucius and Mencius, Augustine is less inclined to public engagement. Particularly, Augustine pays less attention to the public political self even though he also emphasizes community in the formation of moral self. He deals with the formation of moral self in relation to how to channel sexual desire in the search for truth. He highlights the role of friendship in moral learning since it helps search for truth in life.[65] As Augustine, in his youth, used to be led in the wrong direction not all friends made constructive contributions to his moral learning. Before conversion to Christianity, he planned to establish a common household with a group of his friends in the basis of friendship in order to live a life of peace away from the crowd. Friendship seemed to be a comfort in a human society filled with misunderstanding and calamities. After his conversion to faith in Jesus Christ in adulthood, however, his aim of friendship was transformed. For Augustine, the world is no longer

60. *Analects*, 13.3.
61. *Mencius*, 1A1.
62. *Mencius*, 7B33.
63. *Analects*, 16.5.
64. *Mencius*, 4A27.
65. *ep.* 73.3.

pure material and true reality is only comprehended when we know of the transcendent God. In order to seek God he invited a diverse group of friends such as Alypius, Nebridius, and Evodius to join him in friendship in the monastic community.[66] By bringing together such a community, he attempted to pursue the happy life. They became friends in Christ. When Augustine retired to Cassiciacum in September 386 in the aftermath of his conversion, he gathered his friends to focus on spiritual understanding by entering upon a life of creative leisure. And then when he returned to Tagaste he attempted to organize his community, to found the personal relations within it upon a permanent code of behavior, to be responsible for the measure of authority over them. At Hippo, Augustine put his heart and soul in the monastery in order to foster moral learning. The monastery instituted, inspired, and directed by Augustine became a pivotal development in the life of the church of Africa during the last decade of the fourth century and the first quarter of the fifth century.[67] As his monastery became a 'seminary' in the true sense of the word, it came to form an influential group within African church.[68] Augustine's monastery was a community for seeking truth rather than political one.

Marriage is highlighted by both classical Confucians and Augustine in connection with family. Contrary to Confucius and Mencius, who deal with it based on filial piety and public ritual practices such as a funeral, Augustine would uphold the goodness of marriage in the dimension of procreation, fidelity, and sacrament in relation to tackling sexual desire.[69] For Augustine marriage is not a contract but a sacrament. The Manichees taught a dualistic cosmology in which the forces of good and evil were opposed to each other. Under the Manichean scheme marriage and sexuality were evil in that procreation led to the imprisonment of spiritual souls of light in material bodies. Against the Manichees and their rejection of sexual intercourse and procreation as inherently evil, Augustine defended the goodness of the married state and the fact that marriage was instituted by God at the beginning of creation by citing the sayings of Jesus (Matt. 19:3-9) and the letters of Paul (1 Cor. 7; Eph. 5).[70] For Augustine, marriage is the first natural bond of human society, and offspring is

---

66. *conf.* 8.6.13.
67. Beaver, "The Rise of Monasticism in the Church of Africa," 350.
68. Brown, *Augustine of Hippo*, 137.
69. *nupt. et conc.* 1.11.
70. Hunter, "Marriage," 535.

the first social union of the human race.[71] Human nature is social, so God arranged for human beings to be connected to one another not only as members of the same species, but also by the bonds of physical kinship. Fidelity is the commitment to engage in sexual relations only with one's spouse, to avoid adultery. But fidelity also involves the mutual responsibility of married persons to engage in sex with each other by relieving the pressure of sexual desire in order to help the other to refrain from adultery. For Augustine, marriage is a certain sacramental bond. It is a monogamous and indissoluble union until the death of one of the spouses. In the sacramentality of Christian marriage divorce is not allowed. Fundamentally, Augustine's understanding of marriage is not political but sacramental. Both Confucian Augustinianism and Radical Orthodoxy highlight the use of a reading of Augustine, but Confucian Augustinianism is different from Radical Orthodoxy that emerged out of Anglican social thought (especially Christian socialism) as an intellectual, cultural, and ecumenical movement in the late 1980s.[72] In terms of marriage, Confucian Augustinianism is based on the concept of Confucian family and Augustinian sacrament whereas Radical Orthodoxy mainly depends on the Western theology and philosophy. Confucian Augustinianism makes a room for Confucian thinking through virtue ethics.

In a nutshell, Confucian Augustinianism as teleological, constructive, political, public, sacramental and sin-virtue oriented theology can offer a useful via media for the formation of moral self by mutually making up for their weak points. Augustinians can learn public ritual practices and the public political self from classical Confucians whereas Confucians need to attend more to spiritual experience in moral formation of the pubic self. Confucian Augustinianism which is based on virtue ethics as common ground between Confucians and Augustine not only shows methodologies for engaging in public issues with civil society for its articulation of theology in the public sphere, but also provides profound spirituality with the engagement of Augustinian biblical and systematic theology unlike liberation theologies. In contrast to Augustinian realism (hope), Augustinian proceduralism (justice), Augustinian civic liberalism (love), and Radical Orthodoxy (love), Confucian Augustinianism highlights the virtue of humility and sincerity for the practice of love. Confucian Augustinianism offers distinguishing methods for cultivating

---

71. *b. conjug.* 6.6.
72. Gregory, *Politics and the Order of Love*, 125.

self and sanctification by linking the self to family, community, nation, and transcendent God.[73] It can rectify the limit of Protestant individualism. Confucian Augustinianism offers a perspective of Asian Christians on Augustinianism in the rapid growth of Christians in Asia contrary to previous Western Augustinianism. Confucian Augustinianism could make Asian Christians happy in truth. Confucian Augustinianism is to seek true happiness by cultivating virtue and promoting inward, outward, and upward self through moral learning, contemplation, sacramental ritual, and music on the basis of biblical truth in a pluralistic global context. Confucian Augustinianism contributes to the evangelization and social harmony in Jesus' name by showing how to enjoy God, follow Jesus, and live in the Holy Spirit.

Amen.

73. Duara, *The Crisis of Global Modernity*, 2.

Bibliography

CONFUCIUS: PRIMARY SOURCES AND TRANSLATIONS

The Analects. Translated by James Legge. Oxford: Clarendon Press, 1893.
The Analects 論語. Translated by Jong-Yeon Park. Seoul: Eulyu, 2011.
The Analects. Translated by Raymond Dawson. Oxford: Oxford University Press, 2008.
The Doctrine of the Mean. Translated by James Legge in th*e Chinese Classics*, vol. 1. T'ai-pei: Wen hsing shu tien, 1966.
The Doctrine of the Mean 中庸. Translated by Se-Dong Lee. Seoul: Eulyu, 2011.
The Great Learning. Translated by James Legge in *the Chinese Classics*, vol. 1. T'ai-pei: Wen hsing shu tien, 1966.
The Great Learning 大學. Translated by Se-Dong Lee. Seoul: Eulyu, 2011.

MENCIUS: PRIMARY SOURCES AND TRANSLATIONS

Mencius. Translated by Irene Bloom. New York: Columbia University Press, 2011.
Mencius. Translated by D. C. Lau. London: Penguin Books, 2004.
Mencius 孟子. Translated by Jae-Ho Woo. Seoul: Eulyu, 2010.
The Works of Mencius. Translated by James Legge. New York: Dover, 1970.

AUGUSTINE: PRIMARY SOURCES AND TRANSLATIONS

Augustine. *Against the Academicians and The Teacher*. Translated by Peter King. Cambridge: Hackett publishing Company, 1995.
———. *Answer to Faustus, a Manichean*. Translated by Roland Teske in *a Translation for the 21st Century*, vol. I/20. New York: New City Press, 2007.
———. *Against Lying*. Translated by H. Browne in Nicene and Post-Nicene Fathers, vol. 3. Peabody: Hendrickson, 1999.
———. *Arianism and Other Heresies: Heresies, Memorandum to Augustine, To Orosius in Refutation of the Priscillianists and Origenists, Arian Sermon, Answer to Arian Sermon, Debate with Maximinus, Answer to Maximinus, Answer to an Enemy of*

the Law and the Prophets. Translated by Roland Teske in *a Translation for the 21st Century*, vol. I/18. New York: New City Press, 1995.

———. *On Baptism, Against the Donatists*. Translated by J. R. King in *Nicene and Post-Nicene Fathers*, vol. 4. New York: Christian Literature Publishing Co., 1887.

———. *The Catholic Way of Life and the Manichean Way of Life*. Translated by Richard Stothert in *Nicene and Post-Nicene Fathers*, vol. 4. New York: Christian Literature Publishing Co., 1887.

———. *On Christian Belief: True Religion, The Advantage of Believing, Faith and the Creed, Faith in the Unseen, Demonic Divination, Faith and Works, Enchiridion*. Translated by Edmund Hill in *a Translation for the 21st Century*, vol. I/8. New York: New City Press, 2005.

———. *Christian Doctrine*. Translated by James Shaw in *Nicene and Post-Nicene Fathers*, vol. 2. New York: Christian Literature Publishing Co., 1887.

———. *The City of God*. Translated by R. W. Dyson. Cambridge: Cambridge University Press, 2007.

———. *Confessions*. Translated by R. S. Pine-Coffin. London: Penguin Group, 1961.

———. *The Confessions*. Translated by Maria Boulding in *a Translation for the 21st Century*, vol. I/1. New York: New City Press, 1997.

———. *Eighty-Three Different Questions*. Translated by David L. Mosher. Washington, D.C.: The Catholic University of America Press, 1982

———. *Expositions of the Psalms*. Translated by J. E. Tweed in *Nicene and Post-Nicene Fathers*, vol. 8. New York: Christian Literature Publishing Co., 1888.

———. *Expositions on the Psalms 1–32*. Translated by Maria Boulding in *a Translation for the 21st Century*, vol. III/15. New York: New City Press, 2000.

———. *Expositions of the Psalms, 33–50*. Translated by Maria Boulding in *a Translation for the 21st Century*, vol. III/16. New York: New City Press, 2000.

———. *Expositions of the Psalms, 51–72*. Translated by Maria Boulding in *a Translation for the 21st Century*, vol. III/17. New York: New City Press, 2001.

———. *Expositions of the Psalms, 73–98*. Translated by Maria Boulding in *a Translation for the 21st Century*, vol. III/18. New York: New City Press, 2002.

———. *Expositions of the Psalms, 99–120*. Translated by Maria Boulding in *a Translation for the 21st Century*, vol. III/19. New York: New City Press, 2003.

———. *Expositions of the Psalms, 121–150*. Translated by Maria Boulding in *a Translation for the 21st Century*, vol. III/20. New York: New City Press, 2004.

———. *On Free Choice of the Will*. Translated by Thomas Williams. Cambridge: Hackett Publishing Company, 1993.

———. *On Genesis: On Genesis: A Refutation of the Manichees, Unfinished Literal Commentary on Genesis, The Literal Meaning of Genesis*. Translated by Edmund Hill in *a Translation for the 21st Century*, vol. I/13. New York: New City Press, 2002.

———. *Homilies on the First Epistle of John*. Translated by Boniface Ramsey in *a Translation for the 21st Century*, vol. I/14. New York: New City Press, 2008.

———. *Homilies on the Gospel of John 1–40*. Translated by Edmund Hill in *a Translation for the 21st Century*, vol. I/12. New York: New City Press, 2009.

———. *Letters 1–99*. Translated by Roland Teske in *a Translation for the 21st Century*, vol. II/1. New York: New City Press, 2001.

———. *Letters 100–155*. Translated by Roland Teske in *a Translation for the 21st Century*, vol. II/2. New York: New City Press, 2003.

———. *Letters 156–210*. Translated by Roland Teske in *a Translation for the 21st Century*, vol. II/3. New York: New City Press, 2004.

———. *Letters 211–270*. Translated by Roland Teske in *a Translation for the 21st Century*, vol. II/4. New York: New City Press, 2005.

———. *The Manichean Debate: The Catholic Way of Life and the Manichean Way of Life, The Two Souls, A Debate with Fortunatus, a Manichean, Answer to Adimantus, a Disciple of Mani, Answer to the Letter of Mani known as The Foundation, Answer to Felix, a Manichean, The Nature of the Good, Answer to Secundinus, a Manichean*. Translated by Roland Teske in *a Translation for the 21st Century*, vol. I/19. New York: New City Press, 2006.

———. *Marriage and Virginity: The Excellence of Marriage, Holy Virginity, The Excellence of Widowhood, Adulterous Marriages, Continence*. Translated by Ray Kearney in *a Translation for the 21st Century*, vol. I/9. New York: New City Press. 1999.

———. *On Music*. Translated by Robert Catesby Taliaferro in *the Fathers of the Church*, vol. 4. Washington: The Catholic university of America Press, 1947.

———. *On Order*. Translated by Silvano Borruso. Indiana: St. Augustine's Press, 2007.

———. *Answer to the Pelagians: The Punishment and Forgiveness of Sins and the Baptism of Little Ones, The Spirit and the Letter, Nature and Grace, The Perfection of Human Righteousness, The Deeds of Pelagius, The Grace of Christ and Original Sin, The Nature and Origin of the Soul*. Translated by Roland J. Teske in *a Translation for the 21st Century*, vol. I/23. New York: New City Press, 1997.

———. *Answer to the Pelagians, II: Marriage and Desire, Answer to the Two Letters of the Pelagians, Answer to Julian*. Translated by Roland J. Teske in *a Translation for the 21st Century*, vol. I/24. New York: New City Press, 1998.

———. *Answer to the Pelagians, III: Unfinished Work in Answer to Julian*. Translated by Roland J. Teske in *a Translation for the 21st Century*, vol. I/25. New York: New City Press, 1999.

———. *Answer to the Pelagians, IV: To the Monks of Hadrumetum and Provence*. Translated by Roland J. Teske in *a Translation for the 21st Century*, vol. I/26. New York: New City Press, 1999.

———. *Revisions*. Translated by Boniface Ramsey in *a Translation for the 21st Century*, vol. II/1. New York: New City Press, 2010.

———. *Sermons, (1–19) on the Old Testament*. Translated by Matthew J. O'Connell in *a Translation for the 21st Century*, vol. III/1. New York: New City Press, 1990.

———. *Sermons, (20–50) on the Old Testament*. Translated by Edmund Hill in *a Translation for the 21st Century*, vol. III/2. New York: New City Press, 1990.

———. *Sermons, (51–94) on the Old Testament*. Translated by Edmund Hill in *a Translation for the 21st Century*, vol. III/3. New York: New City Press, 1991.

———. *Sermons, (94A–147A) on the Old Testament*. Translated by Edmund Hill in *a Translation for the 21st Century*, vol. III/4. New York: New City Press, 1992.

———. *Sermons, (148–183) on the New Testament*. Translated by Edmund Hill in *a Translation for the 21st Century*, vol. III/5. New York: New City Press, 1992.

———. *Sermons, (184–229Z) on the Liturgical Seasons*. Translated by Edmund Hill in *a Translation for the 21st Century*, vol. III/6. New York: New City Press, 1993.

———. *Sermons, (230–272B) on the Liturgical Seasons*. Translated by Edmund Hill in *a Translation for the 21st Century*, vol. III/7. New York: New City Press, 1993.

———. *Sermons, (273–305A) on the Saints*. Translated by Edmund Hill in *a Translation for the 21st Century*, vol. III/8. New York: New City Press, 1994.

———. *Sermons, (306–340A) on the Saints*. Translated by Edmund Hill in *a Translation for the 21st Century*, vol. III/9. New York: New City Press, 1994.

———. *Sermons, (341–400) on Various Subjects*. Translated by Edmund Hill in *a Translation for the 21st Century*, vol. III/10. New York: New City Press, 1995.

———. *Sermons (Newly discovered)*. Translated by Edmund Hill in *a Translation for the 21st Century*, vol. III/11. New York: New City Press, 1997.

———. *Teaching Christianity*. Translated by Edmund Hill in *a Translation for the 21st Century*, vol. I/11. New York: New City Press, 1996.

———. *On the Holy Trinity*. Translated by Arthur West Haddan in *Nicene and Post-Nicene Fathers*, vol. 3. New York: Christian Literature Publishing Co., 1887.

———. *The Trinity*. Translated by Edmund Hill in *a Translation for the 21st Century*, vol. I/5. New York: New City Press, 1991.

GENERAL WORKS CITED

Allan, Sarah. "On the Identity of Shang Di 上帝 and the Origin of the Concept of a Celestial Mandate (Tian Ming 天命)." *Early China* 31 (2007): 1–46.

Allen, Roland. *Missionary Methods: St. Paul's or Ours?* London: World Dominion Press, 1956.

Anscombe, G. E. M. "Modern Moral Philosophy." In *Virtue Ethics*, edited by Roger Crisp and Michael Slote, 26–44. Oxford: Oxford University Press, 1997.

Aristotle. *The Nicomachean Ethics*. Translated by David Ross. Oxford: Oxford University Press, 2009.

Battenhouse, Roy W. *A Companion to the Study of St. Augustine*. New York: Oxford University Press, 1955.

Begbie, Jeremy. *Music, Modernity, and God Essays in Listening*. Oxford: Oxford University Press, 2013.

Begbie, Jeremy S. *Theology, Music and Time*. Cambridge: Cambridge University Press, 2000.

Behuniak, James. *Mencius on Becoming Human*. Albany: State University of New York Press, 2005.

Bell, Daniel. *China's New Confucianism: Politics and Everyday Life in a Changing Society*. Princeton: Princeton University Press, 2008.

Berthrong, John H. "Chinese (Confucian) Philosophical Theology." In *The Oxford Handbook of Philosophical Theology*, edited by Thomas P. Flint and Michael C. Rea, 575–90. Oxford: Oxford University Press, 2011.

Biggar, Nigel. *Behaving in Public: How to Do Christian Ethics*. Cambridge: W.B. Eerdmans Pub. Co., 2011.

Bonner, Gerald. *St. Augustine of Hippo: Life and Controversies*. Norwich: Canterbury Press, 2002.

Brindley, Erica. "Music, Cosmos, and the Development of Psychology in Early China." *T'oung Pao* 92, no. 1 (2006): 1–49.

Buckley, James Joseph, and David S. Yeago. *Knowing the Triune God: The Work of the Spirit in the Practices of the Church*. Grand Rapids: W.B. Eerdmans, 2001.

Burnaby, John. *Amor Dei: A Study of the Religion of St. Augustine* Norwich: Canterbury Press, 1991.

Butler, Cuthbert. *Western Mysticism; the Teachings of Ss Augustine, Gregory, and Bernard on Contemplation and the Contemplative Life*. London: Constable & company, 1922.

Cahall, Perry. "Saint Augustine and the Communion of Persons: The Relationship of the Bishop of Hippo's Theology of Marriage to His Theology of the Trinity." Ph.D. diss., Saint Louis University, 2001.

Capps, Walter H. *Religious Studies: The Making of a Discipline*. Minneapolis: Fortress Press, 1995.

Cary, Phillip. *Augustine's Invention of the Inner Self: The Legacy of a Christian Platonist*. Oxford Oxford University Press, 2000.

Chan, Chung-Yan Joyce. "Commands from Heaven: Matteo Ricci's Christianity in the Eyes of Míng Confucian Officials." *Missiology* 31, no. 3 (2003): 269–87.

Chang, Carsun. "The Significance of Mencius." *Philosophy East and West* 8, no. 1/2 (1958): 37–48.

Chen, Jia. "How Can One be Perfected by Music?: Contemporary Educational Significance of Chinese Pre-Qin Confucian Thought on Yue Jiao (Music Education)." Ph.D. diss., University of Illinois, 2012.

Chidester, David. "The Symbolism of Learning in St. Augustine." *The Harvard Theological Review* 76, no. 1 (1983): 73–90.

Ching, Julia. *Confucianism and Christianity: A Comparative Study*. Tokyo: Kodansha International in cooperation with the Institute of Oriental Religions, Sophia University, Tokyo, 1977.

Chong, Kim Chong, and Liu, Yuli. *Conceptions of Virtue: East and West*. New York: Marshall Cavendish Academic, 2006.

Chow, Alexander. *Theosis, Sino-Christian Theology and the Second Chinese Enlightenment*. New York: Palgrave Macmillan, 2013.

———. "The East Asian Rediscovery of Sin." *Studies in World Christianity* 19, no. 2 (2013): 126–40.

———. "Calvinist Public Theology in Urban China Today." *International Journal of Public Theology* 8 (2014): 158–75.

Clooney, Francis X. "Comparative Theology." In *The Oxford Handbook of Systematic Theology*, edited by Kathryn Tanner, John Webster, and Iain Torrance, 654–69. Oxford: Oxford University Press, 2007.

———. *Comparative Theology: Deep Learning Across Religious Borders*. Chichester: Wiley-Blackwell, 2010.

Cook, Scott Bradley. "Unity and Diversity in the Musical Thought of Warring States China." Ph.D. diss., University of Michigan, 1995.

Croy, N. Clayton. "Hellenistic Philosophies and the Preaching of the Resurrection (Acts 17:18, 32)." *Novum Testamentum* 39, no. 1 (1997): 21–39.

Deusen, Nacy Van. "De Musica." In *Augustine through the Ages: An Encyclopedia*, edited by Allan Fitzgerald and John C. Cavadini, 574–576. Grand Rapids: William B. Eerdmans Pub., 1999.

Drober, Hubertus R. "Studying Augustine: An Overview of Recent Research." In *Augustine and His Critics: Essays in Honor of Gerald Bonner*, edited by Robert Dodaro and George Lawless, 18–34. London: Routledge, 2000.

Duara, Prasenjit. *The Crisis of Global Modernity: Asian Traditions and a Sustainable Future*. Cambridge: Cambridge University, 2015.

Dunch, Ryan. "Beyond Cultural Imperialism: Cultural Theory, Christian Missions, and Global Modernity." *History and Theory* 41, no. 3 (2002): 301–25.

Evans, G. R. *Augustine on Evil*. Cambridge: Cambridge University Press, 1982.

Feng, Youlan. *A History of Chinese Philosophy*. 2 vols. London: Allen & Unwin, 1937.

Fingarette, Herbert. *Confucius: The Secular as Sacred*. Illinois: Waveland Press, 1972.

———. "The Music of Humanity in the Conversations of Confucius." *Journal of Chinese Philosophy* 10, no. 4 (1983): 331–56.

Franchi, Leonard. "Healing the Wounds: St Augustine, Catechesis, and Religious Education Today." *Religious Education* 106, no. 3 (2011): 299–311.

Fu, Pei-Jung. "The Concept of 'T'ien' in Ancient China: With Special Emphasis on Confucianism." Ph.D. diss., Yale University, 1984.

Gadamer, Hans-Georg. *Truth and Method*. 2nd, rev. Translated by Joel Weinsheimer and Donald G. Marshall. London Continuum, 2004.

Gentz, Joachim. *Understanding Chinese Religions*. Edinburgh: Dunedin Academic, 2012.

Graham, A. C. *Disputers of the Tao: Philosophical Argument in Ancient China*. La Salle: Open Court, 1989.

Greenberg, Michael. *British Trade and the Opening of China, 1800–42*. Cambridge: Cambridge University Press, 1951.

Gregory, Eric. *Politics and the Order of Love: An Augustinian Ethic of Democratic Citizenship*. Chicago: The University of Chicago Press, 2008.

Guarino, Thomas. "Postmodernity and Five Fundamental Theological Issues." *Theological Studies* 57, no. 4 (1996): 654–89.

Guerrant, Mary T. "Three Aspects of Music in Ancient China and Greece." *College Music Symposium* 20, no. 2 (1980): 87–98.

Hagen, Kurtis. "The Propriety of Confucius: A Sense-of-Ritual." *Asian Philosophy* 20, no. 1 (2010): 1–25.

Harmless, William. "Baptism." In *Augustine through the Ages: An Encyclopedia*, edited by Allan Fitzgerald and John C. Cavadini, 84–91. Grand Rapids: William B. Eerdmans Pub., 1999.

Harrison, Carol. "Getting Carried Away: Why Did Augustine Sing?" *Augustinian Studies* 46, no. 1 (2015): 1–22.

———. *Rethinking Augustine's Early Theology: An Argument for Continuity*. Oxford: Oxford University, 2005.

Herdt, Jennifer A. *Putting on Virtue: The Legacy of the Splendid Vices*. Chicago: University of Chicago Press, 2008.

Howie, George. *Educational Theory and Practice in St Augustine*. London: Routledge & K. Paul, 1969.

Huang, Yong. "Confucian Theology: Three Models." *Religion Compass* 1, no. 4 (2007): 455–78.

Hunter, G. David. "Marriage." In *Augustine through the Ages: An Encyclopedia*, edited by Allan Fitzgerald and John C. Cavadini, 535–37. Grand Rapids: William B. Eerdmans Pub., 1999.

Ivanhoe, P. J. *Confucian Moral Self Cultivation*. 2nd ed. Indianapolis: Hackett Pub., 2000.

———. *Ethics in the Confucian Tradition: The Thought of Mengzi and Wang Yangming*. 2nd ed. Indianapolis: Hackett, 2002.

Jenkins, John. "Yearley, Aquinas, and Comparative Method." *Journal of Religious Ethics* 21, no. 2 (1993): 377–83.
Kenney, John Peter. *Contemplation and Classical Christianity: A Study in Augustine*. Oxford Oxford University Press, 2014.
———. *The Mysticism of Saint Augustine: Re-Reading the Confessions*. New York: Routledge, 2005.
Kim, Sebastian C. H. *Theology in the Public Sphere*. London: SCM Press, 2011.
Kolbet, Paul R. *Augustine and the Cure of Souls: Revising a Classical Ideal*. Notre Dame: University of Notre Dame Press, 2009.
Lai, Pan-Chiu. "Chinese Culture and the Development of Chinese Christian Theology." *Studies in World Christianity* 7, no. 2 (2001): 219–40.
Lai, Whalen. "In Defence of Graded Love Three Parables from Mencius." *Asian Philosophy* 1, no. 1 (1991): 51–60.
Lee, Archie C. C. "Cross-Textual Hermeneutics and Identity in Multi-Scriptural Asia." In *Christian Theology in Asia*. Ed. Sebastian C. H. Kim. Cambridge: Cambridge University Press, 2008.
Liu, Xiusheng. *Mencius, Hume, and the Foundations of Ethics*. Aldershot: Ashgate, 2003.
Liu, Yuli. *The Unity of Rule and Virtue: A Critique of a Supposed Parallel between Confucian Ethics and Virtue Ethics*. Singapore: Eastern Universities Press, 2004.
Loewe, Michael. "Imperial China's Reactions to the Catholic Missions." *Numen* 35, no. 2 (1988): 179–212.
MacIntyre, Alasdair C. *After Virtue : A Study in Moral Theory*. London: Duckworth, 1981.
———. *Whose Justice? Which Rationality?* Notre Dame: University of Notre Dame Press, 1988.
Markus, Robert A. *Christianity and the Secular*. Notre Dame: University of Notre Dame, 2006.
Mbanisi, Victor. "Baptism and the Ideal of Unity and Universality of the Church in St. Augustine's Ecclesiology: An Exposition of His Theology of Baptism in Light of Donatist Controversy." Ph.D. diss., Fordham University, 2008.
Miles, Margaret. "Vision: The Eye of the Body and the Eye of the Mind in Saint Augustine's "De Trinitate" and "Confessions"." *The Journal of Religion* 63, no. 2 (1983): 125–42.
Miller, Richard B. "Evil, Friendship, and Iconic Realism in Augustine's Confessions." *Harvard Theological Review* 104, no. 4 (2011): 387–409.
Miyahira, Nozomu. "Christian Theology under Feudalism, Nationalism, and Democracy in Japan," In *Christian Theology in Asia*. ed. Sebastian Kim. Cambridge: Cambridge University Press, 2008.
Mooney, T. Brian and Nowacki, Mark. *Understanding Teaching & Learning Classic Texts on Education by Augustine, Aquinas, Newman and Mill*. Exeter: Imprint Academic, 2011.
Nuyen, Anh Tuan. "Can Morality Be Taught? Aquinas and Mencius on Moral Education ." In *Aquinas, Education, and the East*, edited by Mooney, T. Brian, and Mark R. Nowacki, 103–13. London: Springer, 2013.
Mungello, David E. "Leibniz's Interpretation of Neo-Confucianism." *Philosophy East and West* 21, no. 1 (1971): 3–22.
Nivison, David S. and Norden, Bryan W. Van. *The Ways of Confucianism: Investigations in Chinese Philosophy*. Chicago: Open Court, 1996.

Northcott, Michael S., *The Environment and Christian Ethics*. Cambridge: Cambridge University Press, 1996.

———. "Being Silent: Time in the Spirit." In *The Blackwell Companion to Christian Ethics*, 414–26. Edited by Stanley Hauerwas and Samuel Wells. Oxford: Balckwell Publishing Ltd, 2004.

———. "Christianity in Asia." In *International Encyclopedia of the Social & Behavioral Sciences*, 2nd, 531–533. Edited by James D. Wright. Amsterdam: Elsevier, 2015).

O'Connell, Robert J. *Art and the Christian Intelligence in St. Augustine*. Oxford: Blackwell, 1978.

O'Donovan, Oliver. *Resurrection and Moral Order: An Outline for Evangelical Ethics*. 2nd ed. Leicester: Apollos, 1994.

Panikkar, Raimundo. *The Intrareligious Dialogue*. Rev. ed. New York: Paulist Press, 1999.

Phillips, Tom. "China on Course to Become 'World's Most Christian Nation in 15 Years.'" *The Telegraph* (2014).

Plato. *Plato: Complete Works*. Edited by John M. Cooper. Cambridge: Hackett, 1997.

Rhee, Jong Sung. *Augustine's Doctrine of the Trinity*. Seoul: Korea Institute of Advanced Christian Studies, 2001.

Ricci, Matteo. *The True Meaning of the Lord of Heaven*. edited by Edward J. Malatesta. St. Louis: Institute of Jesuit Sources in cooperation with The Ricci Institute, Taipei, Taiwan, 1985.

Rist, John M. *Augustine: Ancient Thought Baptized*. Cambridge: Cambridge University Press, 1994.

Schumacher, Lydia. *Divine Illumination: The History and Future of Augustine's Theory of Knowledge*. Chichester: Wiley-Blackwell, 2011.

Sharpe, Eric J. *Comparative Religion: A History*. London: Duckworth, 1986.

Shi, Junbo. "A Comparison between the Music Concepts of Confucius and Mencius." *Journal of Guan Zi* 4 (2010): 59–62.

Shun, Kwong-loi. *Mencius and Early Chinese Thought*. Stanford: Stanford University Press, 1997.

Shun, Kwong-loi and Wong, David B. *Confucian Ethics: A Comparative Study of Self, Autonomy, and Community*. New York: Cambridge, 2004.

Smither, Edward L. *Augustine as Mentor: A Model for Preparing Spiritual Leaders*. Nashville: B & H Academic, 2008.

Stalnaker, Aaron. *Overcoming Our Evil: Human Nature and Spiritual Exercises in Xunzi and Augustine*. Washington: Georgetown University Press, 2006.

Sugirtharajah, R. S. *Asian Biblical Hermeneutics and Postcolonialism: Contesting the Interpretations*. Sheffield: Sheffield Academic Press, 1999.

Tan, Leonard. "Towards an Ancient Chinese-Inspired Theory of Music Education." *Music Education Research* (2015): 1–12.

Tian, Xiaojun. "The Musical Pedagogy of Mencius and Xunzi." *Journal of Guizhou University for Ethnic for Ethnic Minorities* 1 (2008): 39–44.

Kent, Bonnie. "Augustine's Ethics." In *The Cambridge Companion to Augustine*, edited by Eleonore Stump and Norman Kretzmann, 205–52. Cambridge: Cambridge University Press, 2001.

Taylor, Charles. *Sources of the Self: The Making of the Modern Identity*. Cambridge: Cambridge University Press, 1989.

Topping, Ryan. *St. Augustine*. London: Continuum International Pub. Group, 2010.

Torchia, N. Joseph. "Contemplation and Action." In *Augustine through the Ages: An Encyclopedia*, edited by Allan Fitzgerald and John C. Cavadini, 233–35. Grand Rapids: William B. Eerdmans Pub., 1999.
Norden, Bryan W. Van. *Virtue Ethics and Consequentialism in Early Chinese Philosophy*. New York: Cambridge University Press, 2007.
Wang, Huaiyu. "Review of a Discourse on Confucius's Music". *Dao* 9 (2010): 115–19.
Wannenwetsch, Bernd. *Political Worship*. Oxford: Oxford University Press, 2004.
Wetzel, James. *Augustine and the Limits of Virtue*. Cambridge: Cambridge University Press, 1992.
Wiest, Jean-Paul. "Matteo Ricci: Pioneer of Chinese-Western Dialogue and Cultural Exchanges." *International Bulletin of Missionary Research* 36, no. 1 (2012): 17–20.
Witte, John. *From Sacrament to Contract: Marriage, Religion, and Law in the Western Tradition*. Louisville: Westminster John Knox Press, 1997.
Wong, Marina. "A comparison between the Philosophies of Confucius and Plato as Applied to Music Education." *The Journal of Aesthetic Education* 32, no. 3 (1998).
Yao, Xinzhong. *Confucianism and Christianity: A Comparative Study of Jen and Agape*. Brighton: Sussex Academic Press, 1996.
———. *An Introduction to Confucianism*. New York: Cambridge University Press, 2000.
Yearley, Lee H. "A Comparison between Classical Chinese Thought and Thomistic Christian Thought." *Journal of the American Academy of Religion* 51, no. 3 (1983): 427–58.
———. *Mencius and Aquinas: Theories of Virtue and Conceptions of Courage*. Albany: State University of New York Press, 1990.
———. "Review of Confucianism and Christianity: A Comparative Study." *Philosophy East and West* 29, no. 4 (1979): 509–12.
Yeo, K. K. *Musing with Confucius and Paul: Toward a Chinese Christian Theology*. Cambridge: James Clarke & Co, 2008.
Xu, Youwei. "Confucius: An Educationalist of Aesthetics in Ancient China." *Journal of Popular Culture* 27, no. 2 (1993): 121–28.
Yu, Jiyuan. *The Ethics of Confucius and Aristotle: Mirrors of Virtue*. New York: Routledge, 2007.
Yue, Ji. 'Confucius on Music Education.' *Nebula* 5, no. 1–2 (2008): 128–33.
Zhao, Yanxia. *Father and Son in Confucianism and Christianity: A Comparative Study of Xunzi and Paul*. Brighton: Sussex Academic Press, 2007.

Index

A

Academic approach, 9, 22, 25
Ambrose, 95–100, 105, 164–65, 175
Anti-Utilitarianism, 154
Ascension, 106, 132, 135
Asceticism, 35, 70–71, 104, 152, 224
Augustinian civic liberalism, 1, 6, 215, 222
Augustinian Orthodoxy, 7
Augustinian proceduralism, 6, 215, 220, 228
Augustinian realism, 1, 5–6, 215, 219–20, 228

B

Baptism, 33–34, 93, 132, 136, 144, 163–78, 192–93, 196, 208, 210, 219
Benevolence, 17, 20–21, 23, 41, 50, 52, 55–59, 61–63, 68–69, 77–78, 82, 106, 109, 111–14, 116–19, 121–22, 124–25, 142, 144–45, 147, 153–55, 157, 162, 166, 195–96, 201, 203, 213, 220, 225, 226
Benevolent Government, 35, 55

C

Community, 7, 19, 31–32, 34, 44, 98, 102, 105, 127, 213, 217, 222, 226–27, 229

Conceptual bridge, 9, 25, 27, 216
Confucian Augustinianism, 1, 5, 8, 32, 215, 216, 217, 219–25, 227–29
Contemplation, 106–7, 109, 111, 113, 115, 117, 119, 121, 123, 125–29, 131–37, 139, 141, 143, 218, 235, 237, 239
Continuity, 32, 236

D

Divine illumination, 34–35, 88, 90, 93, 103, 105, 218

E

Environment, 9, 35, 45, 50, 65–66, 69–70, 72, 93–94, 120, 219

F

Fidelity, 65, 178–79, 183–85, 187, 189, 190, 196, 227–28
Filial piety, 35, 43, 50, 55, 62–64, 71, 79, 80, 83, 103–4, 115, 157, 158–59, 161–62, 196–97, 203, 213, 224, 226–27
Forgiveness, 163, 233
Friendship, 6, 34–35, 43, 53, 73, 96–97, 99, 100–102, 105, 180, 220, 226
Funeral, 144, 154, 156, 158–62, 196, 226–27

G

Government officer, 146, 153–54

H

Habit, 115, 185
Happiness, 1, 35, 46, 52, 57, 68–70, 83–84, 86–87, 104–5, 133, 136, 142, 163, 185, 197–99, 202–4, 209, 213–14, 217–18, 220–221, 223, 226, 229
Harmony, 34, 114, 146, 151, 195, 197–98, 200, 204, 213, 226, 229
Heaven, 4, 13–17, 24, 30, 35, 37, 39–42, 47–48, 55–56, 58, 60–61, 65–66, 68, 72, 74–76, 103–4, 106, 108, 110–12, 124–26, 142, 146, 147–48, 161–62, 198, 217, 220–221, 224–35, 238
Human nature, 6, 15–16, 21, 24, 26, 37, 39–41, 55–56, 65–66, 77–78, 104, 106, 108–14, 119, 129, 139, 142–43, 158, 180, 183, 204, 218, 219–20, 222
Human unity, 35, 61–62, 104, 224

I

Imitation, 29, 35, 98, 141, 221
Inter-textual reasoning, 25, 215–16, 222

L

Liberal discipline, 34, 104, 197, 208, 210–211, 214

M

Man of virtue, 35, 38–40, 43–46, 50, 52, 54–56, 61, 63–64, 68–69, 77, 83, 103–4, 106–8, 111, 115–17, 123, 125–26, 143, 145–46, 148, 150–52, 154–56, 159, 162, 195–96, 204, 220–221, 225–26

Marriage, 34, 71, 134, 140, 144, 155, 163, 177–88, 190–96, 219, 221, 223, 227, 228
Missiological apologetics, 9
Monastery, 95, 103
Monica, 86, 95–96, 100, 105, 133–36, 210
Moral education, 35, 50, 55–57, 62–65, 67, 69–70, 84, 86, 95, 109, 114, 157, 160, 175, 199–200, 221, 225
Moral learning, 8, 26–27, 32, 35, 43–45, 47, 53, 55, 70, 72, 85, 87–88, 91, 93, 95–96, 100, 102–6, 142, 145, 153, 208, 215, 218, 220, 224, 226–27, 229
Music, 8, 25–27, 32, 34, 38–39, 50, 70, 77, 87, 104, 130, 144, 146, 150, 163, 166, 197, 198–204, 206–9, 211, 213–15, 219, 225, 226, 229

N

Naming, 148
New-Confucianism, 9, 18

O

Ostia, 106, 131–34, 136, 143

P

Patience, 123
Poverty, 28, 35, 45–46, 55, 125, 126, 221
Practice, 2, 9, 11, 17–18, 27, 35, 39, 43–44, 50, 54–57, 59, 63, 73–74, 78, 82–83, 104, 110, 117–18, 128, 132, 145–49, 155, 157, 172, 175, 195, 203, 208, 213, 221, 224–28
Procreation, 177

R

Radical Orthodoxy, 1, 5, 7, 215, 228
Relationship, 2, 14, 18, 25, 30, 31, 42, 64, 93, 116, 127, 141, 163, 179, 180–81, 185, 188, 200–201, 207

Index

Ricci, Matteo, 9–17, 20, 23, 25, 33, 216, 235, 238, 239
Righteousness, 16, 23, 38–39, 58–59, 63, 65, 67–69, 82, 106–7, 109, 111–14, 118–19, 121, 123–24, 126, 140, 144, 148, 153–55, 157, 166, 196, 200, 203, 220, 226
Ritual propriety, 25–26, 38–41, 49, 50, 51, 55, 67–68, 104, 106, 111, 114–16, 142, 144, 145–48, 150–56, 159–60, 162–63, 166, 195–96, 199, 201, 203, 224–26

S

Sacrament, 8, 23, 27, 32, 144, 163, 164, 166, 168–74, 176, 178, 179, 183, 186, 187–88, 193–95, 196, 206, 215, 218–20, 227–29
Sacramental bond, 177
Sage, 72, 82, 108
Salvation, 54, 90, 93, 98, 132–33, 136, 164, 167–69, 174, 183, 185, 192, 196, 205, 219
Scripture, 98–99, 102–3, 106, 137, 140, 165, 179, 187, 190
Self-cultivation, 26, 35, 38–39, 43, 53, 55–56, 62–63, 65, 70, 103, 109, 110–11, 114, 118–20, 142, 153, 198–99, 201, 213, 215, 224, 226
Self-reflection, 26, 70, 106–11, 114, 116–17, 120, 122–25, 126, 142–43, 220
Sex, 1, 5, 35, 44, 45, 55, 65, 69, 70, 71, 79, 85, 104, 134, 152, 178, 179–81, 183–84, 186, 188–89, 190, 206, 221, 223, 226–28, 239
Shame, 45, 68, 112–14, 144, 150–51, 154, 184, 189, 196, 220, 226
Sin, 5–7, 34, 55, 101, 139, 141, 144, 163–64, 166–70, 175–76, 184–85, 189, 192–94, 196, 207, 219–22, 228,
Soul, 14–16, 83–84, 88–91, 93–94, 100, 103, 126–37, 141, 143, 163, 165, 175, 178, 185–86, 188–89, 206, 210–215, 218–19, 221–22, 227
Speech, 46, 69, 107, 133, 144, 148–51, 196, 225
Suffering, 46, 68, 106, 113, 123, 125–26, 143, 185

T

Teacher, 34, 51–53, 58, 63, 72, 88–90, 92, 95, 104–5, 108–9, 218, 224
Theological approach, 9, 21, 26
Tradition, 1, 2, 4, 8, 12–13, 15, 19–20, 22, 25–27, 31–32, 35, 42, 47–49, 74, 76, 83–84, 104, 110, 151, 164, 174, 185, 199, 201, 215–17, 223–24
Truth, 12, 27, 38, 40, 43, 45, 47, 50, 62, 83–84, 86–92, 96–97, 99, 104–5, 124, 126, 128, 131, 133–34, 139, 149–50, 166, 174, 190, 197, 204, 209, 212–13, 218, 222, 225–27, 229

V

Virtue, 1, 4–9, 15–17, 19–23, 25–27, 33–34, 36, 40, 42–47, 49–50, 52–57, 59–60, 68–69, 71, 73–75, 81, 83–84, 86, 88, 90, 95, 98, 100, 103–4, 106, 108, 110–15, 118–19, 123, 126, 128, 142–43, 145–46, 151, 154–56, 158, 185, 196–98, 201, 203, 213, 215–17, 219–24, 226, 228–29

W

Weakness, 101, 115, 117, 139, 184, 185
Wisdom, 23, 34, 55, 65, 68, 74, 78, 82–83, 85–86, 89–90, 97, 105–6, 111–14, 116, 128–29, 134–35, 137, 139–40, 142–43, 203, 213, 218, 220, 226